Operators and Nucleus

A Contribution to the Theory of Grammar

CAMBRIDGE STUDIES IN LINGUISTICS

General Editors · W. SIDNEY ALLEN · EUGENIE J. A. HENDERSON · FRED W. HOUSEHOLDER · R. B. LE PAGE · JOHN LYONS · F. R. PALMER · J. L. M. TRIM

Other volumes in preparation

OPERATORS AND NUCLEUS

A CONTRIBUTION TO THE THEORY OF GRAMMAR

PIETER A. M. SEUREN

Fellow of Darwin College and
Lecturer in Linguistics
University of Cambridge

CAMBRIDGE
at the University Press · 1969

Published by the Syndics of the Cambridge University Press
Bentley House, 200 Euston Road, London N.W.1
American Branch: 32 East 57th Street, New York, N.Y.10022

© Cambridge University Press 1969

Library of Congress Catalogue Card Number: 76–85738
Standard Book Number: 521 07476 2

Printed in Great Britain
at the University Printing House, Cambridge
(Brooke Crutchley, University Printer)

DEDICATED TO THE MEMORY OF
PROFESSOR E. W. BETH

ἁρμονίη ἀφανὴς φανερῆς κρείττων

Invisible harmony is stronger than visible harmony

HERACLITUS

Contents

Preface

The present study originated in a research project undertaken in 1962 under contract 062-12-32 CETN for Euratom, under the direction of Professor E. W. Beth, to whose memory this book is dedicated in gratitude. At the earliest stage I profited greatly from the suggestions and criticisms of Dr K. de Bouvère, who gave the first impetus to this work, and Mr R. P. G. de Rijk. The results of the first investigations were laid down in three reports submitted to Euratom in 1963 and 1964.

When, in 1964, the group working under contract for Euratom in the University of Amsterdam was dissolved, I continued the research by myself, first in the University of Groningen, later in the University of Cambridge. It was through the work of Dr A. Kraak, *Negatieve Zinnen* (1966), that I developed the idea of operators in grammar, as appears from my review article of Kraak's book in *Neophilologus 1967*, 'Negation in Dutch'.

I owe a debt to the members of the discussion group 'Generative Grammar' in the University of Amsterdam, with whom I discussed my work in detail. The critical remarks made by Professor J. F. Staal, who presided over this group until his departure for America in 1967, proved particularly helpful. His guidance kept me from many mistakes.

In the later stages of my work a great deal of help, criticism and encouragement came from: Mr J. L. M. Trim, Head of the Department of Linguistics in the University of Cambridge, who followed my work with interest and enabled me on various occasions to present parts of it to linguists in Great Britain; Professor H. Schultink of the University of Utrecht, who enabled me to present this book as a thesis in his University, and whose acute observations and careful reading improved the text considerably; Professor G. Nuchelmans of the University of Leyden, who helped me in gaining some insight into the logical background of operators; Professor A. Vos of the University of Amsterdam, who, in many discussions, let me profit from his vast knowledge of English grammar; Professor A. Cohen of the University of Utrecht and Professor J. Lyons of the University of Edinburgh, who read the

[ix]

Although a number of attempts have been made in the history of our Western civilization to arrive at an all-embracing theory of language, none of these has been entirely successful. Indeed, it must be admitted that we are still very far from such an achievement. As far as the theory of grammar is concerned, however, we are in a relatively better position. The problem of defining the linguistic universal 'grammar' amounts to that of providing a terminological framework in which an adequate grammatical description of any language can be given. Such a framework we call a model. In contemporary linguistics several models are proposed for the grammatical description of languages, some of which one finds discussed in Postal (1964) pp. 18–66; 97–117. Foremost among these is that proposed by Chomsky. This is known as the model of transformational generative grammar and is expounded mainly in his publications (1957), (1964a), (1964b) and (1965). The present study is based on the assumption that Chomsky's model is more successful than those presented by other linguists. The suggestion is made, however, that its degree of success can be raised by the introduction of some modifications.

1.2 Language, sentences, grammar

As will be clear from the above, the core of Chomsky's central notions of language and grammar has been taken over. For the sake of clarity a brief account is given of the points of view adopted from Chomsky. (In chapter 2 his model of grammatical description is described in detail.)

A language is considered to be an infinite set of sentences, each sentence being finite in length and built up out of a finite set of elements.

It must be understood that the term 'sentence' does not refer to an individual, temporally and spatially unique, product of a speaker's activity, which can be heard and recorded. Such individual events are utterance-tokens. The grammarian's primary interest is in sentence-types, rather than in utterance-tokens. Roughly speaking we say that if the members of a speech-community consider different utterance-tokens to be repetitions of each other, or 'the same', we take them to belong to one sentence-type. The concept of type results from a process of abstraction: within the same discourse of grammar we identify some utterance-tokens as the same, disregarding the differences that exist between them.[1] If it is said that a language is an infinite set of sentences, it is implied that 'sentence' is taken as 'sentence-type', not as 'utterance-token' (in which case it would be trivial to speak of an infinite set, since one single type can be repeated in an unlimited number of utterance-tokens).

A grammar, or grammatical description, is essentially a device for defining a language. A grammar of a language L distinguishes the combinations of elements which are sentences of L from those which are not. It moreover assigns a structure to the sentences of L in such a way that they are susceptible of semantic interpretation.

1.3 The form of grammars

A grammar is most conveniently presented in the form of an algorithm. That is, it contains one or more initial strings and a finite number of instructions, or rules, to generate new strings from the initial ones or from any other string generated, except from those which are called terminal strings and from which no rules can generate new strings. In the process of generation elements are introduced from a finite vocabulary of terminal and non-terminal symbols. Every terminal string is interpreted as a sentence, i.e. as a meaningful string of phonetic elements.

A grammar must be as explicit as possible. Its rules must be exact to the extent that nothing is left to the reader's benevolence or possible knowledge of the language described. The reader need only follow the instructions given in the rules in order to arrive at the sentences of the language in question. Or, in other words, the rules must be such that they can be fed into an automaton, which will then generate the terminal strings automatically.

---

[1] We have to do here with the identity that is postulated for indiscernibles. Cf. Quine (1961) p. 71, who speaks of the maxim of ' *the identification of indiscernibles*: Objects indistinguishable from one another within the terms of a given discourse should be construed as identical for that discourse'. The identification of indiscernibles is derived from Leibniz's 'identity of indiscernibles', cf. Russell (1900) pp. 54–63. Although Leibniz's principle seems to be logically untenable for a conception of reality (see Ayer (1954) pp. 26–7), as Leibniz himself recognized (Russell (1900) p. 55), it holds in the realm of theory construction, where factually different objects are classified under the same heading because of a common set of properties (see Bocheński (1962a)). This gives Quine the right to speak of the 'identification' rather than the 'identity' of indiscernibles. See also Ayer (1954) p. 32, where he discusses, in this context, repetitions of strings of what he considers to be the 'same' sounds, without being aware, apparently, of the fact that there are always measurable phonetic differences between different occurrences of the 'same' sound or series of sounds.

A grammatical description of a language consists of three main components: a syntactic component, a semantic component and a phonological component. The syntactic component consists of two subcomponents, the base and the transformational subcomponent. The base generates deep structures, which have a one-to-one correspondence with the meanings of the sentences. The semantic component operates on the deep structures and gives them a semantic interpretation. The transformational subcomponent also operates on deep structures and transforms them into surface structures, whose elements have a one-to-one relationship with the formal elements of the sentences of the language described. The operations of this subcomponent, the transformations, are either obligatory, i.e. prescribed by certain elements in the deep structure, or optional (although the status of optional, i.e. stylistic, transformations is still unclear). In neither case must they result in surface structures with a meaning different from the one that has been established in the semantically interpreted deep structures. Transformations do not affect meaning.[1] The phonological component operates on surface structures and gives them a phonetic interpretation. The rules of the phonological component provide specifications of the phonetic make-up of the surface structures, up to free variation.

The base is the only 'creative' part of the grammar, in that the generative process starts from a general initial symbol, which is developed into a specific (deep) structure, determining the full meaning of the sentence under generation and, within narrow limits, also its form. When it reaches its final stage, a base-terminal string, a sentence has been delimited in principle. After this point its full meaning and most of its form have become predictable in terms of the grammar. The transformational subcomponent and the semantic and phonological components are solely interpretive. Their functioning is determined by the information provided by the deep structures. The only exception is made by the optional transformations, which allow for a certain amount of freedom after the base. As, however, transformations do not affect meaning, sentences derived from the same deep structure but with a different transformational history, must be synonymous in the strictest sense of the term. Optional transformations can only bring

---

[1] The principle of not letting transformations add or delete elements of meaning is comparatively recent in the theory of transformational grammar. See Chomsky (1965) pp. 132–6. For a more detailed discussion see 4.1.

about stylistic variations in what is otherwise 'basically' the same sentence.[1]

1.4 General notions connected with grammar

In order to evaluate the modified model proposed below as compared with the original Chomskian model, something must be said about the standards of evaluation. This implies that some thought must be given to notions underlying the study of grammar. Without going into a detailed discussion of the foundations of linguistic science, we shall select those general aspects which seem to be of direct relevance in the present context.

1.4.1 Discovery procedures. It is an essential feature of method in grammatical studies of the kind inaugurated by Chomsky and pursued here, that no attention is paid to problems of discovering grammatical rules. No straightforward method is presented or implied for arriving at grammatical rules from a corpus of data. It is, in fact, not even assumed that it is possible to develop a rigorous method for establishing grammars, although this possibility is not excluded either. On the whole, linguists are considered to arrive at grammatical descriptions by trial and error, guess-work, on the basis of their previously acquired knowledge of grammatical analysis, etc.[2] The discovery of rules is rather a question of insight than of strict method; it is an art rather than a technique. What is relevant here, is the description as it is presented and as it can be tested as to its adequacy.

1.4.2 Competence and performance. The generative character of the description does not imply any identification with the speaker rather than with the listener. In fact, a generative grammar can have only a limited bearing on the problem how a speaker produces utterances or how a listener understands them. Chomsky distinguishes between competence and performance ((1965) pp. 3 and 4). The actual processes of speaking and understanding are forms of linguistic performance, and their study requires a great deal more than the study of grammar alone. 'To study actual linguistic performance, we must consider the inter-

---

[1] See Chomsky (1965) pp. 136–7. Although on p. 136 it is said of the syntactic component that it constitutes the sole 'creative' part of the grammar, this must be understood to refer strictly to the base, as appears from the whole context, and especially from p. 137: 'The transformational component is solely interpretive.'

[2] See Chomsky (1957) p. 56.

action of a variety of factors, of which the underlying competence of the speaker-hearer is only one' (Chomsky (1965) p. 4). On p. 139 he speaks of the 'absurdity of regarding the system of generative rules as a point-by-point model for the actual construction of a sentence by a speaker'.

Competence, on the other hand, is 'the speaker-hearer's knowledge of his language' (p. 4). According to Chomsky, 'a grammar of a language purports to be a description of the ideal speaker-hearer's intrinsic competence' (p. 4). That is, a grammar is supposed to specify what a speaker-hearer's practical knowledge of his language amounts to, 'not what he may report about his knowledge' (p. 8). For 'any interesting generative grammar will be dealing, for the most part, with mental processes that are far beyond the level of actual or even potential consciousness' (p. 8).

One sees that Chomsky, although emphasizing the distinction between the grammatical process of generation and the psychological processes involved in actual speech, does not distinguish between a grammatical description of a language and a description of the native speaker's knowledge of his language, although they were, and still are, considered distinct by most structural linguists. In fact, he identifies the two, and even goes so far as to say that grammars deal with mental processes. Chomsky has made linguistics 'mentalistic' again, after a period of behaviourism. On p. 25 he says, speaking about the child's acquisition of language: 'As a precondition for language learning, he [i.e. the child] must possess, first, a linguistic theory that specifies the form of the grammar of a possible human language, and, second, a strategy for selecting a grammar of the appropriate form that is compatible with the primary linguistic data. As a long-range task for general linguistics, we might set the problem of developing an account of this innate linguistic theory that provides the basis for language learning.' And on p. 53 we read: 'A general linguistic theory...must therefore be regarded as a specific hypothesis, of an essentially rationalist cast, as to the nature of mental structures and processes.'

It is generally held that there must be certain connections between grammars and whatever mental structures and processes are involved in linguistic competence and performance. Linguistic descriptions will no doubt provide important clues for the psychologist who studies these mental phenomena, since—as far as can be seen—it must be true that 'obviously, every speaker of a language has mastered and internalized a generative grammar that expresses his knowledge of his language' ((1965) p. 8). If, for instance, it appears that the set of sentences of a language L can be described only by means of algorithmical rules, then there is reason to infer that the speakers of L must have at their disposal an algorithmical device of some sort in order to produce (and presumably also to understand) the sentences of L. It seems also that the distinction between deep and surface structures, established purely for reasons of linguistic description, corresponds to a psychological reality. A number of experiments point in this direction.[1]

Chomsky, however, says more. According to him the human mind is a direct object of linguistic study. His view seems to be based on the consideration that the sentence-types which we study are the products of mental processes of abstraction and interpretation. What makes a sentence a sentence, is in the mind. The linguist is primarily concerned with providing the simplest possible answer, i.e. the answer with the highest possible explanatory value, to the problem of why a native speaker judges some utterance-tokens as corresponding to grammatical sentences, and others as not. Any hypothesis aiming at an explanation of the grammaticalness of sentences must necessarily be a hypothesis about the mental principles which make a native speaker distinguish grammatical sentences from ungrammatical type-level configurations. This seems incontrovertible. That the native speaker is quite unaware of almost all structures and processes of his own mind, as indeed of most other parts of his body, is of no concern here.

The decline of mentalism at the beginning of our century is understandable in the light of a mythical concept 'mind' still prevalent at that time, fraught with metaphysical properties which made it insusceptible of scientific treatment. But if we assume that the mind is a physical structure and that its processes are of a physical nature, there is no longer any justification for eschewing discussions about the mind, as the tendency used to be. This does not imply, however, as is pointed out by Katz (1964 b), that the linguist, while dealing with mental structures and processes, has to express himself in neurophysiological terms. The linguist uses notations which are abstract in the sense that it is immaterial in what neurophysiological, physical, or other form the system drawn up by him is realized, 'so long as each [realization] is isomorphic to the representation of linguistic structure given by the theory of the language' (p. 129). That is, the linguist deals not with the brain, but with

[1] See, e.g., Miller (1962); Mehler (1963); Savin and Perchonock (1965); Levelt (1966).

the mind, the distinction being parallel, for instance, to that between the principle of alphabetic ordering of items and its realization in the form of card-files, lists or magnetic tapes.

The recognition of the mentalistic nature of linguistics, far from keeping us from a purely scientific approach, helps us to formulate more precisely the links that undeniably exist between language, logic and the mind.

1.4.3 Adequacy. Chomsky's closely relating, or indeed identifying, the study of language and the study of the mind, although valid and of great importance, may have induced him to formulate the criteria of adequacy for grammars in terms which run the risk of being somewhat opaque to readers trained in the structuralist tradition, and which may also, perhaps, be qualified as unrealistic, in the sense that, if one applies Chomsky's formulation, there is no way of verifying whether a certain level of adequacy is achieved. He distinguishes three levels of success for a grammatical description: the levels of observational adequacy, descriptive adequacy, and explanatory adequacy ((1964a) pp. 28–9).

Observational adequacy is achieved 'if the grammar presents the observed primary data correctly' (p. 28). This could mean that Chomsky takes a grammar to be observationally adequate if it gives a correct description of the utterances of a corpus. But a footnote corrects this impression. An observationally adequate grammar describes sentence-types, not utterance-tokens, but it describes only a limited corpus of sentences and not the infinite set of sentences constituting a natural language.

A grammar is descriptively adequate if it 'gives a correct account of the linguistic intuition of the native speaker, and specifies the observed data (in particular) in terms of significant generalizations that express underlying regularities in the language' (p. 28). In (1965), on p. 24, a grammar is said to be descriptively adequate 'to the extent that it correctly describes the intrinsic competence of the idealized native speaker. The structural descriptions assigned to sentences by the grammar, the distinctions that it makes between well-formed and deviant, and so on, must, for descriptive adequacy, correspond to the linguistic intuition of the native speaker (whether or not he may be immediately aware of this) in a substantial and significant class of crucial cases.'

One understands that a descriptively adequate grammar is not confined to a limited corpus of sentences, but is required to be able to generate all the sentences of a language. It must account for the fact that a native speaker produces and understands throughout his life an enormous mass of utterances which he has never produced or heard before, by assuming that he does so on the basis of an 'internalized' system of rules. If it is required, however, that a grammar 'correctly describes the intrinsic competence of the idealized native speaker', one wonders how anyone could possibly check if this requirement has been fulfilled. Only some enlightened outsider with independent knowledge of the workings of the mind would then be able to evaluate grammars. We presume that an adequate grammar will give a correct account of the native speaker's linguistic intuition. But to use this as a criterion of adequacy sounds tautologous, in much the same way as it would have sounded tautologous for Galileo to defend his theory with the argument that it gave a correct description of our solar system.

It is perhaps more practical to say that if an adequate grammar is to account for the fact that there is no limit to the number of sentences that are accepted by native speakers as perfectly natural, and that some combinations of elements are qualified as unintelligible, ungrammatical, or both,—then it must specify all the sentences of a language in terms of the widest possible generalizations expressing underlying regularities in the language (as Chomsky put it in (1964a) p. 28). If this criterion is applied, a linguist, in order to make judgements about the adequacy of a grammatical description, requires information not so much about the native speaker's mental structures and the processes by which he assigns structural descriptions to the sentences of his language, but rather about this speaker's judgements as to the grammaticalness, acceptability, and deviance of sentences.

As we have seen above, a grammatical description of a language comprises a description of the syntax, the sound-patterns and the meanings of its sentences. For such a description to be adequate, i.e. for a grammar to be descriptively adequate, both the formal and the semantic description must be adequate. Leaving aside the problem of determining the adequacy of a semantic description, we can distinguish several aspects of descriptive adequacy for syntax and phonology. All these aspects are a direct consequence of the structure and the purpose of the grammar as given above.

In order to be adequate, a syntactic and phonological description must, first, be as explicit and exact as possible, so that no disagreement can arise as to what is and what is not generated by the rules and what structural descriptions are assigned to the generated strings.

It must, secondly, generate all combinations of elements which are interpretable as sentences of a language, and only these. This requirement gives rise to the problem of grammaticalness and deviance, about which more will be said below.

It must, thirdly, be as simple as possible. Admittedly, the concept of simplicity is rather elusive and has been much discussed. For our purpose, however, it is sufficient to say that a description meets the requirement of simplicity to the extent that it contains relevant generalizations, or expresses regularities in the language. If two descriptions reach the same degree of generalization, then the description with the smaller number of rules and/or symbols is considered to be the simpler (see also p. 217, note 1).

A fourth requirement of descriptive adequacy is applicable only to syntactic descriptions. It results from the association with a semantic component. We have seen above that the syntactic component of a grammar consists of two parts, the base, generating deep structures, and the transformational part, which converts deep structures into surface structures. The deep structures contain all information necessary for the semantic interpretation, whereas the transformations do not affect meaning. This implies a criterion of adequacy. There must be a level in the description where surface form and meaning meet. We call this the deep structure level. That is, deep structures must not contain any semantic ambiguities. Cases of semantic ambiguity, or homonymy, in surface structures must all be accounted for in later stages of generation, so that either the transformational or the phonological rules lead to accidental merging of originally distinct deep structures. Generally, semantic differences in surface structure must all be traceable back to differences in deep structures. We can regard this concept of a semantically relevant deep structure as a specific answer to the old problem of the relation between form and meaning. Apart from the merits of this particular solution, we impose on grammars, as distinct from other scientific theories, the special requirement that they should somehow define the relation between form and meaning.

We must regard as semantically inadequate a grammar of English where, for example:

(1)   *a*   John didn't eat the two apples

and:

(2)   *a*   John didn't eat two apples

are considered to have the same deep structure, the only difference being in the selection of the article,—and where the same passive transformation applies equally to both, resulting in:

(1) *b* the two apples weren't eaten by John

and:

(2) *b* two apples weren't eaten by John

Such a grammar would be correct for (1*a*) and (1*b*), but not for (2*a*) and (2*b*), since it does not meet the requirement that transformed structures must have the same meaning as their underlying deep structures,—which is clearly not the case for (2*a*) and (2*b*). The semantically regular passive of (2*a*) is:

(2) *c* no two apples were eaten by John

If the grammar, furthermore, generates (2*c*) by a transformation allowing the negation element of (2*b*) to be moved to the position immediately preceding *two*,[1] it becomes even more inadequate from the point of view of semantic interpretation. For it does not allow the semantic component, which operates on deep structures, to distinguish between (2*b*) and (2*c*) despite their different meanings. What is needed is a grammar which contains a passivization rule such that (2*a*) corresponds to (2*c*) and (2*b*) to:

(2) *d* there were two apples which John didn't eat

Chomsky's third level of success for a grammatical description (explanatory adequacy) does not depend directly on the description itself, but on the linguistic theory with which it is associated. In (1964*a*), on p. 28, Chomsky says: 'A third and still higher level of success is achieved when the associated linguistic theory provides a general basis for selecting a grammar that achieves the second level of success over other grammars consistent with the relevant observed data that do not achieve this level of success. In this case, we can say that the linguistic theory in question suggests an explanation for the linguistic intuition of the native speaker. It can be interpreted as asserting that data of the observed kind will enable a speaker whose intrinsic capacities are as represented in this general theory to construct for himself a grammar that characterizes exactly this linguistic intuition.'

In (1965) he distinguishes between the descriptive adequacy of a

---

[1] As is done by Klima (1964) pp. 271–2. Generally, in Klima's article on 'Negation in English' too little account is taken of the necessity of semantic adequacy. See also 4.1.

grammar and that of a linguistic theory (p. 24): 'a linguistic theory is descriptively adequate if it makes a descriptively adequate grammar available for each natural language'. He then proceeds to explanatory adequacy (pp. 25 and 26): 'To the extent that a linguistic theory succeeds in selecting a descriptively adequate grammar on the basis of primary linguistic data, we can say that it meets the condition of *explanatory adequacy*. That is, to this extent it offers an explanation for the intuition of the native speaker on the basis of an empirical hypothesis concerning the innate predisposition of the child to develop a certain kind of theory to deal with the evidence presented to him.'

That is, an explanatory linguistic theory is not simply the set of all grammars of all languages (if such a set were realizable at all), but will explain why these grammars are as they are. And since, ideally, a grammar coincides with, or is a direct description of, the native speaker's linguistic competence, an explanatory linguistic theory will explain any speaker's competence in his language. More specifically, it will specify the apparatus necessary for a human being to acquire full linguistic competence on the basis of a limited amount of primary linguistic data. If such a theory is realized as an automaton, this automaton should be able to discover the, or an, adequate grammar for any human language to which it has been exposed for some time. It is difficult to see how an automaton could be capable of such a formidable task if it did not possess a 'knowledge' of all the universals of human language, so that its task would consist in assigning particular values to universal parameters in a universal structure. This means that a linguist concentrating on linguistic data and formulating rules valid for a language or for language in general, is in fact working at a model which is applicable to the human mind, whether he is aware of this implication or not—in very much the same way as a logician working out rules of valid inference is in fact studying the mind (cf. Miller (1966) p. 93).

We can agree with Chomsky, therefore, when he seems to imply that a linguistic theory that provides the means to decide which of two proposed grammars, both of which meet the requirements of descriptive adequacy, is the better, is more valuable than a theory which does not provide such means. In our terms we shall say that a grammar G_1 reaches a higher degree of descriptive adequacy than a grammar G_2, and is, therefore, preferable to it, when (*a*) it is more explicit, (*b*) it gives a better account of grammaticalness and deviance (see 1.4.4), (*c*) it contains more generalizations, or expresses them with less apparatus, and (*d*) it provides for a more regular and straightforward semantic interpretation to be associated with it. When G_1 requires a model of description different from G_2, we say that the linguistic theory associated with G_1 is more highly valued than the theory associated with G_2.

It is also true, as Chomsky says ((1965) p. 26), that 'it would be utopian to expect to achieve explanatory adequacy on a large scale in the present state of linguistics'. As it is, we can only evaluate a grammar to the standards mentioned under (*a* to *d*) with respect to another grammar on an *ad hoc* basis. In the same way, a relative evaluation of two different models can as yet only be *ad hoc*. Again we can agree with Chomsky, when he goes on ((1965) p. 26): 'Nevertheless, considerations of explanatory adequacy are often critical for advancing linguistic theory. Gross coverage of a large mass of data can often be obtained by conflicting theories; for precisely this reason it is not, in itself, an achievement of any particular theoretical interest or importance. As in any other field, the important problem in linguistics is to discover a complex of data that differentiates between conflicting conceptions of linguistic structure in that one of these conflicting theories can describe these data only by *ad hoc* means whereas the other can explain it on the basis of some empirical assumption about the form of language. Such small-scale studies of explanatory adequacy have, in fact, provided most of the evidence that has any serious bearing on the nature of linguistic structure.' In making a comparative evaluation of Chomsky's model and the modified version proposed here we shall delimit such a complex of data. And although it is not suggested that Chomsky's model handles this complex in an *ad hoc* way, it is claimed that the modified version meets the requirements stated under (*a* to *d*) better than Chomsky's model.

1.4.4 Grammaticalness and deviance. As the second requirement for descriptive adequacy it was mentioned that a description of a language must be able to generate all and only the sentences of that language. In order to test whether a given description meets this requirement one must somehow know from some other source which strings of elements are (interpretable as) sentences of the language and which are not. The problem of deciding which strings are sentences and which are not is known as the problem of grammaticalness.[1]

---

[1] Some opponents of generative grammar maintain that the explicit formulation of the problem of grammaticalness means a step backward with regard to modern structuralism (e.g. Dixon (1963); see also Chomsky's reply in section 2 of *Topics* (1966*b*)). The introduction of a concept of 'correctness' would take linguistics back to the

Generally the native speakers of a language provide the necessary independent information as to the grammaticalness of given strings. In some cases one depends on a limited corpus of written texts, but usually, and preferably, one relies on one or more native speakers. One may raise questions as to the principles and techniques of eliciting judgements of grammaticalness from native speakers so as to get valid results. But I shall not dwell upon this problem here. The point at issue here is that, while questioning native speakers, one will also get only a limited corpus of material. If the description covers only this material, it is observationally adequate. But this form of adequacy is of very limited interest. The description, in order to be descriptively adequate, must cover the infinite set of all sentences that will be accepted as grammatical by native speakers, and only these sentences. That is, the grammar must project the limited corpus of observed sentences on to the whole language. Or, in other words, the grammar must predict the grammaticalness of sentences by asserting, implicitly, that all products generated by it will be accepted by native speakers as grammatical.

The problem of grammaticalness would end here, if the native speakers were able to give unambiguous answers about the grammaticalness of any arbitrary succession of elements. Unfortunately, however, this is not so.

Sometimes a string of elements is too long, or contains too many embeddings of strings that may themselves be sentences, for a speaker to grasp it in its entirety. One may say that, in a sense, such a string is unacceptable to a native speaker, it being structurally too complex, and one might be inclined to exclude such a string from the language. But this sort of unacceptability is not relevant for the grammarian, since he wants to find the system, or—if one wishes—to express the relevant generalizations, underlying those sentences which present no structural problems to the native speaker. There is no reason to suspect that this system ceases to be valid at any given sentence length or at any degree of complexity. Indeed, any upper limit to sentence length or com-

stage of normative grammar. Generative grammar would thus cease to be a descriptive science, and become a normative science, as before. For Dixon, 'whatever is, is right' (p. 79). If linguistics were to become a normative science, we would have to accept the consequence: there is nothing disreputable about that. But this is not even the case. In order to see this it is sufficient to understand the difference between a man prescribing rules of behaviour and setting norms for other people, who recognize his authority, and a man without such authority, who patiently tries to discover which norms are current in a society. In short, it is sufficient to distinguish between imposing norms and describing them.

plexity must be arbitrary. And if we say that the set of sentences of a language is infinite (which it is precisely because there is no upper limit to sentence length), we mean by this that 'for theoretic purposes, the utterances of a natural language may be thought of as constituting an infinite set' (Ziff (1964) p. 392).

From the point of view of grammaticalness, a speaker's hesitation or incapacity to give a judgement of grammaticalness on the grounds of length or complexity need not cause any difficulty. Having established systematic rules for unambiguous cases, and having tested these up to the limits of the native speaker's grasp, we say that the grammar is structurally correct: it generates the sentences which are still within the limits of the speaker's capacity to grasp and, moreover, an infinite set of sentences which are outside these limits. To judge the grammaticalness of the strings which lie beyond the speaker's capacity we will rely on the grammar itself, thus following Chomsky, who says ((1957) p. 14): 'In many intermediate cases we shall be prepared to let the grammar itself decide, when the grammar is set up in the simplest possible way so that it includes the clear sentences and excludes the clear non-sentences. This is a familiar feature of explication.'

Even here, however, the problem of grammaticalness does not end. For there are many cases where the native speakers are uncertain, although there is no question of excessive length or complexity. When asked if, for example,

(3)   the cigarette spoke two apples under the yellow hour

is grammatical in English, some speakers will give a positive answer, others will answer negatively, and still others will not know what to answer. On the whole, they will try to think up some, possibly far-fetched, context or situation, in which such a sentence would fit. And if they succeed in doing so, they will answer that it *could* be used, although with some difficulty.

Attempts have been made to develop a notion of degrees of grammaticalness[1] in order to cope with this problem. But they have not been

---

[1] Chomsky's attempt (1961) and (1964*b*) must be considered unsuccessful, since it depends upon a nesting system of categories at different levels of description. Rough syntactic categories may fit into such a system, but selection restriction classes are better described in terms of matrix-like cross-classifications. Quirk and Svartvik (1966) conducted a number of experiments to establish degrees of acceptability and of effort of reconstruction. Acceptability, however, is not the same as grammaticalness, and the process of reconstruction is linguistically not very significant (see below). They do not relate the degrees of acceptability to any specific model of grammar, nor do they claim that their results are final. Interesting though these results may be, they will not be given further attention here.

successful. One of the reasons is, probably, that if one wants to establish a system of degrees of grammaticalness, one must distinguish different scales of degrees, according to whether a sentence is structurally or semantically more or less well-formed. But instead of trying to establish, or of adopting, any such system here, we shall follow a different procedure. We shall assume that in submitting (3) to a native speaker with the purpose of eliciting a judgement of grammaticalness, we were not sufficiently specific, so that we really asked him the wrong question.

From a purely structural point of view (3) is faultless. Its 'fault' is rather semantic, in that it is difficult to imagine how it could possibly be used with good sense in any context or situation. Let us call such sentences semantically anomalous, or simply deviant. The deviance of (3) is due to the fact that not all nouns can, with good sense, be selected as a subject, or as an object, to any verb, or be combined with any preposition, etc. For a sentence having *speak* as its main verb to be semantically regular, an animate subject is required, and an object containing the semantic feature 'linguistic'. And the noun *hour* can be combined in a semantically regular way with a preposition of time and with an adjective containing, for instance, the semantic feature 'time', or 'degree of pleasure', but not, at any rate, 'colour'.

The concept of semantic anomaly, or deviance, thus implies that rules can be formulated for semantically regular collocations. Chomsky speaks of rules of selectional restrictions. These rules are intended to establish the semantic characteristics of sentences which contain only lexical items in their 'literal' or 'proper' sense. Apart from Chomsky's proposal ((1965) pp. 75–106) there is hardly any literature (Matthews (1965)) on how to formulate exactly rules of selectional restrictions. Such rules are nevertheless of great importance in a linguistic description, since they give a formal specification of what is generally recognized as 'proper usage'. They are a necessary prerequisite to any precise delimitation of stylistic figures such as metaphor and metonymy.

We want to draw the distinction between grammaticalness and un-grammaticalness in such a way that semantic anomaly does not make a sentence ungrammatical in the sense that it would not belong to the language. Such a decision would lead to the somewhat undesirable consequence of excluding most literature and many sentences used in daily life from the language. Deviant sentences are taken to constitute a proper subset of the set of grammatical sentences. The deviant and non-deviant sentences together thus form the set of grammatical sentences.

This is essentially the distinction drawn by Bazell (1962) and Ziff (1964). Ziff speaks of syntactically non-deviant and syntactically deviant utterances, both constituting together the set of grammatical utterances. His syntactically deviant utterances correspond to what are called here semantically anomalous or deviant sentences. Although the anomaly of deviant sentences is due to the co-occurrence of certain incompatible elements and can thus be regarded as syntactic, it seems better to avoid the term 'syntactic' here, because the incompatibility of co-occurrence is due to semantic reasons, and because the rules ensuring the non-deviant co-occurrence of elements may be looked upon as providing a partial semantic analysis of lexical meanings (see 5.4).

The point of view adopted here is, again, that the set of grammatical sentences can be considered to consist of two mutually exclusive subsets of semantically non-deviant and deviant sentences, all of which have a meaning (although it often seems difficult to make the meaning of deviant sentences fit a possible context or situation), and that no structurally defective, or ungrammatical, string has a meaning. In the following a justification of this position will be given on what are mainly *a priori* and speculative grounds, and it will be defended against Katz, who advocates a different classification. It must be understood, however, that the ultimate justification of this principle does not lie in these speculative considerations, but rather in the degree of success and the number of relevant results that can be obtained on the basis of it. The justification given here is merely intended to show that the principle is not completely arbitrary and that there are good reasons for its being adopted as a basis for research.

Katz (1964a) classifies deviant sentences as ungrammatical. But he asserts that nonetheless an account must be given of them by relating them to one or more grammatical sentences (in his sense of grammaticalness). Amongst what he calls ungrammatical sentences he distinguishes 'two exclusive and jointly exhaustive proper subsets: the set SS of semisentences and the set NS of nonsense strings' (p. 402). His way, however, of delimiting SS and NS is inconsistent. It appears that SS must be taken to coincide with our set of deviant sentences.

Nonsense strings he defines as those ungrammatical strings which are not understood by native speakers, that is, which are incomprehensible. Semi-sentences are those ungrammatical strings which can nevertheless be understood (p. 400), provided that they are 'comprehensible to each speaker according only to his linguistic abilities' (p. 415). That is, he

2

excludes ungrammatical strings which are understood by virtue of one's skill in 'performance with intelligence', rather than one's 'purely linguistic skill' (p. 415). Thus he excludes from SS, for example:

(4)   the a man a that a I a saw a is a here a

or

(5)   find nation the nationalize hidden national sentence nationally

One reason for excluding these from SS is that the discovery of the 'hidden sentence' depends largely on individual skill of intelligence of some sort, whereas he justifiably states that 'a necessary condition for something to be part of the subject matter of a linguistic theory is that each speaker be able to perform in that regard as much as every other does' (p. 415).

Thus for Katz SS includes some but not all deviant sentences, and also structurally ill-formed strings, such as:

(6)   scientists truth the universe
(7)   the chair who annoyed me found here
(8)   the ball hit by the man
(9)   ten dollars was cost by the book
(10) man bit dog

He excludes from SS deviant sentences which he says are incomprehensible, such as:

(11)   the beef cut sincerity

There seem to be some inconsistencies here, however. First, it is hard to maintain that the strings (6–9) are understood by virtue of only the speaker's (or listener's) 'purely linguistic skill'. Clearly, some amount of syntactic reconstruction is involved, which will be more or less easy to perform according to the degree of ill-formedness and the listener's skill in reconstructing defective strings. The strings (8) and (9) are relatively easy to reconstruct for any native speaker of English, although different reconstructions are possible. But the strings (6) and (7) are more problematic and their reconstruction is, in fact, more ambiguous. Katz claims that (6) is understood as 'scientists study the universe', or 'scientists discover facts about the universe' (pp. 401–2). But one may as well reconstruct (6) as:

(12)   scientists make the universe a true universe

or perhaps as:

(13)   scientists test the universe.

Or one may be unable to reconstruct it at all.

He also claims that (7) means 'the chair annoyed me, and someone found the chair here' (p. 406), this being, presumably, the underlying structure of:

(14) the chair which annoyed me was found here

But this is to some degree arbitrary, since one may very well reconstruct (7) as:

(15)   I found the annoying chair here

or, again, be unable to reconstruct it at all.

Generally one may state the principle that structurally ill-formed strings need reconstruction in order to be understood, and that a listener fails to understand when a given string is too difficult for him to reconstruct. The activity of reconstruction is certainly not a 'purely linguistic skill'. It rather resembles the riddle-solving needed for (4) and (5). Accordingly, there is not sufficient uniformity in performance with regard to these strings to take their being 'understood' as a relevant fact for a linguistic theory. They should, therefore, be excluded from SS on the same grounds as (4) and (5).

Sentence (10) presents a different case. One may maintain that it is immediately understood (in the linguistic sense of 'understanding'), although it is structurally defective according to the rules of an adequate grammar of English. That is, it does not, apparently, need any reconstruction requiring skill in solving puzzles. As it seems, in fact, it is perfectly well-formed according to a grammar 'derived' from the grammar of English, namely the grammar of newspaper headlines.[1] Speakers of English usually know the language of headlines and understand (10) as a sentence of this language. Although the relation of 'derived' languages, such as are found in headlines or telegrams, to the 'mother'-language are by no means clear, enough is known to exclude sentences of such languages from general statements about ungram-

---

[1] See Straumann (1935). The language of headlines and telegrams is, in some sense, parasitic upon the normal language, and can be derived from it by means of transformations involving deletion and reordering of elements. These transformations will necessarily lead to highly ambiguous strings in the derived language.

maticalness. We know, for example, that the most likely 'full' English sentence corresponding to (10) is:

(16)   a man bit a dog

and not, as Katz has it (p. 411), to a set of sentences:

(17)   *i*   the man bit the dog
       ii   a man bit a dog
       iii   the man bit some dog
       iv   some man bit a dog
              etc.

(Katz holds that the sentences of (17) are paraphrases of each other, which would account for the unambiguousness of (10). This is untenable, however, since it disregards the semantic difference between the definite and the indefinite article, which are clearly distinguished from both a syntactic and a semantic point of view, as will be shown in chapter 4, when the category of operators is introduced. If (10) is unambiguous, this must be due to a grammar of headlines assigning it the 'full' form of (16).)

The conclusion must be, therefore, that if SS is to be a set of strings which are understood on the basis of a purely linguistic skill (i.e. without any problem-solving), then all structurally ill-formed strings must be excluded from it. (Strings are referred to here at type level: they are not taken as ill-formed utterance-tokens in actual speech, about which below.) This makes SS a proper subset of the set of deviant sentences, such as (11), which Katz wants to exclude from SS on the ground of their alleged incomprehensibility or meaninglessness.

Here we hit upon a second inconsistency. On p. 401 we read: 'it is the aim of grammar construction to discover what a speaker knows about grammatical structure that enables him to understand utterances in his language'. This implies that the grammatical structure of a sentence is at least in part responsible for the meaning of this sentence. This point is hardly debatable. But the rules in the grammar which determine the structural well-formedness of sentences have precisely *not* been broken in the generation of (11). The deviance of (11) is due to a violation or non-observance of selection restriction rules, which do not determine grammatical structure. The grammatical structure of (11) is, in fact, impeccable. Therefore, (11) must have at least as much meaning as is conveyed by its grammatical structure. That is, it must have at least as much meaning as Ogden and Richards' famous 'the gostak distims the doshes'.[1] But it has more meaning than just this, because it has meaningful lexical items in proper functional positions: *the beef* is the subject, *cut* is the finite verbal form, *sincerity* is the object.

There can be no doubt that (11) has some meaning, although we may be unable, given the present state of our knowledge (see 4.1 and 5.4), to describe it. In view, however, of the absence of any sufficiently developed semantic descriptive language, we must not be astonished when our highly *ad hoc* means for semantic description prove inadequate for more difficult cases. It seems, therefore, that in a linguistic theory claiming to account also for the meaning of sentences, (11) should not be treated on a par with nonsense strings.[2]

What, then, does Katz mean when he says that (11) is 'quite incomprehensible to speakers of English' (p. 406)? And what does he mean in general when he speaks of the understanding or the comprehension of sentences? To answer the former question first, for Katz to be right in asserting that (11) is incomprehensible,—and there is some point in it—, he must mean that he cannot think up a situation in which it could

---

[1] Ogden and Richards (1923) p. 46.

[2] The meaningfulness of deviant sentences appears also from the fact that they are false if they are not negative, and true if they are denied. Truth and falsity are properties of information. If there is information, there must be meaning and form carrying it. Therefore, if anything is said to be true or false, it must have a meaning. Drange (1966) discusses this aspect of deviant sentences at length. He quotes (p. 19) Ewing ((1937) p. 360) and Prior ((1954) pp. 159–60), who show how negative deviant sentences can be derived logically. The falsity of their positive counterparts then follows automatically. Again, it is not clear how anything that can be derived logically as being true could possibly be meaningless. Although Drange accepts the falsity of deviant sentences and the truth of their denials, he comes to the somewhat curious conclusion that positive deviant sentences are both false and meaningless, but that their denials are true and meaningful (p. 23). He believes, apparently, that there is a sentence *s* such that *s* is meaningless in 'it is true that *s*', but meaningful in 'it is not true that *s*': 'Thus, a sentence could be meaningless even though its negation is not meaningless' (p. 23). He also seems to believe that meaningless includes analytically false. While discussing Pap (1960), he says: 'Pap's definition [of meaningless as neither true nor false] is a poor one, because when philosophers assert that false sentences are not meaningless, they invariably have in mind *empirically* false sentences. Therefore, a better definition of "meaningless" would be "neither true nor empirically false". By this definition a sentence could be meaningless even though its negation is not meaningless. And type crossings [i.e. positive deviant sentences] would be meaningless, since they are neither true nor empirically false' (p. 23). This restriction to 'empirically false', however, can only be qualified as highly arbitrary. It seems to have been introduced only for the sake of saving the predicate 'meaningless' for positive deviant sentences. What is gained by this procedure is not clear, whereas it is easily seen that it must lead to some very disturbing and undesirable consequences in any theory of meaning.

possibly be used with good sense. If he means that it carries no information at all, he is surely wrong, because it carries the, doubtless absurd, information that the beef cut sincerity, so that, if one wishes, sincerity was cut by the beef. He must refer, therefore, to the comprehension involved in the actual speech process, or, as Chomsky put it, in performance.

But if we take this to be the comprehension, or understanding, underlying Katz's definition of semi-sentences, we run into difficulties. For then the set SS should include also all grammatically ill-formed utterance-tokens so often found in actual speech (false starts, half-finished sentences, interjections, etc.) and understood, or comprehended, without any effort of reconstruction, i.e. on the sole basis of the listener's speech-comprehension skill. But the understanding of grammatically defective utterance-tokens depends largely on the specific context or situation in which they occur. In a different context, or out of context, they may be incomprehensible. A theory of semi-sentences would therefore have to account for all different possible contexts or situations, which is clearly far beyond our reach at present, and also far from Katz's own intention. He does not discuss this problem, however. He only says (p. 415, note 23), without further explanation, that ill-formed but (apparently in some context) intelligible strings occurring in actual speech are 'not fruitfully taken as semi-sentences', which must imply that he intends 'understanding' to be the understanding of the information conveyed by a string regardless of any specific speech-situation. The indiscriminate use of the same set of terms, viz. 'understanding', 'comprehend', for two distinct concepts is a third inconsistency found in Katz's paper.

This paper has been discussed at some length, because some important conclusions emerge from it. Katz's set of semi-sentences, consisting of what he calls ungrammatical strings which are nevertheless understandable on the basis of a purely linguistic competence, seems to coincide with the set of structurally well-formed but semantically anomalous sentences. If we correlate this linguistic understanding to meaning, by saying that a sentence is understood linguistically if and only if it has a meaning, we may further assert that non-deviant and deviant sentences are all meaningful, although our still *ad hoc* means of semantic description may not always be sufficient to describe exactly what meaning a sentence has.

Structurally ill-formed strings are strictly speaking meaningless. They may sometimes be related to, or converted into, sets of one or more structurally well-formed strings (non-deviant or deviant), which are substituted for them. The well-formed strings are all meaningful, and the original ill-formed strings are thus sometimes replaced by meaningful well-formed strings in the process of understanding. If such a reconstruction, or substitution, takes place, the process of understanding is no longer a purely linguistic process.

As the ability to reconstruct defective strings (i.e. to replace them by well-formed strings) is not a purely linguistic ability and varies a great deal according to the individual, it is not really an interesting linguistic problem to find out how structurally ill-formed strings can be related to well-formed sentences, or where reconstructibility ends. (One would not deny that this problem may well be interesting and relevant from other points of view, such as the stylistic characterization of ungrammatical poetry.) The important point is that an ill-formed string can only be understood if it has been related to and replaced by a well-formed sentence. And the meaning correlated with this understanding is the meaning of a well-formed sentence. The linguist may, therefore, justifiably turn away from ill-formed strings, and concentrate upon the set of meaningful, well-formed, sentences, which is divided into two subsets, consisting of the non-deviant and the deviant sentences. There is little point in calling only the non-deviant sentences grammatical, and letting the term 'ungrammatical' cover both the deviant and the structurally ill-formed strings. We shall rather follow Ziff, and call the sentences in which the linguist is interested, i.e. the structurally well-formed and meaningful sentences, grammatical, and the uninteresting structurally ill-formed strings ungrammatical.

We can now give more substance to the second requirement of descriptive adequacy (1.4.3), which says that a grammar should generate all strings corresponding to sentences of a language and only these. Equating these strings with grammatical strings, we require from the grammar that it generate all and only the grammatical strings. If the grammar is adequate in this respect, it will never generate a structurally ill-formed, and therefore meaningless, string. It will generate all non-deviant and all deviant strings. But how are we to delimit the set of all deviant sentences? Or, more specifically, how are we to establish a formal relationship between the set of non-deviant and the set of deviant sentences?

Ziff and Katz are both concerned with establishing formal relation-

ships between deviant and ungrammatical strings on the one hand, and
the set of non-deviant sentences on the other. We have seen that the
relations of ungrammatical strings to their possible reconstructed
grammatical relata (which are the relations on which Katz largely con-
centrates) are not interesting from a grammatical point of view, so that
we may disregard them. But the deviant sentences do interest the
linguist, and he wishes to give a description of them. The problem of
determining the relationship of deviant to non-deviant sentences, i.e., of
specifying formally how deviant sentences deviate from non-deviant
sentences, is therefore important and remains to be solved. It is on this
problem that Ziff mainly focuses his attention, although he intends his
suggestion to be valid also for ungrammatical strings.

In order to relate a deviant sentence, such as:

(18)   he expressed a green thought

to the set of non-deviant sentences, or, equivalently, to the grammar of
non-deviant sentences, he invokes a rule, which would make (18) non-
deviant if it were a rule of the grammar (p. 395): 'Let E_i be the class of
elements that can occur without syntactic deviation in the environment
"he expressed a...thought": then we can relate the utterance to the
regular grammar by invoking the rule $E_i \rightarrow green$.' (In order to relate
structurally ill-formed strings to the grammar, he invokes rules of a
transformational character, bringing about inversions, deletions, permu-
tations, additions, as if they were part of the grammar.)

We see now, however, that we can relate deviant sentences to the
grammar in a much more natural and less laborious way. We construct
the grammar in such a way that it contains a distinct set of selection
restriction rules ensuring the proper collocation of specific lexical items
in specific functional positions. If a grammar observes these rules, it will
generate all and only the non-deviant sentences. We stipulate, however,
that it must be possible for the grammar to ignore these rules without
the process of generation being blocked or leading to ungrammatical
strings. If the grammar ignores these rules, it will generate both the
non-deviant and the deviant sentences, i.e. all and only the grammatical
sentences. We thus establish a formal relationship between deviant and
non-deviant sentences by imposing a condition on the form of grammars,
rather than by invoking spurious rules.

In addition, therefore, to the second requirement of descriptive
adequacy, namely that the grammar should generate all and only the

grammatical sentences of a language, we posit the further requirement that it should contain a distinct set of selection restriction rules which, when observed, lead to non-deviant sentences, and, when disregarded, to grammatical sentences.

Our point of departure has thus been defined and a justification has been given, as far as possible, on more or less *a priori* and speculative grounds. But its ultimate validity depends on the question whether it helps us to find a significant quantity of homogeneous and intuitively appealing results.

2 Chomsky's model of grammatical description

2.0 Introduction

Although it would be possible to refer the reader to Chomsky's own publications for a detailed account of his model of grammatical description, it is perhaps useful to sum it up in concise form here, especially since some important innovations were introduced as recently as in (1965). Moreover, his expositions in (1965) are not always easy to follow, particularly in the section devoted to selection restriction rules (pp. 75–106).

2.1 The base

The algorithmical device which was developed by Chomsky for his base grammar is called *phrase structure grammar* (PSG). A PSG generates strings of symbols. More precisely, the output of a PSG consists of a series of non-terminal strings, each series leading up to a terminal string, which consists exclusively of (base-) terminal symbols and is interpreted as a deep structure (with one proviso, formulated in (1965) pp. 138–9, about which more will be said in chapter 3). A *derivation* consists of an initial string, the non-terminal strings derived from it, and a terminal string. A derivation can be condensed to a *phrase marker* (P-marker) of a terminal string. Suppose, for example, we have a PSG containing the following rules:

(1) *i* $S \rightarrow NP + VP$
  ii $VP \rightarrow T + VP_1$
  iii $VP_1 \rightarrow V + NP$
  iv $NP \rightarrow A + N$
  v $A \rightarrow$ the
  vi $N \rightarrow \{man, dog\}$
  vii $T \rightarrow$ Past
  viii $V \rightarrow$ see

(The arrow → means: 'replace the symbol on the left-hand side by the symbol or string of symbols on the right-hand side'. The braces imply that any one, but not more than one, of the symbols enclosed may be chosen. The rules are not ordered, apart from the intrinsic order imposed on them by their applicability.)

This PSG permits, among a few others, the derivation:

(2) *i* S
   ii NP + VP   by rule *i* of (1)
  iii NP + T + VP$_1$ *ii*
  iv NP + T + V + NP   *iii*
   v A + N + T + V + NP   *iv*
  vi A + N + T + V + A + N   *iv*
 vii the + N + T + V + A + N   *v*
viii the + man + T + V + A + N   *vi*
  ix the + man + Past + V + A + N   *vii*
   x the + man + Past + see + A + N   *viii*
  xi the + man + Past + see + the + N   *v*
 xii the + man + Past + see + the + dog   *vi*

This derivation can be condensed to a phrase marker by the following general procedure:

(3) In order to obtain a P-marker, write down the initial string of the derivation. Then take its extreme left symbol (*a*) and check off through the following strings of the derivation whether and by which string *a'* of one or more symbols *a* has been rewritten. If *a'* can be determined uniquely, write down *a'* as the beginning of the second string of the P-marker. If *a'* cannot be determined uniquely, write down only the first symbol of *a'*. Now check the next right symbol (*b*) of the initial string, try to determine its replacing string *b'*. If *a'* has not been determined, it will be determined now, so that *a'* can be written down. If *b'* has been determined uniquely, write down *b'* to the right of *a'*. If not, write down only the first symbol of *b'*, and wait for the rest of *b'* until *b'* has been determined during the checking of *b*'s next right symbol in the initial string (*c*), which has been replaced by *c'*, and so forth, until all the symbols of the initial string have been checked off. Draw connecting lines between any symbol rewritten and the symbol(s) replacing it. Repeat with the now available second string

of the P-marker, so that a third string is written down, and so on, until there is no non-terminal symbol left in the derivation.

One notices that this procedure, which converts derivations into P-markers, is in itself an algorithmical procedure, the initial strings of which are provided by the derivations. Applying this procedure of condensation to (2) we obtain the set of strings:

(4) *i*   S
  ii   NP + VP
  iii   A + N + T + VP$_1$
  iv   the + man + Past + V + NP
  v   the + man + Past + see + A + N
  vi   the + man + Past + see + the + dog

which, with the connecting lines, results in the P-marker (a so-called *tree*):

(5)

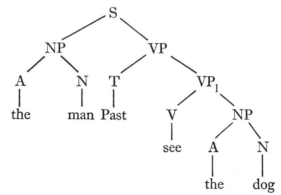

In order to ensure that the condensation algorithm reducing derivations to P-markers works without being blocked by insoluble ambiguities regarding the determination of the strings that have been rewritten for every non-terminal symbol, the rules of a PSG must comply with certain restrictions, which have been phrased most clearly by Bach (1964) pp. 35–6. Avoiding unnecessary technicalities we may sum up these restrictions as follows:

(*a*) Only one symbol may be written at a time. That is, even if there is a string of more than one symbol at the left side of the arrow, only one of these symbols may be rewritten by virtue of one rule.

(*b*) There must be no recursion of elements. That is, no symbol occurring on the left of an arrow, with the exception of the initial symbol *S*, may be rewritten in a string containing the same symbol.

(*c*) There must be no deletion of elements. That is, a symbol may never be rewritten into a zero-element.

(*d*) There must be no permutation of elements. That is, a series of one or more rules must never have the effect of reversing the order of elements in either an initial string or a derived string. Thus a PSG must not contain a rule like:

$$x+y \rightarrow y+x$$

Neither must it contain a series of rules like

$$x+y \rightarrow a+y$$
$$y \quad \rightarrow b$$
$$a \quad \rightarrow y$$
$$b \quad \rightarrow x$$

Rules which remain within the limits set by these restrictions are called *phrase structure rules* (PS-rules).

Thus, the output of a PSG consists of P-markers, each of which contains a terminal string. The P-markers reflect the linguist's analysis of their terminal strings. They are intended to be interpreted as the *structural descriptions* of their terminal strings. P-marker (5), for example, is meant to be interpreted in grammatical terms as follows:

(6)   In the string of terminal elements

the + man + Past + see + the + dog,

the article *the* plus the noun *man* form a noun phrase, followed by a verb phrase consisting of the tense affix *Past* followed by a derived verb phrase, which, in its turn, consists of the verb *see* followed by the noun phrase composed of the article *the* plus the noun *dog*.

In principle, the structural descriptions of a PSG are a formalization of *immediate constituent analysis,* as introduced by Bloomfield (1933) and further developed, among others, by Wells (1947) and Harris (1951). (For further comment, see 5.0.)

2.2   The transformations

The structural description expressed in a P-marker is required both for the semantic interpretation that will be attached to the corresponding terminal string by the semantic component and for the transformational subcomponent through which PSG-terminal strings must pass before receiving phonetic interpretation.

Grammatical transformations (T-rules) are also rewrite rules, but of a different character. Whereas PS-rules operate on single symbols, without being able to take into account any other symbols from which they may have been previously rewritten (their derivational history), T-rules operate on P-markers. That is, they map, or convert, basic P-markers into derived P-markers.

In order to explain the functioning of T-rules it is necessary to define the relation 'is dominated by', or 'is a'. This relation can be read immediately from P-markers. We say that a string or part of a string (terminal or non-terminal) is dominated by X, or is an X, if it has been expanded from X by one or more rewrite operations, or if it is X itself. Thus, in (5), *the man* is dominated by *NP* (is an *NP*), *Past see the dog* is a *VP*, *see the dog* is a VP_1, *the dog* is again an *NP*, A plus N is an *NP*, *NP* plus *VP* is an *S*, and the whole terminal string is an *S*.

A T-rule consists essentially of two parts, a *structural analysis* (SA) and a *structural change* (SC). The SA defines the domain of the T-rule, i.e. defines on which basic strings a specific T-rule may operate. It does so by giving just so much structural information, expressed in terms of underlying P-markers, as is essential for a specific domain to be delimited. The SC's specify what treatment an underlying basic string (within the domain defined by the SA) undergoes, thus determining the form of the resulting surface string. SC's may delete, replace, expand, add and permute elements (see Bach (1964) pp. 73–82).

Some examples will be useful here. Let us assume a PSG slightly more elaborate than (1):

(7)   *i*   S → (QU) Nucleus[1]
    ii   Nucleus → NP + PredP
    iii   PredP → T + VP
    iv   VP → V (NP) (Manner)
    v   NP → (A) N (S)
    vi   A → the
    vii   N → {dog, man}
    viii   T → {Pres, Past}
    ix   V → {see, frighten, bark}
    x   Manner → by + Passive

(The brackets indicate optional inclusion of the enclosed element or elements. *QU* stands for 'question', *PredP* for 'predicate phrase' and *Manner* for 'adverbial expression of manner'.)

---

[1] This first rule in the rewriting of *S* was introduced by Katz and Postal (1964) p. 103 in order to deal with questions.

The following P-marker may be generated by (7):

(8)

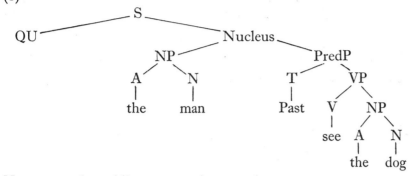

Now we need an obligatory question transformation:

(9) SA: QU $-$ NP $-$ T $-$ VP
     SC: $X_1 - X_2 - X_3 - X_4 \Rightarrow X_1 - X_3 - X_2 - X_4$

The SA of (9) defines the domain of this T-rule in the following way:

Any PSG-terminal string which, when being read from left to right, can be split up exhaustively into parts dominated by *QU*, *NP*, *T* and *VP* respectively, falls within the domain of T-rule (9).

It is seen that the terminal string of (8) does, in fact, belong to the domain of (9), for it can be split up exhaustively into *QU*, *the man* (*NP*), *Past* (*T*) and *see the dog* (*VP*). The SC numbers the elements of the SA from left to right, and has the effect of (double arrow) arranging them in a different order. The resulting derived string will thus be: *QU Past the man see the dog*, which will undergo further transformational treatment and phonetic interpretation, to become: (*question intonation*) *did the man see the dog*.

Or suppose the following P-marker has been generated by (7):

(10)

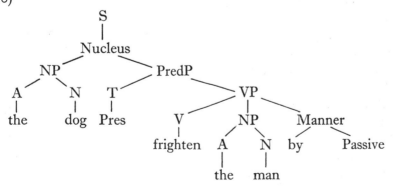

Then we want an obligatory passive transformation:

(11) SA: $NP - T - V - NP - by - Passive$
      SC: $X_1 - X_2 - X_3 - X_4 - X_5 - X_6 \Rightarrow$
$$X_4 - X_2 - be - en - X_3 - X_5 - X_1$$

converting the terminal string of (10) into: *the man Pres be en frighten by the dog*, which will become: *the man is frightened by the dog* in phonetic representation.

One notices that rule v of (7) contains the only recursive element that is allowed according to restriction (*b*) on PS-rules, namely the symbol S. In the latest version of Chomsky's transformational model the recursion, which is necessary for the generation of an infinite set of strings, is restricted to S. In (1965) p. 137, Chomsky says; 'Now the recursive property is a feature of the base component, in particular of the rules that introduce the initial symbol S in designated positions in strings of category symbols. There are, apparently, no other recursive rules in the base. The transformational component is solely interpretive.' And in (1966*a*) pp. 41–2, we read: 'We see, moreover, that, in the examples given, the recursive devices meet certain formal conditions that have no a priori necessity. In both the trivial cases (e.g. conjunction, disjunction, etc.) and the more interesting ones discussed in connection with relatives and infinitives, the only method for extending deep structures is by adding full propositions of a basic subject–predicate form. The transformational rules of deletion, rearrangement, etc., do not play a role in the creation of new structures.'

The restriction of recursion in language to a basic sentence type is emphasized and elaborated in Chomsky (1966*a*), where he shows that this same view was held by the grammarians of Port Royal. One cannot escape from the impression that Chomsky has here, once again, hit upon an essential feature of human language, although (as will be seen in chapter 5) recursion of the symbol S alone does not seem sufficient for all cases of embedded subject–predicate constructions, which can be full sentences, propositions or nuclei (see chapter 4).

Such a restriction also drastically simplifies grammatical descriptions in any sense of the term simplicity. The infinitely many sentences of a language can now be generated by a device which may reiterate an unlimited number of times the embedding of fundamentally similar and relatively simple basic structures. And as semantic analyses of sentences in any language invariably support this hypothesis, in that they reveal a relation of predication in all those parts of surface structures which we want to reduce to embedded basic sentences, its incorporation in a grammatical model means an important step forward towards semantic adequacy (see 1.4.3).

Making use of this recursion (7) may generate:

(12)

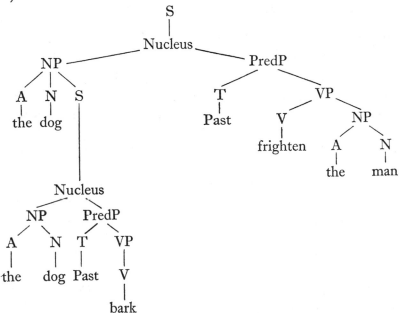

We may now follow two transformational paths. The first path leads to a surface structure containing a relative clause:

(13)   SA: $Y - A - N - NP - PredP - Z$
       SC: $X_1 - X_2 - X_3 - X_4 - X_5 \quad -X_6 \Rightarrow$
       $\qquad\qquad\qquad X_1 - X_2 - X_3 - wh - X_5 - X_6$

which yields: *the dog wh Past bark Past frighten the man*, underlying a phonetic representation of *the dog which barked frightened the man*. (*Y* and *Z* are variables for any structures, possibly null, preceding and following the structure affected by the transformation.)

The second path involves a number of T-rules:

(14) *i* SA: $Y - A - N - NP - T - V - Z$
         SC: $X_1 - X_2 - X_3 - X_4 - X_5 - X_6 - X_7 \Rightarrow$
         $\qquad\qquad\qquad X_1 - X_2 - X_3 - X_4 - X_6 - ing - X_7$

which converts *the dog the dog Past bark* into *the dog the dog barking*
(word boundaries are not accounted for here). Then we apply:

(14) *ii* SA: Y $-$A $-$N $-$S $-$Z
           SC: $X_1-X_2-X_3-X_4-X_5 \Rightarrow X_1-X_2-X_4-X_3-X_5$

Now the string *the dog the dog barking* has become: *the the dog barking
dog*. Next a deletion transformation is required:

(14) *iii* SA: A $-$NP$-$V $-$ing$-$N
            SC: $X_1-X_2 -X_3-X_4-X_5 \Rightarrow X_1-X_3-X_4-X_5$

giving us, finally: *the barking dog Past frighten the man.*

Needless to say, these T-rules are not meant to cover all analogous
cases in English. They have been simplified to fit these particular
examples, and are therefore very much *ad hoc*. They are meant only to
demonstrate in a simple and straightforward way the transformational
principle as worked out by Chomsky.

Since the semantic interpretation is required to operate on base-
terminal strings, the sentence that will ultimately be generated by the
grammar must not undergo, after the base stage, any treatment that
would affect its semantic content. That is, the transformations must not
add any new semantic element or take away any semantic element
connected with the terminal string of the base. This condition imposes
certain additional requirements on the base and certain limitations on
the transformations. If there is a risk of their affecting the meaning of
the base-terminal string, then there must be some symbol in the base-
terminal string, which entails the obligatory application of the pertinent
transformation in the transformational subcomponent. Semantic elements which would otherwise be introduced by optional transformations
are now attached to transformational markers in the base-terminal
strings. These markers put into action the same, now obligatory, transformations. There will, presumably, still be optional transformations
for the generation of semantically equivalent but stylistically different
sentences.

The rôle of optional transformations, however, is still problematic. It
is not clear, especially, how optional stylistic differences of order are to
be accounted for adequately. Chomsky writes ((1965) pp. 126–7): 'It
should be emphasized that grammatical transformations do not seem to
be an appropriate device for expressing the full range of possibilities for
stylistic inversion. It seems, rather, that there are several underlying

generalizations that determine when such reordering is permissible, and what its semantic functions are. For one thing, richly inflected languages tolerate stylistic reordering much more extensively than languages that are poor in inflection, for obvious reasons. Second, even richly inflected languages do not seem to tolerate reordering when it leads to ambiguity... If this is universal, it suggests the generalization that in any language, stylistic inversion of "major constituents" (in some sense to be defined) is tolerated up to ambiguity—that is, up to the point where a structure is produced that might have been generated independently by the grammatical rules...Something of this sort seems to be true, and it is not statable in terms of the theory of transformations.'

A further limitation on transformations is that elements may only be deleted if no semantic information is lost. This is the requirement of recoverability. It is particularly crucial in cases of deletion of lexical items. The base must provide for the possibility of selecting lexical 'dummy' items, as in the case of object deletion: 'he eats (something) ⇒ he eats'. Or else, deletion of a lexical entry is only permitted if the same lexical entry occurs in the terminal string in some other position defined for each particular deletion, as in the case of (14) *iii*.

One notices that a proper functioning of the transformations presupposes the selection of lexical items in the base grammar. This means that all problems connected with selectional restrictions of individual items with regard to each other in the same sentence must have been solved in the base, i.e. before transformational treatment.

2.3 Selection restriction rules

The problem of describing selectional restrictions was not tackled by Chomsky before (1965) pp. 75–127. There he proposes a method of introducing rules for the description of these restrictions. It must be understood, however, that he does not present this method as a definitive answer to all problems connected with them. He rather suggests lines along which a solution may possibly be arrived at and does not conceal the remaining difficulties. The pages he devotes to the subject are perhaps best regarded as a report on research in progress, rather than as a final result. Unfortunately, however, he presents a text which is extremely difficult to read. An attempt will be made here, therefore, to give a short but adequate account of his suggestions, which will then be subjected to a more critical treatment in chapter 3.

As Chomsky points out on pp. 79–80, lexical subcategories cannot be adequately represented by branching rules of the type exemplified in (7). For, if we take the category of nouns as being divided into, for example, proper nouns and common nouns, and moreover find that the distinction *human/non-human* applies equally to both, any description in terms of PS-rules will involve an arbitrary priority to one of the two distinctions. We may set up rules like the following:

(15)   N → Proper
       N → Common
       Proper → Pr-Human
       Proper → Pr-nHuman
       Common → C-Human
       Common → C-nHuman

or, with equal justification:

(16)   N → Human
       N → nHuman
       Human → H-Proper
       Human → H-Common
       nHuman → nH-Proper
       nHuman → nH-Common

Moreover, there is no way of expressing in (15) that the distinction *human/non-human* applies equally to proper and common nouns, or in (16) that the distinction between *proper* and *common* applies equally to human and non-human nouns.

In order to avoid these inadequacies Chomsky introduces a system of matrices or cross-classifications. In drawing up this system he is largely led by a supposed formal analogy with phonological rules (pp. 81–2):

Each lexical formative is represented as a sequence of segments, each segment being a set of features. In other words, each lexical formative is represented by a *distinctive-feature matrix* in which the columns stand for successive segments, and the rows for particular features. An entry in the ith column and the jth row of such a matrix indicates how the ith segment is specified with respect to the jth feature. A particular entry may indicate that the segment in question is *unspecified* with respect to the feature in question, or that it is *positively specified* with respect to this feature, or that it is *negatively specified* with respect to this feature. We say that two segments are *distinct* just in case one is positively specified with respect to a feature with respect to which the other is negatively specified, and, more generally, that two matrices with the same number of columns are distinct if the ith segment of one is distinct in this sense from the ith segment of the other, for some i.

Suppose that

(17) $A \rightarrow Z/X\text{—}Y$

is a phonological rule, where A, Z, X, and Y are matrices, and A and Z are, furthermore, segments (matrices with just a single column). This is the typical form of a phonological rule. We shall say that the rule (17) is applicable to any string $WX'A'Y'V$, where X', A', Y' are matrices with the same number of columns as X, A, Y, respectively, and $X'A'Y'$ is not distinct from XAY (actually, qualifications are necessary that do not concern us here...). The rule (17) converts the string $WX'A'Y'V$ to the string $WX'Z'Y'V$, where Z' is the segment consisting of the feature specifications of Z together with all feature specifications of A' for features with respect to which Z is unspecified.

As an illustration of some of these notions, consider this phonological rule:

(18) $[+\text{continuant}] \rightarrow [+\text{voiced}]/\text{—}[+\text{voiced}]$

This will convert [sm] into [zm], [fd] into [vd], [šg] into [žg], etc., but it will not affect [st] or [pd], for example. These conventions (which can be simplified and generalized in ways that do not concern us here) allow us to apply rules to any class of segments specified by a given combination of features, and thus to make use of the cross-classification of segments provided by the feature representation.

(Throughout the present book the numbers of examples given in quotations are not those of the original text; quoted examples are numbered according to their order in the present text.)

Chomsky moreover introduces the notion of *complex symbol* (CS), 'each complex symbol being a set of specified syntactic features, just as each phonological segment is a set of specified phonological features' (p. 82). Complex symbols are enclosed by square brackets. A complex symbol being a set of syntactic features, any complex symbol consisting of more than one feature can be considered to contain several subsets, each of which is, in its turn, a complex symbol. The symbols of the base grammar representing lexical categories (N, V, etc.) are rewritten as complex symbols. There will also be a *lexicon* associated with the rules of the base grammar. The lexicon is

a set of *lexical entries*, each lexical entry being a pair (D, C), where D is a phonological distinctive feature matrix 'spelling' a certain lexical formative and C is a collection of specified syntactic features (a complex symbol). The system of rewriting rules will now generate derivations terminating with strings that consist of grammatical formatives and complex symbols. Such a string we call a *preterminal string*. A terminal string is formed from a preterminal string by insertion of a lexical formative in accordance with the following *lexical rule*:

> If Q is a complex symbol of a preterminal string and (D, C) is a lexical entry, where C is not distinct from Q, then Q can be replaced by D' (p. 84).

One notices that this lexical rule is not so much a rule as a rule schema: it is a cover formula for a large number of individual rules, each of which would apply to a particular complex symbol and a particular lexical item. Chomsky's remark ((1965) p. 112), that 'The lexical rule need not be stated in the grammar since it is universal and hence part of the theory of grammar', is true but incomplete.

The principle of rewriting matrix features and the application of the lexical rule are perhaps best demonstrated by an example. Chomsky gives a simple grammar on p. 85, where he leaves out, for the moment, the treatment of the verb, which will be taken care of later on:[1]

(19) $S \rightarrow NP + Aux + VP$
        $VP \rightarrow V + NP$
        $NP \rightarrow (Det) \, N$
        $Aux \rightarrow M$

(20)   *i* $N \rightarrow [+N, \pm Common]$
       ii $[+Common] \rightarrow [\pm Count]$
       iii $[+Count] \rightarrow [\pm Animate]$
       iv $[-Common] \rightarrow [\pm Animate]$
       v $[+Animate] \rightarrow [\pm Human]$
       vi $[-Count] \rightarrow [\pm Abstract]$
       vii $M \rightarrow [+M]$

(21)   (*sincerity*, $[+N, +Common, -Count, +Abstract]$)
        (*boy*, $[+N, +Common, +Count, +Animate, +Human]$)
        (*may*, $[+M]$)

The lexicon of this small grammar is represented by (21). 'It is to be understood, here and later on, that the italicized items stand for phonological distinctive feature matrices, that is "spellings" of formatives' (p. 85). Although Chomsky does not present the lexicon in the form of matrices consisting of actual columns and rows, there is no danger of misrepresentation if we do so. We may replace, therefore, (21) by the following matrix, adding some entries on the basis of p. 83.

---

[1] A misprint has been corrected and some necessary details added.

(22)

	sincerity	dog	boy	book	virtue	dirt	John	Fido	Egypt	may
M										+
N	+	+	+	+	+	+	+	+	+	
Common	+	+	+	+	+	+	−	−̥	−	
Count	−	+	+	+	−	−				
Animate		+	+	−			+	+	−	
Human		−	+				+	−		
Abstract	+				+	−				

This grammar can generate, for example, the preterminal string:

(23) $Det + [+N, +Common, -Count, +Abstract] + [+M]$
$+V + Det + [+N, +Common, +Count, +Animate, +Human]$

It can now be seen that the first complex symbol is not distinct from the column associated with *sincerity*, or with *virtue*, that the second complex symbol is not distinct from the column associated with *may*, and that the third CS is not distinct from the column associated with *boy*, so that the application of the lexical rule will yield:

(24) sincerity may V the boy

or:

(25) virtue may V the boy

(assuming that *Det* may be developed into the definite or the indefinite article, and that the indefinite article is deleted transformationally before non-count nouns; see 3.2.2.)

So far the grammar provides only a subcategorization of nouns and modal auxiliaries, and a subsequent rewriting into lexical formatives. No restrictions have been imposed, as yet, upon the selection of matrix features in CS's in view of other complex symbols occurring in the same string. Thus it is possible to generate a string like:

(26) $Det + [+N, -Common, +Animate, -Human] + [+M] + V$
$+ [+N, +Common, +Count, -Animate]$

leading to:

(27) the Fido may V book

which is ungrammatical, whatever item is selected for *V*. (We might assume that the definite article is deleted transformationally before proper names, but Chomsky does not seem to follow this course. Moreover, common nouns, like *book*, do require an article.) The analysis in matrix features and the introduction of CS's is intended to enable one to eliminate strings like (26) and to select a proper verb given the rest of the string. For such selections, which are necessarily subject to heavy contextual restrictions, there must be general conventions, stated in the theory of the grammar (as in the case of the lexical rule mentioned above), about the reading and application of rules. Moreover, contextual features must be added to the syntactic features already present in the CS's associated with each lexical item.

That is, apart from the syntactic features as exemplified in (21), the CS will also contain specifications of the form $+X—Z$, where X and Z stand for the contiguous context in which a particular entry may occur, and where X or Z, or both, may be null. Thus, for instance, *sincerity* now has the associated complex symbol (p. 107) $[+N, +Det—, -Count, +Abstract...]$ which specifies that it may occur only if preceded by a symbol dominated by *Det*. (This feature makes it no longer necessary to specify the feature $[+Common]$, which only means that the noun in question must be preceded by a determiner.) Or the verb *frighten* will now have an associated CS $[+V, +—NP, +[+Abstract]Aux—Det [+Animate], +Object-deletion...]$ (p. 107), specifying that this verb may only occur if followed by a string dominated by *NP* (i.e. it is transitive), and if preceded by a string containing the syntactic feature $[+Abstract]$ followed by an auxiliary verb (i.e. it must have an abstract subject) and followed by a determiner plus a string containing the syntactic feature $[+Animate]$ (i.e. its object must be animate). (Presumably, *Det* must be optional here, since we want to be able to generate, for example, *sincerity may frighten Fido*.) The feature $[+Object -deletion]$, furthermore, will put into action, in the transformational subcomponent, a transformation deleting the object if this contains a dummy symbol indicating that no particular lexical item has been selected,—for which provision must be made in the grammar. The presence of syntactic features in the context restriction features of the verb makes it necessary that the rewriting and subsequent selection of V take place after the selection of preceding and following parts of the string. Chomsky, in other words, chooses to select verbs in terms of nouns (p. 115), and not *vice versa*. He argues this point on pp. 113–15, and more will be said about this in 3.2.2.

The proper order of selection and the proper selection are to be ensured by two different kinds of subcategorization rule. We have, first, *strict subcategorization rules*, and, second, *selectional rules*. The strict subcategorization rules 'subcategorize a lexical category in terms of the frame of category symbols in which it appears' (p. 113), category symbols being the symbols introduced by the preceding PS-rules as exemplified in (7) *i*–(7) *v*. A strict subcategorization rule is of the form:

(28) $A \rightarrow CS^1$

which must be read and applied in the following way, according to instructions phrased in the grammatical theory: *A* stands for any symbol ready for rewriting through strict subcategorization rules, such as *N*, or *V*. *CS* stands for any partial matrix in the CS of a lexical entry of the form $[+A, +X—Z]$, where the contextual feature $[+X—Z]$ acts as a context restriction. Thus, for example:

(29) $N \rightarrow CS$

is expanded as:

(30) $N \rightarrow [+N, +Det—]$

if and only if the *N* in question is preceded by a string dominated by the category symbol *Det*. Or:

(31) $V \rightarrow CS$

is only carried out as:

(32) $V \rightarrow [+V, +—NP]$

if this *V* is followed by a noun-phrase. It is thus impossible to generate a noun-phrase like *the Fido*, since *Fido* will be associated in the lexicon with a CS $[+N, +—, ...]$. It is also certain that no intransitive verb will be selected in a sentence containing an object. The feature $[+—]$, which figures in Chomsky (1965) p. 107 rule (57) *xi* must be taken to mean that there is no context immediately dominated by the same node as dominates *N*. That is, there is no context under what will be called here the *local condition*.

The local condition is an additional general instruction given by Chomsky for the reading and application of rules of the type (28). The context restriction *X—Z* applies only to those strings *XAZ* which are

---

[1] On pp. 120–3 Chomsky suggests a possible way of eliminating the strict subcategorization rules, i.e. rules of the type (28), by incorporating the general conditions associated with them into the lexical rule. The branching rules would then generate preterminal strings consisting of occurrences of the dummy symbol and of grammatical formatives. The lexical rule would replace the dummy symbols by (phonological) lexical items according to the context restrictions expressed in each CS. As this modification implies no essential change in the total concept, and as it has not been worked out in detail, it will not be considered here.

dominated by the category symbol immediately dominating *A*, i.e., by the category symbol σ that appears on the left in the rule σ → ...A... that introduces *A* (p. 99). This further condition is necessary to avoid the action of context restrictions in cases where this is undesirable. It is, in fact, necessary if one adopts a base grammar containing the following rules:

(33) *i*   S → NP + Predicate-Phrase
    ii   Predicate-Phrase → Aux + VP (Place) (Time)
    iii VP → $\left\{ \begin{matrix} be + \text{Predicate} \\ V \left\{ \begin{matrix} \text{(NP) (Prep-Phrase) (Prep-Phrase) (Manner)} \\ \text{Adj} \\ S' \\ (like) \text{ Predicate-Nominal} \end{matrix} \right\} \end{matrix} \right\}$
    iv   Prep-Phrase → $\left\{ \begin{matrix} \text{Direction} \\ \text{Duration} \\ \text{Place} \\ \text{Frequency} \\ \text{etc.} \end{matrix} \right\}$
    v   V → CS   (Chomsky (1965) p. 102)

with a lexicon containing such entries as:

(34) (*dash*, [+V, +—Direction, ...])
    (*last*, [+V, +—Duration, ...])
    (*remain*, [+V, +—Place, ...])
    (*laugh*, [+V, +—, ...])
    (*sleep*, [+V, +—, ...])

From (33) we can generate a P-marker:

(35)

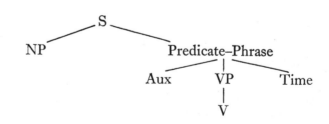

But for the local condition, rule (33) *v* would not allow for the selection of, for example, *sleep*, because it is followed by *Time*. The local condition, however, confines the context restriction for *sleep* to the string dominated by *VP*, so that, in fact, *sleep* may be selected, which is a necessary condition for the generation of such sentences as:

(36)   John slept three hours

On the other hand, (35) excludes the selection of, for example, *last*, although:

(37)   the ceremony lasted three hours

is a perfectly grammatical English sentence. But the element *three hours* in (37) is better considered as part of the verb phrase. It can be derived from:

(38)

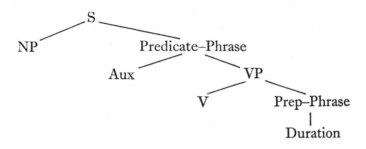

which can also be generated from (33). Here (33) *v* allows for the selection of *last*; the context restriction imposed by the feature [+—Duration] in the CS of *last* in (34) is fulfilled, since both *V* and *Duration* are dominated by the same symbol *VP*. In this case there is a 'stronger' cohesion between the verb and the adverbial phrase than in (35).

Chomsky gives a number of good reasons for distinguishing between degrees of 'cohesion' between the verb and the accompanying adverbial phrase (pp. 101–6). 'The point can be illustrated clearly by such ambiguous constructions as:

(39)   he decided on the boat

which may mean "he chose the boat" or "he made his decision on the boat". Both kinds of phrase appear in:

(40)   he decided on the boat on the train

that is, "he chose the boat while on the train"' (p. 101). In fact, this difference in cohesion, expressed in (33) *ii* and (33) *iii*, accounts for homonymous sentences like:

(41)   John lived in England

which is interpretable as either 'John resided in England', with a prepositional phrase introduced by rule (33) *iii*, or roughly as 'in England, John really lived' or 'in England, John remained alive', with a place adverbial introduced by (33) *ii* and thus part of the predicate phrase. (Cf. 'John will surely die on the Continent, but he may live in England' —Chomsky (1965) note 27, pp. 217–18.) A grammatical description that distinguishes between these two sorts of adverbial phrase will thus have a higher degree of semantic adequacy (see 1.4.3, 4.1).

One notices that the general instructions regarding strict subcategorization rules of the type (28), especially the definitions of the context restrictions and the local condition, imply information about the constituent structure of the strings generated by the PS-branching rules. Strict subcategorization rules can only be applied if it is known which symbols dominate which partial strings. These rules involve a certain amount of structural analysis expressed in the P-marker and are, therefore, to be regarded as transformational at least from the formal point of view. Chomsky calls attention to this fact and gives a justification for it on pp. 88–90, and 98–9. Nothing more essential seems to be involved here than the simple admission that, apparently, PS-rules alone are not sufficient for a description of deep structure. The distinction between the base and the transformational subcomponent does not rest primarily on a formal difference between the two types of rule: there are independent grounds for such a distinction (see 4.1 and 5.0).

Apart from the strict subcategorization rules Chomsky has *selectional rules*, which apply after them, and 'subcategorize a lexical category in terms of syntactic features that appear in specified positions in the sentence' (p. 113). A selectional rule is of the form:

(42) $[+V] \rightarrow CS/\alpha + Aux - (Det + \beta)$, where α is an N and β is an N.

which must be read as follows:

> The syntactic feature $[+V]$ (developed by the rewriting of V) confers a new contextual feature on the CS of which $[+V]$ is a part. This contextual feature consists itself of a CS, namely the preceding context $\alpha + Aux$— and the following context $-Det + \beta$ (if any), where α and β are both dominated by N.

That is, the CS's developed by rewriting the N of the subject and the N of the object are incorporated in their entirety into the CS into which V is developed. 'The rules abbreviated by the schemata (42) assert, simply, that each feature of the preceding and following Noun is assigned to the

Verb and determines an appropriate selectional subclassification of it' (p. 97). If we have generated, for instance, a string:

(43)   Det + [+ N, + Det—, − Count, + Abstract] + Aux
$\qquad$ + [+ V, + —NP] + Det + [+ N, + Det—, + Count,
$\qquad\qquad\qquad\qquad\qquad\qquad\qquad\qquad$ + Animate, + Human]

then the selectional rule (42) permits us to carry over as a contextual feature into the CS[+ V, + —NP] the whole subcategory specification of the preceding and following noun plus *Aux* and *Det*. Instead of [+ V, + —NP] we thus write:

(44)   [+ V, + —NP, + [+ N, + Det—, − Count, + Abstract]
$\qquad$ + Aux—Det + [+ N, + Det—, + Count, + Animate, + Human]]

Let us call this new contextual feature by the general name of *matrix contextual feature*, since it defines context in terms of matrix features and not in terms of category symbols as was the case with the contextual features introduced by strict subcategorization rules. Matrix contextual features act as a context restriction for the selection of the verb. This selection presumably takes place according to the following procedure (Chomsky is not explicit on this point):

> We go through the lexicon and look for a lexical entry (V, C)—where *V* is a phonological 'spelling' of a verb and *C* an associated CS—such that *C* is not distinct from (44) as far as the syntactic and (non-matrix) contextual features are concerned, and such that the CS's incorporated in the matrix contextual features of *C* are not distinct from the CS's in corresponding positions in (44). Having found such an entry, we replace (44) by *V*.

Suppose that we have a lexicon containing the entry:

(45)   (*frighten*, [+ V, + —NP, + [+ Abstract] + Aux—Det
$\qquad\qquad\qquad\qquad\qquad\qquad\qquad\qquad$ + [+ Animate], ...])

then we see that the CS of (45) is not distinct from (44) as far as the syntactic and contextual features are concerned: both have [+ V] and [+ —NP]. We see furthermore that the matrix contextual feature of (45) is not distinct from that in (44) in corresponding positions. We may, therefore, select *frighten* as a verb in this sentence. Application of the lexical rule to the two nouns and the auxiliary of (43) according to the lexicon (22)—where *Common* is replaced by *Det*— —will finally yield:

(46)   sincerity may frighten the boy

as the final form of (24).

The base subcomponent of a Chomskian generative grammar is thus seen to consist of a number of PS-rules (branching rules), which are probably context-free, strict subcategorization rules, some of which are context-sensitive, and selectional rules, which are context-sensitive. Application of the base rules takes place in this order. The terminal strings resulting from application of the base rules are ready for semantic interpretation in the semantic component and for transformational treatment in the transformational subcomponent described earlier. The strings produced by the transformational subcomponent enter into the phonological component for phonetic interpretation.

3 *Criticisms of Chomsky's model*

3.0 Introduction

In this chapter it will be shown that Chomsky's model, although very valuable and probably the best that is available, does not meet the requirements of descriptive adequacy in a satisfactory way. In pointing out the weaknesses of Chomsky's model we shall deal in turn with the four aspects of descriptive adequacy outlined in 1.4.3, viz. explicitness, grammaticalness and deviance, simplicity, and semantic adequacy.

3.1 Standards of explicitness

It is required of a grammar that it should be as explicit as possible. That is, it must specify exactly which strings it can generate and which it cannot, and it must also unambiguously assign a structural description to the strings which it generates. In the latter respect Chomsky's model shows a deficiency, which has already been pointed out by Bach ((1964) pp. 79–81). As Chomsky has not so far given an answer to this problem, the question is raised here again. The point at issue is that Chomsky's model does not give sufficient information about the structure to be assigned to transforms, i.e. about derived constituent structure.

Transformations are defined as operations, converting deep structures into surface structures, or underlying P-markers into derived P-markers. As Katz and Postal put it ((1964) p. 10): 'Given a particular P-marker, bracketed in a certain way in terms of a structure index, there must be a unique output P-marker, given the application of a particular elementary transformation. Thus each type of elementary transformation must have associated with it a particular condition stating how it affects P-markers to produce new P-markers. These principles of *derived constituent structure* must be stated in the general theory of linguistic descriptions. They are the analogue in the transformational part of the syntax of the algorithm which permits the construction of underlying P-markers from phrase structure rule derivations.'

It appears, however, that the effect of transformations upon underlying P-markers is not clearly specified, and that in most cases the derived P-marker does not follow from the underlying P-marker plus a given transformation.

Bach gives several examples. On p. 79 he gives the following (simplified) P-marker:

(1)

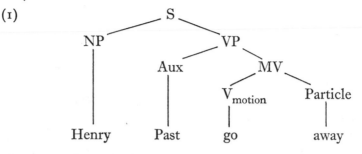

plus a transformation:

(2) SA: $NP - Aux - V_{motion} - Particle$
     SC: $X_1 - X_2 - X_3 \quad -X_4 \Rightarrow X_4 - X_2 - X_3 - X_1$

yielding a series of diagram nodes:

(3) $Particle - Aux - V_{motion} - NP$

The general theory (grammatical metalanguage) states that not only the nodes are affected by transformations, but also whatever is dominated by them, so that we have, in fact, a succession of nodes plus their downward extensions:

(4) $Particle - Aux - V_{motion} \quad - NP$
      | | | |
     away   Past   go   Henry

But neither the transformation itself nor the general theory explains how these nodes are to be connected in an upward direction so as to form a complete derived P-marker. Bach suggests two alternatives:

(5) *i*   or   (5) *ii*

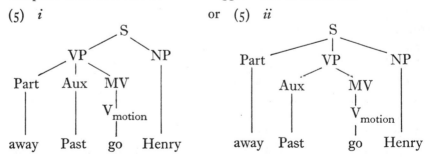

to which a third possibility may be added (if we allow for discontinuous
constituents in surface structures):

(5) *iii*

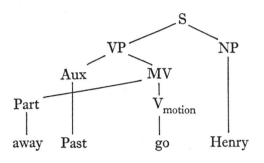

Another example is provided by the passive transformation. If we let
transformation (11) of 2.2 operate on the underlying P-marker (10), the
result is, strictly speaking:

(6)

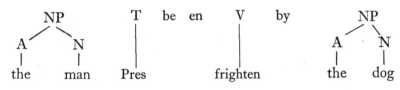

We lack any precise information as to the underlying structure of (6). It
could be:

(7) *i*

or (7) *ii*

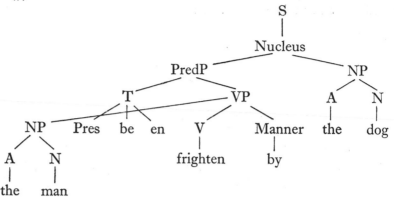

or even, perhaps, some other structure.

This lack of information about derived and constituent structure leads to difficulties when we want a succession of transformations to apply. Suppose that (10) of 2.2 is generated from an embedded *S* in an *NP*, as in:

(8)   the man (the dog Pres frighten the man by Passive) runs away

According to Chomsky ((1965) pp. 128–31), the passive transformation must be applied first, giving (6) for the bracketed part of (8). Now we want to apply the relative transformation (13) of 2.2, in order to generate

(9)   the man, who is frightened by the dog, runs away

But as we have not sufficient information as to whether or in what way the derived P-marker (6) contains a *PredP*, this relative transformation is strictly speaking not applicable.

In general terms this means that if a number of transformations are to be applied consecutively, the process is in danger of being blocked through lack of sufficient information about the derived constituent structure.[1]

---

[1] It must be noted that a possible answer to this difficulty is found in Hockett (1966) pp. 194–5. Here Hockett proposes a different formulation of transformational rules. He does not give a structural analysis and a structural change, but sums up the whole relevant structure in bracketed strings. Thus, the passive transformation (cf. (11) of 2.2) could be formulated as follows:

S(NP$_1$, PredP(T, VP(V, NP$_2$, Manner(by, Passive)))) $\Rightarrow$
      S(NP$_2$, PredP(T(δ, be, en), VP(V, Manner(by, NP$_1$))))

where *a(b, c)* stands for '*a* dominates *b* and *c*', and δ stands for any string dominated by the immediately dominating symbol *T* in the underlying P-marker (e.g. *Pres* or

3.2 Standards of grammaticalness and deviance

It follows from 1.4.4 that the second requirement, descriptive adequacy, incorporates two distinct but closely related requirements: the grammar must distinguish grammatical from ungrammatical strings, and within the set of grammatical strings must distinguish between deviant and non-deviant sentences. Let us consider these two requirements separately.

3.2.1 Grammaticalness: parasitic growth of deep structures.

There is no doubt that Chomsky's model enables a linguist to draw up a grammar which separates clearly and unambiguously grammatical from ungrammatical strings. It does so, however, in a rather roundabout way: a Chomskian base grammar is allowed to generate a vast number of structures which will never be developed into surface structures because they are not well-formed. The transformational part acts as a 'filter', so that only certain basic structures reach the status of surface structures. Although the grammar as a whole delivers only grammatical sentences, the majority of the products generated by the base are not grammatical at the level of deep structure. The base does not separate grammatical deep structures from ungrammatical ones. Chomsky himself draws attention to this difficulty ((1965) pp. 137–41), but it may be argued that his answer is unsatisfactory.

A base grammar may generate a string like:

(10)   the dog (the dog Past be angry) Past frighten the man

but also, for example:

(11)   the dog (the man Past be angry) Past frighten the man

which cannot be further developed into a surface structure, since any transformation incorporating the bracketed clause into (11) requires that the remaining and the deleted element should be identical,—a condition arising from the general requirement of recoverability of deleted elements. As there is no way of dictating the grammar to select

Past). In this way the whole relevant P-marker is transformed, and there seems to be no ambiguity as to derived constituent structure.

An attempt is made by Koutsoudas ((1966) pp. 27–35) to establish conventions for derived P-markers. Although this is a step forward, there are still too many deficiencies and inconsistencies in his proposals for them to be a satisfactory answer to the problem.

the lexical item *dog* as the subject of the embedded sentence, we cannot prevent the base from generating strings like (11).

A matter of principle is involved here. We can consider two ways of characterizing the sentences of a language. One can either allow structures to shoot up freely within the most general limits set for structures and use grammatical rules as calibres, or filters, rejecting the structures that do not fit. Or one can predetermine the growth of structures in such a way that only such structures will be generated as can end up as well-formed sentences. Chomsky's grammar is essentially of the latter type. Deviant collocations, intransitive verbs with objects, etc., could be sorted out and rejected by filter-rules, but they are not: the subcategorization rules aim at ensuring the survival of the structures generated. This type of competence description would seem psychologically more plausible in that it would be more easily relatable to an account of the production and understanding of sentences. It is not clear why one should resort to filter-rules in order to eliminate structures such as (11).

There seems to be some lack of specification in the function of the rules here. It must be possible, in principle, to overcome this difficulty by adding further refinements to the base, more specifically, by restricting somehow the applicability of the base rules for embeddings. How this can be done is not a simple matter: the answer to this problem may require some drastic modifications in the base grammar. But the matter seems worth investigating. It will be shown below that the addition of such restrictions to a Chomskian base leads to unacceptably complicated procedures. It will also become clear that, if such restrictions are not added to the base grammar, a certain kind of regularity in language remains essentially beyond the grasp of description. Quite generally, the inability of a system of description to come to terms in a satisfactory way with these difficulties may be taken as an indication that this system has not reached the highest possible degree of simplicity. In chapter 5 some possible improvements on this state of affairs, will be suggested but it does not seem that a decisive answer can be provided as yet.

Chomsky's answer to this difficulty is as follows ((1965) pp. 138–9):

Putting aside questions of formalization, we can see that not all generalized Phrase-markers generated by the base will underlie actual sentences and thus qualify as deep structures. What, then, is the test that determines whether a generalized Phrase-marker is the deep structure of some sentence? The answer is very simple. The transformational rules provide exactly such a test, and there is, in general, no simpler test... A deep structure is a generalized

Phrase-marker underlying some well-formed surface structure. Thus the basic notion defined by a transformational grammar is: *deep structure* M_D *underlies well-formed surface structure* M_S. The notion 'deep structure' itself is derivative from this. The transformational rules act as a 'filter' that permits only certain generalized Phrase-markers to qualify as deep structures.[1]

If we take it that the 'filter' of the transformations is necessary for base products to qualify as deep structures, we are faced with some complications. Not only must we accept that it is no longer appropriate to speak of the base as generating deep structures (since most of its products will not pass the transformational test), it also follows that most base products are not susceptible of semantic interpretation. Katz and Postal say ((1964) p. 47): 'it is obviously necessary to provide one single interpretation for the sentence as a whole.' It is clearly impossible to provide one single interpretation for, for example, (11). One must, therefore, accept the conclusion that a semantic interpretation can only be imposed after the transformations have been operative, but that it is still imposed on the structure as it was before transformational treatment.

Both the generation of an overwhelming proportion of parasitic base structures, and the delay in the application of the semantic component, make one wonder whether 'this is precisely what we want' (Chomsky (1965) p. 138). At any rate, a Chomskian base will generate much more than a set of semantically interpretable deep structures. Only with the help of the transformations can one make sure that a string generated by the base is, in fact, well-formed and semantically interpretable.

---

[1] In Hockett's terms ((1966) p. 260) the assignment of a filtering function to the transformations amounts to saying that they form an output-monitored conversion grammar. A conversion grammar is essentially a mapping of a set of inputs on to a set of outputs. More precisely, a conversion grammar G consists of a set of inputs C, each $c \in C$ being a network (roughly, an ordered set of nodes) over a finite input alphabet A, a set of outputs L, each $l \in L$ being a network over a finite output alphabet B, and a mapping g of C on to L such that for each $l \in L$ there is a finite set of $c \in C$ such that g(c) = 1. G is input-monitored if C is given in advance. G is output-monitored if the determination of C depends on the computability of each if $c \in C$ by G. That is, if a given network s over A can only be said to belong to C if there is an l such that g(s) = 1, then G is output-monitored. We may take the transformational part of a grammar to be G, the transformational rules to be g, the set of deep structures C, the set of surface structures L. In Chomsky's model C is not determined in advance: in order to make sure whether a given network (deep structure) over the input alphabet belongs to C we must know whether the computation g leads to an actual output in L. Although Hockett does not say that he intends his distinction to be applied in this way, it is interesting to see that it can. We can now say that, for reasons of descriptive adequacy, we want the transformational part to be input-monitored.

One may consider the possibility of eliminating this difficulty by devising subcategorization rules in the base which permit the extension of conditions of context-restriction of lexical selection beyond a single S into the embedding clause. But even then the problem would not be solved. For we should also need context restrictions extending over several embeddings, as appears from, for example:

(12)   I saw the game you wanted to make him lose

which has three embedded clauses. Its deep structure can be summed up as follows:

(13) S_0
       |
       I saw the game S_1
                      |
                      you wanted S_2
                                 |
                                 you make S_3
                                          |
                                          he loses the game

Here lexical identity is required for *game* in S_0 and S_3.

Moreover, several negative conditions must be met for embedded clauses. Thus, for example, none of the embedded clauses of (13) must contain the element QU, which transforms it into a question. S_3 must not contain the constituent *by + Passive*, which transforms it into a passive sentence. S_2 and S_3 are not allowed to contain a constituent *Aux* dominating a modal auxiliary verb (*may*, *must*).

Subcategorization rules of the Chomskian type, however, would be, if possible at all, very complicated, *ad hoc* and non-predictive for bases such as (13). One is naturally led to think that a simpler and more revealing solution would consist in a formula determining the choice to be made by the grammar during the generative process. Such a formula would have to be generated along with the deep structure and would, ideally and among other things, stipulate for the embedded relative clause S_1 of (13) the following instructions:

(14)   *a*   that it contain a noun phrase with *game* as the noun,
or   *b*   that it contain an embedded object-clause, which is subject
             to the same instructions (*a*) and (*b*).

S_1 is then seen to satisfy instruction (*b*), S_2 is likewise seen to satisfy (*b*), and S_3 satisfies instruction (*a*).

If it proves possible to develop an algorithm which, from the P-marker of the noun phrase *the game S* of (13), generates a formula, to be connected with S, and ensuring the rewriting development of S according to the instructions stated in (14), then that formula will embody a recursive rule of some kind, let us say a selection instruction rule, determining the well-formedness not only of (13), but also, for instance, of:

(15) S_0
     |
  I saw the game S_1
        |
       you wanted S_2
           |
          you make S_3
             |
            I think S_4
               |
              he lost the game

corresponding to the sentence:

(16)   I saw the game you wanted to make me think he lost

Let us see now whether a Chomskian base allows for the generation of choice-determining formulae. In order to simplify the question, we may restrict ourselves, for the moment, to formulae giving instructions of the type (14*a*) for the development of an embedded clause, leaving aside the recursive instructions as found in (14*b*). We shall then see that it is possible to generate from Chomskian P-markers formulae giving non-recursive instructions for the development of embedded clauses, although slight adjustments of the model will then be necessary. But at the same time this generation involves an unduly complicated apparatus which calls for simplification.

Let us try to construct a formula F giving instruction (14*a*) for the development of S_1 of (13). F would have to specify which rules of the base may be used in rewriting this S and which are excluded. Suppose the base has a rule:

(17) $NP \rightarrow \begin{Bmatrix} (Det) \ N \ (S) \\ (Det) \ S \end{Bmatrix}$

which, without the consolidating notation of braces and brackets, is resolved into:

(18)   *i* $NP \rightarrow Det + N$
    ii $NP \rightarrow N$

   iii NP → Det + N + S
   iv NP → N + S
    v NP → Det + S
   vi NP → S

Suppose also that the base has the following set of strict subcategorization rules (cf. Chomsky (1965) p. 85):

(19)   *i* N → $\left\{ \begin{array}{l} [+\text{N}, +\text{Det}\!-\!] \\ [+\text{N}, +\!-\!] \end{array} \right\}$
    ii [+Det—] → [±Count]
   iii [+Count] → [±Animate]
    iv [+—] → [±Animate]
    v [+Animate] → [±Human]
   vi [−Count] → [±Abstract]

(which can be resolved into twelve different rules), and the lexicon (22) of 2.3, but enlarged with the entry:

(20) (*game*, [+N, +Det—, +Count, −Animate])

The noun phrase *the game S* of (13) has been generated by application of the rules (18) *iii* and, subsequently:

(21)   *i* N → [+N, +Det—]
    ii [+Det—] → [+Count]
   iii [+Count] → [−Animate]

which are contained in (19). The application of (21) results in a CS:

(22) [+N, +Det—, +Count, −Animate]

which is not distinct from the CS in (20), so that the lexical rule may replace (22) by *game*. The relevant part of the P-marker of *the game S* can be represented as follows:

(23)

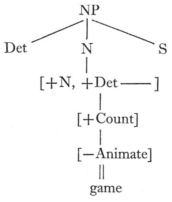

(where the square brackets contain the elements used in building up the matrix (22), and the double derivation line indicates the operation of the lexical rule.)

F must specify the set of all rules permitting a development of S under instruction (14*a*), and F must be constructed on the basis of the partial P-marker (23). The set of rules which led to the partial P-marker (23) is:

(24) {(18) *iii*, (21) *i*, (21) *ii*, (21) *iii*, Lexical Rule}

But the strict subcategorization rules (21) *i* – (21) *iii* are irrelevant for the construction of F, since we are not interested in subcategorization features, but in the selection of *game*, with the exclusion of all other lexical items: not even a synonym of *game* would do. On the other hand, the mention of *Lexical Rule* is not sufficiently specific: it must be specified so as to lead directly from N to *game* and to be applicable only to *game*. Let us call the lexical rule thus specified 'LR(*game*)'. We see now that F must contain at least the rules:

(25) {(18) *iii*, LR(*game*)}

Yet (25) is not sufficient, since (18) *iii* in it would entail the obligatory generation of a new embedded S, whereas we want to be able to generate also NP's without a new S. It is not necessary to generate the S of (23) again. On the other hand, we need the constituent *Det* for the transition from N to *game* to be grammatically correct. F must contain, therefore, all PS-rules of the form:

(26) $NP \rightarrow Det + N + Y$ (where Y is a string of null, one, or more category symbols)

There are two rules satisfying this condition, namely (18) *i* and (18) *iii*. Thus we see that we must construct:

(27) $F = \{(18)\ i,\ (18)\ iii,\ LR(game)\}$

How can this be done? More generally, how can we construct an algorithm A, based on partial P-markers dominated by NP, and leading to an F such that F ensures the generation of a new NP containing the same lexical item as has been selected in the original NP? One might expect A to instruct us to read upwards from bottom to top through the original P-marker and to go directly from the lexical item at the bottom (i.e. *game* in (23)) to the dominating category symbol (N), bypassing the intermediate square-bracketed feature symbols. But this would not do, since in the highest square-bracketed feature symbol a context restriction is stated which is necessary for the determination of those PS-rules that may be used to generate the new *NP*. That is, in our case we need the feature $[+\text{Det}\!-\!]$ generated by (21) *i*, in order to establish that only those PS-rules may be used that yield *Det* immediately on the left of the noun, viz. (18) *i* and (18) *iii*. *A* will instruct us, therefore, to bypass all square-bracketed feature symbols but the last one, which is immediately dominated by a category symbol, and it will begin the generation of *F* (as yet empty) by putting into it 'LR(*x*)', where *x* stands for the lexical item concerned. Reading upwards from the highest feature symbol [a] to the category symbol *N* immediately dominating it, we infer that the grammar must have a rule N → [a]. We check the grammar, find this rule, and retain it for the further construction of *F*. In the case of (23) this means that we infer that the grammar must have a rule

$$\text{N} \rightarrow [+\text{N}, \ +\text{Det}\!-\!];$$

we find this in the grammar under (21) *i*, and retain it. The rule N → [a] contains a context restriction, which will tell us how to select those PS-rules that yield strings conforming to this restriction. If the context restriction is, for instance, $[+\text{Det}\!-\!]$, we check the grammar on all rules of the form:

(28)   X → Det + N + Y (where *X* is a category symbol, and *Y* as in (26))

(The local condition on (28) of 2.3 excludes the possibility of a context restriction connected with a category symbol other than the one, *X*, from which *N* is immediately rewritten.)

For (23) this gives us the rules (18) *i* and (18) *iii*. We add these rules to *F*. When we have worked our way up through the original P-marker as far as the category symbol *NP*, to which instruction (14*a*) applies (as we have now for (23)), we have finished the construction of *F*. Applying this procedure to (23) we see that *F* contains precisely those rules specified in (27). We still must specify in *F* that it applies to only one *NP* in *S*, no matter which. But for the purpose of the present discussion, we can disregard this further complication, assuming simply that such a specification can be devised for *F*.

One notices that for *A* to work we need information as to the underlying P-marker, which makes *A* exceed the strict limits of base rules. But as the local condition and the selection rules have already done the same, we can disregard this difficulty here: Chomsky seems to intend these strict limitations to apply only to part of the base.

We must now associate F with S of (23). This can be done in the following way. We modify (18) *iii* as follows:

(29) $NP \rightarrow Det + N + S : F$

where $S : F$ is read as: '$S : F$ puts algorithm A into action, and S is subject to the instruction rule F generated by A.'

Thus we can accept that it is, in principle, possible to generate an F imposing instruction (14*a*) on the development of S in (23). Although (14*b*) does not interest us directly in the present discussion, we may assume that it is possible to let A work in such a way that F may alternatively be developed into {(18) *vi*}, with the extra specifications that (18) *vi* apply only to the object of the newly generated embedded S, and that the second embedded S generated by application of (18) *vi* carry with it the instruction applying to the S dominating it. That is, instructions are to be hereditary.[1]

It will have become clear by now that in order to overcome the difficulty of parasitic growth of deep structures in Chomsky's model of grammar, one needs a fairly elaborate apparatus, which has only been sketched in outline above. Viewing the problem in a wider perspective, however, we see that the complication of this apparatus is largely due to the fact that the selection of the individual lexical items takes place at the very end of the base development. The selection of an individual noun thus depends on the environment created by the previous development of the noun phrase. Generally speaking, the formulation of instruction rules such as (14) in a formalized grammar would be considerably simpler if the individual nouns were selected at an earlier stage, so that the noun phrase would be developed after the selection of the noun, and the presence of, say, *Det* would depend on the noun selected instead of *vice versa*. It would then be possible to incorporate (14) into the grammar by simply instructing the grammar to select a particular given noun, and the grammar would then automatically provide a suitably developed noun phrase. In 3.2.2 this possibility will be discussed again and further arguments will be advanced in support of such a solution. In chapter 5 a solution of this kind is proposed and worked out in some detail. It is

---

[1] Chomsky said once in a private communication that this problem could not be solved. The construction of F outlined above shows that there is, perhaps, a possible way of solving it in terms of his model, and also that an attempt to solve it brings to light a grammatical regularity which otherwise remains unnoticed.

clear, at any rate, that the realization of such a principle in a Chomskian base grammar would have far-reaching consequences and, in fact, necessitate considerable modifications in the model.

3.2.2 Deviance: no clear distinction between deviant and non-deviant sentences.

In 1.4.4 it was stated as a requirement that a grammar should contain a distinct set of rules to ensure proper selections in such a way that the grammar will still generate all and only grammatical (=structurally well-formed) sentences even when these rules are disregarded. Observance of these rules will then lead to non-deviant sentences, whereas neglect of some or all of these rules will lead to sentences which are grammatical but which may be either deviant or non-deviant.

In Chomsky's model of the base the function of the selection restriction rules is fulfilled by the subcategorization rules (i.e. the strict subcategorization rules and the selectional rules—see Chomsky (1965) p. 120). The question is, therefore, whether a Chomskian base can generate all and only deep structures leading to grammatical sentences (supposing that the difficulty of parasitic growth has been met), when the subcategorization rules are neglected.

Suppose we have the rules (17) to (19) with the corresponding lexicon. Elimination of the subcategorization rules here means elimination of (19). An additional rule is now required permitting a direct path from N to the lexicon. The lexical rule could be modified for this purpose so as to become:

(30)   If Q is a category symbol, and (D, C) is a lexical entry where C is not distinct from $[+Q]$, then Q can be replaced by D.

The grammatical metalanguage could now specify that the grammar follows either rule (30) or a rule of the type (28) of 2.3, in which case it enters the subcategorization rules and finally arrives at the lexical rule as formulated in Chomsky (1965) p. 84.

We now have a direct rewriting of, for example, N into *game*. But, just as in 3.2.1, we must now also accept that there is no means of avoiding the generation of a noun phrase containing *game* without a determiner, which is ungrammatical. In order to avoid ungrammaticalness in the case of noun phrases we must leave at least one subcategorization rule intact, viz. (19) i, which puts a contextual restriction on the selection of the noun.

For the direct selection of the verb, i.e. without the intervention of the subcategorization rules, the situation is very much the same with respect to transitive and intransitive verbs. Rule (30) would allow an intransitive verb to be selected when followed by a noun phrase, which is clearly ungrammatical. At least one subcategorization rule is required in order to establish the necessary context, viz. a rule:

(31)　$V \rightarrow [+V, +\text{—NP}]$

for transitive verbs, and a rule:

(32)　$V \rightarrow [+V, +\text{—}]$

for intransitive verbs. This means, generally, that the strict subcategorization rules of the type (28) of 2.3 must be preserved for the generated products to be grammatical.

Thus one could propose the distinction of two sets of rules in the grammar:

a　the categorial PS-rules plus the strict subcategorization rules of the type $A \rightarrow CS$;
b　the remaining subcategorization rules.

One could now state that elimination of (*b*) would lead to the set of all and only grammatical sentences, and provide an appropriate lexical rule as an optional alternative to Chomsky's lexical rule:

(33)　If Q is a complex symbol immediately rewritten from a category symbol, and (D, C) is a lexical entry where C is not distinct from Q, then Q can be replaced by D.

The CS's of the lexical entries would thus be disregarded except for the first two features, which establish the 'rough' category (noun, verb, adjective, etc.) of the entry and the context required for its being selected.

This would leave a fairly regular picture, if there were no further complications. As it is, however, the remainder of the CS of a lexical entry cannot be totally disregarded without the grammar leading either to ungrammatical sentences or to the exclusion of grammatical sentences. Some further features of the CS must still be generated by the grammar if it is to generate all and only the grammatical sentences.

In 2.3 ((24) and (25)) it was seen that the feature [− Count] provided the necessary information for the transformational part to delete obligatorily the indefinite article. Hence the indefinite article cannot be deleted if the feature [−Count] does not appear in the P-marker (i.e. has not been generated),[1] and the transformational part will deliver sentences containing either a phrase like [*–Definite*] *sincerity*, which is unfinished, or *a sincerity*, which runs the risk of being ungrammatical.

Grammatical sentences are excluded when the feature (+Object −deletion] occurs in the CS of a verb, as is the case with *frighten* (Chomsky (1965) p. 107):

(34)   (*frighten*, [+V, +—NP, +[+Abstract]+Aux—Det
                                  +[+Animate], +Object−deletion, ...])

This feature contains the information for the transformational part to allow for an optional deletion of the object of some verbs, such as *eat*, *drink*, etc. Dispensing with subcategorization rules means that this feature is not generated, so that there will be some verbs which cannot occur without an object, although such an occurrence is perfectly regular.

We must assume, furthermore, that the feature [+—S], or [+—that S], will occur in the CS of some verbs and nouns in the lexicon, indicating the occurrence of an embedded object-clause, sometimes preceded by *that*. Chomsky touches upon this in (1965) p. 94. In some cases this occurrence is optional, in others it is obligatory. For verbs this difficulty need not be more serious than the transitive–intransitive distinction. We may adopt rule (33) *iii* of 2.3 in the base. Thus, for example, for the verb *explain*, which is followed by a noun phrase or by an embedded object-clause, we might give the double lexical entry:

(35)   (*explain*, {[+V, +—NP, ...]}
                          {[+V, +—S, ...] })

so that the rule V → [+V, +—S] (of the type (28) of 2.3) would prevent an inappropriate verb from being selected in the context '—S'.

For nouns the problem of embedded object-clauses is more serious. Here their occurrence is always optional, and they cannot be made part of a context generated before the application of (33). There is no way of avoiding the occurrence of [+—S], or [+—that S] further down in the

---

[1] See Chomsky (1965) p. 107: 'Adding the rules that realize Definite as *the* and non-Definite as null before a following non-Count Noun, we derive the sentence "sincerity may frighten the boy".'

CS so as to bring it to the position of the contextual features. Thus we must have a CS of the sort:

(36)   [+ N, + Det—, ... +—that S, ...]

for nouns as *story, rumour, opinion*, etc. The subcategorization rules must contain a rule:

(37)   [X] → [±—that S] (where X is a matrix feature preceded by a positive or negative specification)

Elimination of the subcategorization rules would lead to the generation of noun phrases containing object-clauses irrespective of the preceding noun.[1]

It seems clear that in Chomsky's subcategorization rules the rules ensuring syntactic well-formedness and those ensuring proper selection of lexical items are not kept sufficiently apart. Consequently, it is not possible to draw a clear and general line through the rules of the base so as to set apart the rules for non-deviance from the other rules in the base.

In Chomsky's system the selection of the individual lexical items takes place at the end of the base development, and is made dependent at the same time on immediate context already generated and on selection restriction features such as *Count, Animate*, etc. Clearly, however, the regularities of proper selection of lexical items are quite independent of the regularities of immediate context restrictions. That is, the fact that *believe* must have an animate subject is quite separate from the question whether or not this subject must be preceded by a determiner. For we have both *John believes* and *the Englishman believes*. This suggests that the two sorts of regularities should be dealt with by two different sets of rules.

Furthermore, there is not only the absence of a connection between regularities of non-deviant selection and regularities of immediate context restrictions (which help to secure the grammaticalness but not the non-deviance of the phrase in which they occur). There is also, within

---

[1] Prof. J. F. Staal calls my attention to the fact that a possible solution would consist in introducing items such as *explanation* (*that*...) only after a nominalization transformation has been applied to deep structures containing the verb *explain* (*that*...). Although this seems to be a very natural procedure, it would raise other problems, such as the introduction of some lexical items after certain transformations, which would, anyhow, imply a considerable modification of the model presented by Chomsky. Quite outside the present context, however, the suggestion of introducing specific lexical items during or after the transformational treatment, leaving to the base only the specification of lexical semantic features, is well worth considering. This would, among other things, make the base more universal.

the regularities of non-deviant selection, a dependency relation between the proper selection of the nouns and the verbs. The proper selection of a noun does not depend so much on the presence or absence of a determiner as on the verb to which it is subject, object, or with which it is otherwise connected, or else on the preposition, if it occurs in a prepositional phrase. Limiting ourselves to the verbs, we can say that the main verb of a sentence states the conditions for the selection of the nouns in the subject and the object. On the other hand, it is the noun in a noun phrase which determines whether there must be, or may be, a determiner or not. It seems advisable, therefore, to let the grammar first select a particular verb, then particular nouns for subject, object, etc. depending on the verb, and let it subsequently develop appropriate noun phrases in terms of the chosen noun. As far as nouns and noun phrases are concerned, this is exactly the suggestion which emerged from 3.2.1.

As for the order of selection of the verbal and nominal parts, two approaches are possible: either verb selection is dependent on the selection of the nouns (if any) in subject, object, etc., or the latter are selected according to the restrictions stated by the verb. The former course is taken by Chomsky. He lets his grammar select freely, but with corresponding sets of selection restriction features, a subject-noun, an object-noun (which may be null) and one or more (or possibly null) prepositions each followed by a noun. Then the grammar selects a verb which tallies with the previously selected nouns and/or prepositions followed by nouns. This system has at least two disadvantages. For one thing, one incurs the risk of not finding any verb satisfying the requirements imposed by the already selected items. For another, the selection of the verb does not depend, in this system, only on the sets of selection restriction features associated with each selected item, but also on the presence or absence of, for example, an object-noun, so that the selection of the verb depends at least in part on features of syntactic structure. This is exactly what we want to avoid, because this will make it impossible to set apart and disregard a distinct set of selection restriction rules so as to be able to generate deviant, but not ungrammatical, strings as well. P. H. Matthews ((1967) p. 131) mentions the same point.

Chomsky's motivation for this procedure is given on pp. 113–15. His conclusion is (p. 115): 'In short, the decision to choose the complex symbol analysis of Verbs independently and to select Nouns by a selectional rule in terms of Verbs leads to a quite considerable complication of the grammar. The problems are magnified when we bring into account the independent Noun-Adjective selectional rules. In much the same way we can rule out the possibility of allowing Subject to select Verb but Verb to select Object.' His argument is based on the following considerations. The CS associated with a verb does not have any selection restriction features of its own, but contains matrix contextual features for the selection of subject, object, etc. Thus a verb may have the associated CS:

(38) $[+V, +\text{—NP}, +[\text{Abstract}]+\text{Aux—Det}+[+\text{Animate}], \ldots]^1$

(cf. (45) of 2.3)

Suppose we let the grammar generate (38) by means of a number of context-free subcategorization rules. We would then need selectional rules for the choice of the subject and object, such as:

(39) $[+N] \rightarrow CS/ \begin{Bmatrix} \text{—Aux}+\alpha \\ \alpha+\text{Det—} \end{Bmatrix}$ (where α is a V)

This would carry over into the CS of both the subject-noun and the object-noun the whole CS (38) of the verb, so that the subject-noun would contain also information which is only relevant to the object, and *vice versa*. Application of (39) to the subject would lead to a double 'embedding' of matrix features:

(40) $[+N, +\text{Det—}, +\text{—Aux}+[+V, +\text{—NP},$
$+[+\text{Abstract}]+\text{Aux—Det}+[+\text{Animate}], \ldots]]$

which would require a lexicon entry such as:

(41) $(sincerity, [+N, +\text{Det—},$
$+\text{—Aux}+[+V, +[+\text{Abstract}]+\text{Aux—}], \ldots])$

And as *sincerity* must also be allowed to figure as the object in some sentences, the entry would have to be expanded for a possible object-position, in which the feature $[+\text{Abstract}]$ would also have to occur in a double embedding indicating its object-position with respect to the verb. All this would, obviously, complicate the grammar enormously and, among other things, conceal the fact that a noun is abstract, animate, etc. by itself, and not by virtue of its occurrence in the position of object, subject, etc.

---

[1]   I do not adopt here Chomsky's abbreviated notation involving the symbols *Subject* and *Object*. The full Chomskian notation illustrates his point rather more clearly.

This argument, however, does not say anything about the question whether context-free selection of the verb and subsequent selection of the subject-noun and object-noun in terms of the chosen verb is preferable or not for reasons of descriptive adequacy. It only shows that prior selection of the verb does not fit into Chomsky's model of the base, so that it says more about this model than about independent prior verb-selection. But even so, it does not say much about the model of the base either, because it hinges on the reading given to the selectional rules of the type (39), or (42) in 2.3. By adapting this reading slightly one can easily avoid the obviously absurd consequences shown in (40) and (41). One can, for instance, read (39) as follows: The syntactic feature $[+N]$ (developed by the rewriting of N) assigns a new feature to the CS of which $[+N]$ is a part, namely that feature in α (which is dominated by V) which is found in the context indicated. In this way, application of (39) to the subject of the sentence *sincerity may frighten the boy* would yield:

(42) $[+N, +Det—, +Abstract]$

and application to the object would give:

(43) $[+N, +Det—, +Animate]$

so that all problems would be solved. This system would, in fact, be more economical than the one worked out by Chomsky, because the grammar would now no longer have to contain rules of the type (19) generating CS's for nouns with a large number of features irrelevant to the ultimate selection of the verb. Chomsky's procedure is, in fact, counter-productive, in that, on the one hand, it appears from the form in which verbs are specified in the lexicon that it is the verb that determines the selection of certain nouns in various positions in the sentence, whereas, on the other, the nouns are selected first. This point will be mentioned again in 3.3.2.

Thus it remains true that, quite generally, prior context-free selection of the main verb permits the grammar to avoid the introduction of features of syntactic structure in the selection restriction rules. Such prior selection of the verb is, therefore, preferable from the point of view of descriptive adequacy.

From 3.2.1 and from the present section it follows that we need in the base component of a grammar selection restriction rules which

a   can be put aside and replaced by an instruction to select a *particular* lexical item (so as to avoid the parasitic growth of deep structures);

b   can be put aside and replaced by an instruction to select an *arbitrary* lexical item within certain 'rough' categories such as *noun, verb, adjective*, etc. (implicitly defined in the grammar), without, however, permitting the grammar to generate ungrammatical strings; or

c   can be observed, thus leading to the set of all and only non-deviant grammatical sentences.

We need, therefore, a clear distinction between rules which assign structure and those which select items. Furthermore, it follows from the present section that with regard to the rules which select items it is preferable to let the verb be selected first and without context restrictions, and to let the selection of the remaining lexical items depend on the verb chosen.

3.3   Standards of simplicity

It appears on various grounds that Chomsky's model of the base does not achieve the highest possible degree of simplicity. In one respect it does not express certain generalizations which are grammatically relevant and can be expressed. In some other respects it can be shown to involve unnecessary apparatus for the expression of certain generalizations.

3.3.1 Instructions for lexical selection and structure in embedded clauses.

In 3.2.1 it was shown that a Chomskian base grammar does not account for recursive regularities of instruction on lexical choice in embedded relative clauses. One such regularity was formulated in (14) with respect to (13) and (15). It was also shown that a Chomskian base could perhaps account for such regularities, i.e. formulate them in formal and explicit selection instruction rules, but only by means of an elaborate additional algorithm, which was briefly outlined. One can conclude, therefore, that a Chomskian base grammar does not easily or naturally lend itself to the description of selectional instruction in embedded clauses. Yet selection instruction rules are of importance in the grammatical description of a language, since they are indispensable for the generation of such recursive structures as (13) and (15).

It is still doubtful whether a Chomskian base can be made to account for regularities of structural restrictions in embedded clauses, such as the impossibility of the question element (QU) in some embedded clauses. And if it proves possible to set up structural instruction rules, the question still remains whether these rules, too, do not involve a needlessly complex apparatus. But it does not seem necessary to go into these questions here, since the failure to account adequately for certain lexical regularities which would, ideally, be described by selection instruction rules, calls for such radical modification that the question of structural restrictions is best postponed until it can be reconsidered in the light of the resulting new grammatical model.

3.3.2 Redundancy in subcategorization rules. In 3.2.2 it was shown that prior context-free generation of the noun phrases of subject, object, etc., followed by the selection of the main verb in terms of these, is counter-productive and unfortunate from the point of view of distinguishing deviant from non-deviant sentences, and that Chomsky's argument for this procedure does not hold. It is easily demonstrated that this procedure involves a redundant apparatus of rules and generated strings (counter-productivity), so that we must conclude that prior context-free selection of the verb is preferable from all points of view.

From 2.3 it resulted that the subcategorization rules for nouns generate CS's containing a number of features, such as, for example, (43) of 2.3. But only one of these features in the subject and only one in the object were seen to be relevant for the selection of the verb, namely [+Abstract] in the subject and [+Animate] in the object, whereas the only reason for the generation of these CS's of nouns was precisely the selection of a proper verb. The remaining features must therefore be regarded as redundant (although the feature [+Count] is syntactically relevant for the transformational rewriting of the indefinite article as *a*—see 3.2.2). This redundancy can be avoided, as was shown in 3.2.2, by giving precedence to the selection of the verb, and by consequently changing the reading of the selectional rules.

3.3.3 Relational constituents. Traditionally there are two ways of analysing a sentence. There is, first, the kind of analysis which labels the constituents of the sentence according to their relations with the other constituents. This we might call syntagmatic, functional, or relational, analysis. It distinguishes such positions, or relational constituents, as *subject, main verb, object, indirect object*, etc. Second, there is what we might call categorial or paradigmatic analysis, which classifies the constituent parts of the sentence according to the class-membership of some of their constituents as noun phrase, verb phrase, etc. and which classifies the lexical items which occur into rough classes such as *noun, verb, adjective, preposition,* etc., or into more refined classes such as *animate noun, verb with animate subject,* etc. In modern linguistics these two types of analysis are seen to be interrelated in such a way that certain classes of lexical items can occur only in certain relational constituents. These restrictions of occurrence are, in fact, the criterion by which the categorial classes are distinguished.[1] The rough classes can be defined by the possible occurrence of their members in certain positions in the sentences of a language, irrespective of what specific lexical items occupy the other positions. The more refined selection restriction classes are defined by the possible occurrence of their members in certain positions, given the occurrence of at least one specific lexical item in another position. (Incidentally, since relational constituents such as *main verb, subject, object,* seem to figure universally in the deep structure of all languages, and since there seem to be also universal restrictions on the occurrence of classes of lexical items in any, or any set of, these positions, there are good grounds for taking the rough classes of *verb, noun, adjective,* as universal for all languages, in spite of language-bound surface differences in morphological and syntactic rules.)

It is worth noticing that the relational constituents do not play a rôle in Chomsky's generative model. As can be seen from the account given in chapter 2, sentences are generated solely with the help of categorial notions. Chomsky does not, however, deny the relevance of relational constituents for the description of a language. In his more recent work they are frequently mentioned. In (1965) pp. 63–4, he distinguishes three kinds of information provided by a traditional grammar, the first and the third of which are based on categorial analysis. The second kind of information is relational:

(44)

> the NP *sincerity* [in: *sincerity may frighten the boy*] functions as the Subject of the sentence, whereas the VP *frighten the boy* functions as the Predicate of this sentence; the NP *boy* functions as the Object of the VP, and the V *frighten* as its Main Verb; the grammatical relation Subject-Verb holds of the pair (*sincerity, frighten*), and the grammatical relation Verb-Object holds of the pair (*frighten, the boy*).

He then devotes a section *Functional notions* to this type of information (pp. 68–74). Here he stresses that a relational analysis is to be sharply distinguished from a categorial analysis. He points out, reiterating

---

[1] See Bloomfield (1933) pp. 185, 265.

Postal's argument (Postal (1964) pp. 34–8), that confusion of these two types of analysis and a treatment of relational constituents as if they were categorial leads to undesirable redundancy in the description. He gives as an example (p. 69):

(45)

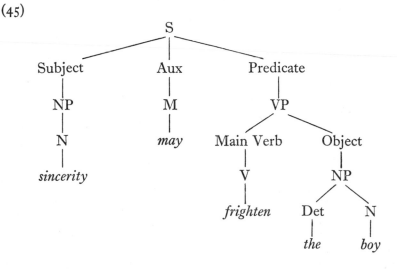

where the nodes *Subject, Predicate, Main Verb*, and *Object* are considered to be redundant for the generation of the deep structure of *sincerity may frighten the boy.*

Instead, Chomsky wants the relational information to be read from the P-marker as follows. One may set up ordered pairs of nodes of the form [Y, Z], where the left-hand element is a node directly dominated by the right-hand element. Each relational constituent can then be defined by such a pair (p. 71). Thus the subject will be defined as [NP, S] (i.e. noun phrase of sentence), the predicate as [VP, S] (i.e. verb phrase of sentence), the object as [NP, VP] (i.e. noun phrase of verb phrase), and the main verb as [V, VP] (i.e. verb of verb phrase).

Assuming that this can be done, there still remain some arguable points. It is not clear what the importance is of relational constituents if they play no rôle at all in the generation and description of sentences. Chomsky seems to use the terms *subject* and *object* only as abbreviations. In (1965) p. 107, he introduces 'object-deletion' as a feature of *frighten*, presumably as the name of a transformation. And on pp. 114–15 we find these terms again in an abbreviative notation. The only place where they may, perhaps, be fruitfully used in a Chomskian framework is the semantic component, but Chomsky does not say anything precise about this. He does compliment Pike on his introduction of relational constituents into the tagmemic model of description ((1964) p. 61): 'It is the great merit of Pike's recent work in tagmemics to have focussed attention on the importance of these traditional motions, although the tagmemic method of analysis of these relational notions is both redundant and (since it is a strictly categorial interpretation) not adequate—see Postal (1964, section VII).' But this compliment would seem void of meaning in view of the way in which he himself treats these notions.[1] In fact, he asserts ((1966*b*) p. 58): 'The important point is that a phrase structure grammar need not be supplemented in any way for it to assign these properties to the strings it generates. Once we recognize the relational character of these notions, we see at once they are already assigned, in the appropriate way, with no further elaboration of the rules.' It would certainly be worth our while to examine whether this is true.

In point of fact, the truth of this assertion depends on the question whether or not there is another way of representing relational constituents, different from Chomsky's and more appropriate, i.e. more adequate. It will be maintained below that there is, in fact, such a different representation, which from the points of view of simplicity and semantic interpretation, is more adequate than Chomsky's. There are three main objections to Chomsky's rejection of explicit mention of relational constituents in the rules and derivations, and his introduction of subsidiary definitions based on his phrase structure analysis.

First, if introduced into the grammar in an appropriate way, symbols for relational constituents can simplify the grammar considerably. It also makes a semantic interpretation more straightforward. (One way of doing this will be shown in chapter 5.)

Secondly, Chomsky's definitions of deep structure subject, object, etc. by means of definitions of the type [Y, Z] do not play any part in the generation of sentences: they remain disconnected from the main body of the grammar.

Thirdly, these definitions depend on the actual phrase structure analysis given in Chomsky's deep structure model. If, for any valid reason, this model has to be modified, these definitions will fall with it. Yet, it is clear that the notions of object, subject, etc. do not themselves

---

[1] I have discussed the tagmemic method of handling relational constituents in the light of Postal's criticism in my review of Longacre (1964) in *Foundations of Language 2* (1966) pp. 200–12.

depend on Chomsky's particular PS-analysis: the same notions occur in quite different models of grammar.

In a different base model these notions may or may not be definable in categorial terms. If they are not, they must be expressed separately, which in itself is no reason for considering such a model inadequate. If they are, their definition will be different from the one they receive in Chomsky's model. Chomsky gives no indication that the definitions he proposes do, in fact, reflect their real nature. It is not clear, for example, why there is no relational definiens for [Aux, Predicate-Phrase] or [Manner, V]. We shall see below that this can possibly be explained by assuming that the relational constituents are those elements in the sentence whose lexical selection depends on the verb chosen. That is, they are specified in the lexicon and are relevant for that part of the sentence which will be called the nucleus. It must be recognized that, contrary to Chomsky's assertion, Pike does not treat relational constituents as categorial, but keeps the two sorts of constituents strictly apart. For him, as for all tagmemic writers, the relational constituents are 'slots', functional positions in the sentence, which can be filled by categorial constituents.[1] In tagmemic terminology, a slot filled by one or more categorial items forms a tagmeme in a sentence. A tagmeme is represented in the form $A : a$, where A is the slot and a the filler. Longacre, in his attempt to present a generative tagmemic apparatus (1964), also keeps the two sorts of constituents apart, and says so explicitly on p. 28, footnote: 'Such substitution in two stages does not in itself indicate two nodes in the tree of a construction. There is but one node, viz. a grammatical point with this particular construction manifesting it. From this node there is multiple branching as indicated in the formula of the included construction.' Although, as was pointed out in Seuren (1966) (see p. 71, note 1), the author is not sufficiently specific here as regards the precise form of the structural descriptions he has in mind, so much is clear that one cannot impute to the tagmemicist writers a confusion of categorial and relational constituents. Postal's criticism, therefore, which is based on the assumption that 'it is clear that these [i.e. tagmemic formulae] may be looked upon simply as a method of collapsing distinct phrase structure rules' (p. 33), does not hold water. To say that 'a

[1]   See Pike (1967) pp. 194–251; 490–2; especially p. 282: 'Thus the present theory is *neither* that of relationships apart from substance *nor* of substance apart from relationships, but a theory in which the "relationships" into which units enter are interpreted as conceptualized hypostatic constructs viewed by the analyst as components of those units.' Also: Elson and Pickett (1962) pp. 57–81.

formula like $A = B:b\ C:c$ is to be viewed simply as a notational variant of $A \rightarrow BC$; $B \rightarrow b$; $C \rightarrow c'$ (p. 33), is a serious misrepresentation of some fundamental tagmemic notions. Disposal of relational constituents on the sole ground that they can be expressed in terms of categorial constituents given certain P-markers, not only implies severe restrictions on the form of P-markers—restrictions which lack any other, independent motivation—but seems also to eliminate the possibility of simplifying the grammar in various respects.

The tagmemic way of handling relational constituents can be properly described as follows: in $A:a\ A$ is a parameter whose value is a. A central and valid criticism of tagmemics, however, is that the concept of deep structure is not taken into account. All surface structures are meant to be described exhaustively by tagmemic formulae. That this is, to say the least, an uneconomical way of describing sentences, is a fact that has been confirmed conclusively by work in transformational grammar. Some attempts have been made to introduce the concept of deep structure into tagmemics (Longacre (1964), Cook (1964)), but these attempts lack sufficient specificity and elaboration (see also 5.0).

Accepting Chomsky's and Postal's point that little is gained and much is lost by a categorial treatment of relational constituents, we can still consider the question whether anything is gained or lost by an introduction of relational constituents in such a way that they are kept clearly distinct from the categorial constituents and, at the same time, play a constitutive rôle in the generation of sentences, i.e. by introducing them as parameters. Let us leave until chapter 5 the question whether and how this can be done, and see if there is any point in attempting to do so. It becomes clear then, first, that both the base and the transformational component can be simplified by such a procedure, and, second, that this will enable us to distinguish formally between such traditional concepts as logical subject, object, predicate, etc., i.e. in deep structure, and grammatical subject, object, predicate, etc., i.e. in surface structure.[1] That is, the grammar will then provide more relational information than a Chomskian grammar does, in that it will also specify the relational constituents in surface structures, which, in spite of Chomsky's statements to the contrary, is relevant grammatical information, belonging, and justifiably so, to the traditional lore of grammar. The theory of transformational grammar in its present form, where the introduction of relational constituents is rejected as leading to redundancy, is thus seen

---

[1] Chomsky touches upon this point in (1966b) p. 56, and elsewhere.

to be open to the same charge of redundancy, precisely for its neglect of relational constituents. And this neglect, moreover, is thus shown to lead to a lack of relevant grammatical information.

To illustrate the first point for the transformational part, it is sufficient to point to the fact that many, or even most of, the transformations involve operations on relational constituents. This fact is so obvious that it hardly needs further illustration. It is perhaps most evident in the passive transformation, where object becomes subject, etc. or in the case of object-deletion. Not to make a formal use of the names of these relational constituents in transformational processes means, at least, an unnecessary complication of the formalism, since these constituents must now be indicated by their categorial denomination plus their position. As we have seen, Chomsky uses the term *object-deletion* himself ((1965) p. 107), and it is difficult to see why this natural and useful notation should not be used throughout and consistently. In general terms we say that, since most transformations operate on parameters rather than on their values, there is no point in excluding these parameters from the descriptive system.

As for the base grammar, redundancy through avoidance of relational constituents becomes apparent in the subcategorization rules and the lexicon. Specifically, the subcategorization features of the verbs can be presented in a clearer and simpler way by stating that they require subjects, objects, indirect objects, prepositional phrases of a certain kind. Again, Chomsky does something of this sort in (1965) on pp. 114–15, 'to simplify the reading'—as he says in the pertinent note 31 on p. 220, where he goes on to say: 'There is nothing essential involved in this change of notation.' What is involved, however, is that there seems to be no cogent reason why this simplification should not be incorporated into the formalism.

The second point is also fairly simple. In Chomsky's system of defining relational constituents by means of ordered pairs associated with categorial base rules it is, presumably, possible to define these constituents in deep structure. But this system does not allow for their definition in surface structure. Yet it is this sort of information which is implied in (44) and which is provided by traditional grammars. Chomsky's relational definitions define relational constituents in deep structure, not in surface structure. Chomsky argues ((1964) p. 65) that the 'primary motivation for the theory of transformational grammar lies in the fact that the significant grammatical functions and relations are expressed, in a natural way, only in underlying elementary Phrase-markers'. (The same argument is found in (1965) p. 70.)

Taking Chomsky's point that grammatical relations are, in fact, explicitly expressed in underlying P-markers ((1967*b*) p. 113, note 13), one is still in doubt whether they are expressed in a natural way. As indicated above, there seems to be no need to define the relation of, for instance, *Auxiliary* to *Predicate-Phrase*, or of *Modal* to *Auxiliary*. Why this is so, is not immediately clear, but it may well have to do with the nature of these relations. It is reasonable to assume that the grammatical relations of the type under discussion are relevant in so far as they are involved in the proper selection of lexical items in relation to the main verb. In Chomsky's terms this means that relational definitions are only provided for those constituents which occur in matrix contextual features (see p. 45) in the complex symbol associated with a verb in the lexicon. In more general terms we can say that those constituents are relational whose lexical selection is entailed by the main verb and which are, therefore, part of the specification of that verb in the lexicon. This assumption underlies the whole of chapter 5, where the nucleus is purely lexical and relational. And since it is not *a priori* clear that the relational constituents can be defined in terms of internal nucleus-structure, they are mentioned explicitly in the actual representation.

If it is true that the transformational component can be simplified by the introduction of relational parameters, then these parameters must be preserved in the transformed structures so as to allow for the application of other transformations. That is, the simplifying effect can only be guaranteed if the relational parameters are retained throughout, up to the ultimate surface structures. If, in a surface structure, some constituent must be interpreted grammatically as the subject, or the object, or the subject and object, of two or more embedded sentences in the deep structure simultaneously (see (46) in 3.4), then such an idiosyncrasy must somehow be expressed in the surface structure. Traditional grammar has always done so, although in an intuitive way.

Furthermore, if the grammar is to establish relationships between deep and surface structures, and if the relational constituents are recognized as being essential in deep structure (viz. for a semantic interpretation), then quite naturally one wishes to see what becomes of them in surface structure, or, in other words, how the significant semantic relations of deep structure are expressed in surface structure. In fact, this relationship has never been sufficiently clarified in traditional grammar, mainly because of a lack of explicitness and formalization. The clash which is found to be there, sometimes, between grammatical and logical relational constituents has always been a puzzle both to philosophers and to linguists. Perhaps we shall be led to conclude that surface relational constituents are essentially different from their deep structure namesakes. The problem, however, is real, and we shall not gain an understanding of the phenomenon 'language' by simply dodging the issue.

Almost as an afterthought, Chomsky says something about this question in his note 32, on pp. 220–1 of (1965). From this note it is clear that Chomsky is not entirely satisfied with his own way of handling relational constituents, and that his thoughts tend in much the same direction as has been suggested in the preceding paragraph. This rather lengthy note deserves quoting in full:

For example, if we were to adapt the definitions of universal categories and functions so that they apply to such sentences as 'in England is where I met him', which are often cited to show that phrases other than NP's can occur as Subjects, these proposals would fail completely. This sentence, however, is obviously transformationally derived. It would be perfectly correct to say that 'in England' is the Subject of 'in England is where I met him', extending the grammatical relation *Subject-of*, that is, [NP, S], to the *derived* Phrasemarker (the surface structure). In the basis, however, 'in England' is an Adverbial of Place, associated with the VP 'meet him' in the Predicate-Phrase 'met him in England', and the sentence is interpreted in accordance with the grammatical relations defined in this underlying deep structure.

This extension to surface structures of such functional notions as Subject-of is not an entirely straightforward matter. Thus in base structures, there is apparently never more than a single occurrence of a category such as NP in any structure immediately dominated by a single category (cf. note 1, p. 69), and our definitions of these notions relied on this fact. But this is not true of surface structures. In the sentence 'this book I really enjoyed', both 'this book' and 'I' are NP's immediately dominated by S. Apparently, then, order is significant in determining the grammatical relations defined by surface structures (not surprisingly), though it seems to play no role in the determination of grammatical relations in deep structures. Consequently, somewhat different definitions are needed for the surface notions.

It might be suggested that Topic-Comment is the basic grammatical relation of surface structure corresponding (roughly) to the fundamental Subject-Predicate relation of deep structure. Thus we might define the Topic-of the Sentence as the leftmost NP immediately dominated by S in the surface structure, and the Comment-of the Sentence as the rest of the string. Often, of course, Topic and Subject will coincide, but not in the examples discussed. This proposal, which seems plausible, was suggested to me by Paul Kiparsky. One might refine it in various ways, for example by defining the Topic-of the

Sentence as the leftmost NP that is immediately dominated by S in the surface structure and that is, furthermore, a major category (cf. p. 74—this will make *John* the Topic in the cleft sentence 'it was John who I saw'). Other elaborations also come to mind, but I shall not go into the question any more fully here.

One has the feeling that this topic–comment distinction, enigmatic enough in itself, would not account for a surface distinction between subject and predicate. At any rate, if 'topic' is defined in the way Chomsky defines it, it is different from both deep and surface structure subject, as appears from Chomsky's own example *it was John who I saw*, where *John* may be taken as the topic, but cannot be taken as the subject of the sentence. The same appears from, for example, *without his father he will not come*, where *without his father* cannot be taken as the subject in any accepted sense of the term.

However, the difficult problem of describing the relationship between deep and surface structure relational constituents, and of assessing the precise rôle of surface structure relational constituents, will not be elaborated further in this study, which largely confines itself to deep structure.[1] But one may expect that this problem will be brought nearer to a solution when the relational constituents in deep structure, at least, are accounted for as adequately as is possible at the present moment.

3.4 Standards of semantic adequacy

The semantic adequacy of a Chomskian grammar will be discussed in this section from two points of view. First, it will be shown that this form of adequacy can be enhanced by adequately handling relational constituents. Secondly, the notion of semantic interpretation and the status of the semantic component will be discussed.

3.4.1 Semantic relevance of relational constituents. The question of relational constituents in deep structure is closely connected with considerations of semantic interpretation. Chomsky agrees with this. In (1965) p. 70 he gives the examples:

(46) *a* John was persuaded by Bill to leave
     b John was persuaded by Bill to be examined
     c what disturbed John was being regarded as incompetent

---

[1] For suggestions regarding surface relational constituents and the topic–comment distinction, see Staal (1967) pp. 75–87.

on which he makes the following comments:

In (46a), *John* is simultaneously Object-of *persuade* (*to leave*) and Subject-of *leave*; in (46b), *John* is simultaneously Object-of *persuade* (*to be examined*) and Object-of *examine*; in (46c), *John* is simultaneously Object-of *disturb*, Object-of *regard* (*as incompetent*), and Subject-of the predication *as incompetent*. In both (46a) and (46b), *Bill* is the ('logical') Subject-of the Sentence, rather than *John*, which is the so-called 'grammatical' Subject-of the Sentence, that is, the Subject with respect to the surface structure (cf. note 32). In such cases as these, the impossibility of a categorial interpretation of functional notions becomes at once apparent; correspondingly, the deep structure in which the significant grammatical functions are represented will be very different from the surface structure. Examples of this sort, of course, provide the primary motivation and empirical justification for the theory of transformational grammar. That is, each sentence of (46) will have a basis consisting of a sequence of base Phrase-markers, each of which represents some of the semantically relevant information concerning grammatical function.

There seem to be very few authors in linguistics or philosophy who deny the semantic relevance of relational constituents, although a precise semantic description of these has never been given—due, one would say, to the lack of any satisfactory theory of linguistic meaning.

Fillmore (1966) questions 'the linguistic validity of the notions "subject" and "object"' (p. 19). He argues that in, for instance, *the door opened* and *the janitor opened the door* 'the semantically relevant relation common to the two sentences is that between the subject of the intransitive verb and the object of the transitive verb, not between the subjects of the two sentences' (p. 21). Since the relevant semantic relations must be reflected in deep structure, and since, here at least, these relations seem to be independent of a distinction between subject and object, Fillmore concludes that such a distinction is irrelevant for deep structure analyses.

We have known for some time that the surface distinction between, for instance, subject and object is not regularly applicable to deep structure. Fillmore may well be right in positing that we will have to recognize a still deeper, and more universal, layer of structure. Much of the present work of Lyons (see, for instance, Lyons (1966)) points in the same direction.

Fillmore proposes two fundamental deep structure rules, the first being $S \rightarrow Mod + Aux + Prop$ (Sentence is to be rewritten as *Modality* plus *Auxiliary* plus *Proposition*), the second $Prop \rightarrow V(Erg)(Dat)(Loc)$ $(Inst)(Ag)$,—where V stands for *verb*, *Erg* for *ergative*, *Dat* for *dative*,

Loc for *locative*, *Inst* for *instrumental*, and *Ag* for *agentive*. He thus proposes the relational constituents of ergative, etc. as a 'deeper' and more adequate alternative to deep structure subject, object, etc.—that is, he does not reject the notion of relational constituent, but denies that the traditional concepts of subject, object, etc. are adequate to account for relational constituents in deep structure.

Fillmore seems to make an important point here. But it must be recognized, on the other hand, that our knowledge of deep structure is still very limited. The deep structure relations among lexical items, in particular, are still almost completely unknown. It seems that, in our present state of knowledge, investigations into 'deeper' structure are bound to be too speculative to be fruitfully pursued. We shall have to wait until more is known about 'less deep' structure before we can venture into greater depth.

Another author who denies the semantic relevance of relational constituents, although on less fundamental grounds, is Postal. But we shall see that a discussion of his argument leads again to speculations about a still 'deeper' structure. Postal sees the semantic motivation underlying proposals for introducing relational constituents, but he denies its validity. In (1964) p. 36 he says:

Why does Pike feel that this [=tagmemic] formulation is superior to the NVN [=noun-verb-noun] formula? The reason is, I think, the assumption that an attempt to describe the semantic features of sentences requires in some sense a semantic interpretation of the nonterminal constituents, that is, of elements like 'Verb', 'Subject', etc., as well as of the terminal constituents or morphemes. Thus in English if we take *John likes Bill*, *Bill likes John*, and all similar sentences which are NVN, we would presumably find that the class of items which occurs in the postverbal position is the same as that in the preverbial position. Yet it would appear that the former is in some sense associated with the meaning of 'subject', the latter with that of 'object'.

To this he adds a note (64), to be found in (1964) p. 88:

This is, of course, not really the case and the whole assumption of a semantic interpretation of nonterminal elements is, I think, mistaken. Thus the subject in *John pushes Bill* has nothing very obvious in common semantically with the subject in *John remembers his appointment*, *John received a blow*, *John suffered a defeat*, etc. At this point, however, the tagmemic linguist is, of course, free to set up many different higher order tagmemes, including Subject versus Actor, etc. But this course, if followed to its natural conclusion, will lead to enormous complication of the description by requiring the recognition of dozens of grammatically equivalent constituents. First steps along this unhappy path have in fact been taken by Longacre, 'String Constituent Analysis'

70–3. Note that the semantic difference between subject in the above cases, as well as all analogous ones, is entirely due to the character of the verb. Thus marking it in terms of tagmemes is redundant even from the point of view of semantics. For a semantic conception which can take advantage of this fact and avoid redundancies see Jerrold Katz and Jerry Fodor, 'The Structure of a Semantic Theory', to appear in *Language*.

Although it is admittedly true that no general definition has as yet been given for the meanings of relational constituents, it is certainly not self-evident that there is none to be given. In fact, an argument completely analogous to the one given by Postal would then hold for such concepts as 'sentence', 'noun', 'verb'. But there is every reason to believe (see Katz and Postal (1964) p. 163 *et passim*) that Postal regards these concepts as semantically relevant. It is also quite understandable why relational constituents have never been defined semantically. Their semantic definition must be given in universal semantic terms, and too little is known about universal semantics as yet to assign an adequate deep structure syntactic status to these constituents.

It is wiser, therefore, to reckon with the possibility that semantic definitions of relational constituents can and will be given. Postal asserts that 'the semantic difference between subject in the above cases...is entirely due to the character of the verb'. But perhaps it is also true that some common semantic feature in these different subjects is also due to some common character of verbs. It is not difficult to adduce grammatical evidence that most verbs have a common semantic factor 'do'. This appears, for instance, from the following set of sentences:

(47) *a* John pushes Bill, and so does Mary
      b John remembers his appointment, and so does Bill
      c John received a blow, and so did Bill
      d John suffered a defeat, and so did Bill

However, not every form of *do*-substitution is possible for every verb. Some verbs do not allow for certain forms of *do*-substitution:

(48) *a* what John does is (to) push Bill
      b *what John does is (to) remember his appointment
      c *what John did was (to) receive a blow
      d *what John did was (to) suffer a defeat

Various forms of *do*-substitution, usually not coextensive with the English forms, are found in other languages. In Dutch, for instance, the object and the main verb may be placed at the beginning of the sentence, but the verb must then be taken up, 'proverbially' rather than 'pronominally', by the verb *doen* (to do):

(49) *a* Wim duwen doet Jan nooit
           (pushing Bill is something John never does)
      b zijn afspraak onthouden doet Jan nooit
           (remembering his appointment is something John never does)
      c een klap krijgen deed Jan nooit
           (receiving a blow was something John never did)
      d een nederlaag lijden deed Jan nooit
           (suffering a defeat was something John never did)

While in Italian we have:

(50) *a* Giovanni non fa altro che spingere Pino
           (John does nothing but push Joe)
      b Giovanni non fa altro che ricordarsi del suo appuntamento
           (John does nothing but remember his appointment)
      c Giovanni non fece altro che prendere un colpo
           (John did nothing but receive a blow)
      d Giovanni non fece altro che subire una sconfitta
           (John did nothing but suffer a defeat)

In ancient Greek many verbs may be replaced by their corresponding nouns plus ποιεῖσθαι (to do). Thus[1] we find πλοῦν ποιεῖσθαι (to make a boat-trip) for πλεῖν (to sail, go by sea); λήθην ποιεῖσθαι ('to do forgetfulness') for λανθάνεσθαι (to forget); βουλὴν ποιεῖσθαι ('to do consultation') for βουλεύεσθαι (to deliberate); τὰς μάχας ποιεῖσθαι ('to do the fightings') for μάχεσθαι (to fight), etc.

The English 'translations' of the sentences (*b*), (*c*) and (*d*) of (49) and (50) are not, or hardly, grammatical, although these sentences seem correct in Dutch and Italian. It appears that copula-verbs cannot be replaced by *do*-forms in any language. The consequences of this with regard to subcategorization of verbs are not immediately clear. But there is reason to assume that verbs can be grouped into a very limited number of main subcategories, possibly only two, characterized by the semantic factors 'do' and 'be'.

Another consideration to be taken into account is that there seems to be grammatical evidence (see Gruber (1967)) to support the view that not

---

[1] I quote Liddell and Scott, *A Greek–English Lexicon*, Oxford.

all verbs belong to the lexicon of deep structure. In particular, the verb *have* seems to be transformationally derivable from *be* plus an indirect object.[1] (This would, among other things, account for the fact that *have* is excluded from the passive.) Generally, there are relations obtaining between lexical items which have not, as yet, been studied in detail, but which suggest that there may be a relation of derivability between such items as *send/give to* or *receive/obtain from*, or *sell to/buy from*, or *follow/ precede, like/please, above/under*.[2] Too little is known about deep structure to say anything more definite here. But we know enough not to be disturbed here by the ungrammaticalness of referring to verbs such as *receive* or *suffer* by the substitute form *do*. In view of the possibility that these verbs might, perhaps, not belong to the deep vocabulary, this evidence only reinforces our hypothesis that in most deep structure verbs there is a semantic factor 'do', another class of deep structure verbs being perhaps characterized by the factor 'be' (copula-verbs).

If this is true, an approximate semantic characterization of, for example, the relational constituent *subject* would not be too far to seek. It would consist in the specification of *who* or *what is* or *does*. Such an interpretation would be in complete agreement with the conception of subject as a parameter.

All this is admittedly tentative. But the outcome is, at least, that we are well justified in discarding Postal's objection to relational constituents, and in taking the side of the majority of linguists, who recognize the relevance of these constituents and, at the same time, their inability to say anything more precise about them.

At the end of his note (64), Postal refers to Katz and Fodor's article in *Language* (1963). This article was followed by Katz and Postal's *An Integrated Theory of Linguistic Descriptions* (1964), in which a theory of semantic interpretation is proposed in outline. A detailed discussion of this work would fall outside the scope of the present study,[3] although

---

[1] See Lyons (1966) pp. 229–30.   [2] See Staal (1967a) pp. 66–74.

[3] A detailed discussion is found in Staal (1965). It is to be noted that the projection rules type 1 and type 2, which form the basis of the procedure of semantic interpretation envisaged by Katz and Postal, have meanwhile become outdated. The authors themselves suggest eliminating the rules of type 2 (pp. 67–8) together with the generalized transformations. The rules of type 1 are inadequate insofar as they are based on a factorial analysis of the meanings of lexical items in terms of branching. We know now that such an analysis must be given in terms of matrix features rather than in terms of branching: see Chomsky (1965) pp. 79–80, especially p. 79: 'The difficulty is that this subcategorization is typically not strictly hierarchic, but involves rather cross classification.'

some criticism will be advanced in 3.4.2. But it is worth noticing that here the relational constituents have been reinstated, although the semantic account given of them remains defective. They devote some pages (33–9) to the problem of relational constituents, or grammatical relations, and conclude, on p. 39:

The meaning of a sentence is a function not only of the meanings of its lexical items but also of the grammatical relations between them. In the simplest case this is illustrated by

(51) John loves Mary
(52) Mary loves John

where the difference in meaning cannot be attributed to a difference in the meanings of the lexical items because they are the same in both cases. But since the meaning of a sentence is in part determined by the grammatical relations in it, and since, furthermore, these relations are uniquely characterized syntactically only in underlying P-markers, it follows that P 1 [i.e. projection rules type 1] must obtain the meanings of a sentence from the meanings of its lexical items by operating on underlying P-markers. Otherwise, P 1 will not have the grammatical relations needed to determine the combinations of lexical information that give the correct meaning for the sentence as a whole.[1]

The projection rules type 1, however, are not illustrated very clearly (see also 3.4.2 below). On p. 22, for instance, the reading:

(53) (Physical Object) → (Globular Shape) → (Colour) →
              [Abounding in contrast or variety of bright colours]

is assigned to the partial noun phrase *colourful ball* in:

(54) the baby is playing with a colourful ball

But the relation of *colourful ball* to the rest of the sentence is not gone into. On pp. 34–5 the authors propose a definition for relational constituents in terms of P-marker configurations:

Thus for English at least the 'subject' relation can be defined in terms of the configuration (Sentence: Noun Phrase + Verb Phrase), in which case it holds between any string of morphemes dominated by such a Noun Phrase and the string dominated by the following Verb Phrase if the sequence of such strings is dominated by Sentence.

Assuming that such a set of relational definitions in terms of P-marker configurations would belong to the general theory, so that the subject, object, etc., could be read from the semantically interpreted P-marker,

---

[1] On pp. 158–9 the authors underline the universal character of relational constituents.

then these definitions would still not tell us anything about the semantic characteristics of these relational constituents. They would remain, in fact, uninterpreted, as before. One recalls that Chomsky gives an almost identical way for 'reading' the relational constituents from deep structure P-markers, with the sole purpose of providing syntactic information without, as yet, a semantic interpretation. This syntactic information is thus left uninterpreted in Katz and Postal's theory.

It is doubtful whether a semantic interpretation of relational constituents can be given at all in the framework of Katz and Postal's semantic component. A first and obvious difficulty is raised by the terms in which a semantic description can be given. In order to provide semantic descriptions in general there must be a set of universal semantic primes related in some way with the human mind. The establishment of such a set can only be the result of painstaking research and intelligent hypotheses. Only the very first steps have been taken on this difficult path. What the semantic primes could be for an adequate description of deep structure relational constituents can only be guessed at. A suggestion, but no more than that, was made on p. 82. Fillmore (see pp. 78–9 above) may well be right in assuming that other relational constituents than subject, object, etc. must be taken as basic. And it seems beyond doubt (see p. 82 above) that the lexical items of, for instance, English are derivable from underlying composite forms, about the nature of which we are still very much in the dark. Furthermore, even with a set of universal semantic primes given for relational constituents, it is not clear how these can be incorporated into Katz and Postal's semantic component.

3.4.2 The status of the semantic component. Apart from the question of relational constituents there is another, more general difficulty in transformational grammar as it exists nowadays: it is not at all clear what precisely the relationship is between the base grammar and its resulting deep structure on the one hand, and the semantic component on the other. No doubt the deep structures are meant to be input to the semantic component, just as the surface structures are input to the phonological component (both the semantic and the phonological components are 'interpretive'). The output of the phonological component will be phonetic representations in terms of some set of sound-specifying features. But what will the output of the semantic component look like? According to Katz and Postal ((1964) p. 22), it will consist of a set of semantically interpreted P-markers, each of which is 'a set of pairs with respect to the P-marker, one member of which is a node of the P-marker and the other of which is a set of readings, each reading giving one of the meanings of the string dominated by that node in the P-marker'. Yet not a single illustration of such a semantically interpreted P-marker is to be found in the book, nor, for that matter, anywhere else in the literature. In fact, Katz and Postal's book is a study in syntax, rather than in semantics. They show how syntactic descriptions can be simplified by the adoption of the principle of a semantically relevant deep structure. This has been an important contribution to the study of syntax. But the semantic component performing a semantic interpretation is invoked rather than described: the instances given of lexical meaning are very scarce indeed, and the projection rules are hardly illustrated at all.

This would be less alarming if one did not have grave suspicions about the viability of a semantic component as envisaged by Katz and Postal. They speak lightly about 'a dictionary that provides a meaning for each of the *lexical items* of the language', and of projection rules which 'assign a *semantic interpretation* to each string of formatives generated by the syntactic component'. They then expect that 'the semantic interpretation that a string of formatives has assigned to it provides a full analysis of its cognitive meaning' (p. 12).

It is not quite clear what their position is here. One might infer that they dodge the old and vexed issue of *how*, or *in what terms* to describe meanings. That is, one might think that they are not disturbed by the question what descriptive terms are going to be used in their semantic component. They do not, at any rate, discuss the problem whether meanings can be described at all in any form of language. This language again has its meaning: any definition in terms of the same or another language leads to an infinite regress. (In some cases meanings can be defined ostensively, but never in words.) This argument, if correct, would lead to the then inescapable conclusion that meanings can only be clarified by means of synonyms. If we are right in interpreting Katz and Postal in this way, then the output of their semantic component would be just a set of synonymous expressions for every sentence generated, without any indication that these synonyms have some explanatory value. The addition of a semantic component to the grammar would then be pointless.

But it is perhaps fairer to lend more weight to their term 'cognitive meaning' in the quotation above. This may be taken to imply that the terms for describing meanings are, in fact, terms for describing knowledge. Semantic description will then be directly related to a description of knowledge. The synonymy relation of the output of the semantic component with the sentences generated will then have the explanatory value of relating sentences with knowledge. In fact, the very few examples given by Katz and Postal show a Leibniz-type analysis of the way some philosophers think knowledge is organized in our minds.

A link-up between meaning and knowledge is certainly far from absurd: if it is successful it will have considerable explanatory power. But one has to recognize that any analysis of the contents and organization of human knowledge has so far been highly speculative and heavily dependent on assumptions of all kinds about language, about the structure of the human mind, and about what one imagines to be 'bare reality'. Moreover, no analysis of this kind has ever been complete. One wonders whether any attempt at completeness would not yield an unwieldy and unmanageable apparatus.

The human mind is not open to direct observation. If we want to gain some insight into its structure and contents, we must construct a model, a theory, which is compatible with all known facts and with valid theories about them. One category of such facts are the facts of language. Consequently, an adequate theory of language must provide the investigator of the human mind with important clues. In his *The Philosophy of Language*, Katz points out quite correctly (p. 8) 'that the philosopher of language should begin with and draw his linguistic information from the theory of language as developed in descriptive linguistics. Thus, the theory of language is the first step toward an account of conceptual knowledge in terms of its mode of expression and communication in natural languages. It supplies the philosopher with generalizations about the form and content of languages upon which he can base inferences to revealing truths about the form and content of conceptual knowledge'. He seems, however, to overestimate somewhat the results of linguistic theory that are sufficiently unequivocal and well established to serve as a basis for a theory of the human mind. It is only realistic to admit that we have hardly started work in linguistic theory, and that, particularly in the field of deep structure, which is most relevant for the study of the mind, most problems still await solution. In their analysis of the meanings of *bachelor* ((1964) p. 14), however, Katz and Postal do not, or only to a very limited extent, rely on information provided by a linguistic theory. They follow the opposite way, applying a Leibnizian philosophical, speculative, theory to the description of particular meanings, without indicating how this theory can be linguistically motivated.

Then, if meanings are to be related to knowledge, it must be made clear why and how we can say things that we do not know, in the form of questions, wishes, suggestions, or unfounded assertions. We can also introduce new concepts which are not necessarily part of our knowledge. In general, we can say that we express *thoughts* in language, and thoughts comprise much more than knowledge. It will be necessary, therefore, to set up a model of the human mind in which thoughts are accounted for in a satisfactory way, and the connection would be between deep structures and thoughts, rather than between deep structures and knowledge.

Lastly, if one wants to apply existing philosophical theories of knowledge to language, one would be interested to know how they are applicable. One would like to see, for instance, the question of extension and intension solved. It seems that neither extension nor intension, nor both taken together, could account for certain peculiarities of linguistic reference. The word *good*, for example, may have different extensions and intensions for different speakers (see Ziff's *Semantic Analysis* (1960)). Yet there is undoubtedly a common element of 'goodness' in their understanding of the word *good*. If semantic interpretations are to provide a full analysis of *cognitive* meanings, one would expect these points to be clarified. One fears, however, that this would constitute a utopian programme: one can hardly pretend to solve these old problems without the help of completely new insights and methods, which Katz and Postal do not provide, and which have not, as yet, been sufficiently developed.

In 5.4.2 it will be argued that fruitful results can be obtained by setting our sights much lower than the linking up of meaning with knowledge or thought, and by eliminating the concept of a semantic component as an interpretive device for deep structures. We can regard the base itself as a semantic generator and the expressions it generates, i.e., the deep structures, will be synonymous with the sentences of the language (account being taken of synonymous and homonymous sentences of the language). The deep structure language will then be a language of so-called 'favourite synonyms', since they permit the simplest transformational derivation of surface structures. The principle of the primacy of form in linguistic analysis will thus be saved, since the semantic descriptions will only be set up on grounds of derivability of formal structures. And we honour, at the same time, the old Medieval and Humanist principle of the logical priority of meaning, that is, of meaning as a, presumably universal, source from which sentences are derived. But we must first go into problems of syntax, before we are entitled to say anything more about meaning.

3.5 Conclusion

Concluding this chapter we can summarize the requirements we expect a grammar to fulfil, apart from those already fulfilled by a Chomskian grammar. We wish, then, a grammar

(55) *i*   to give a clear specification of derived constituent structure (3.1);

  ii   to avoid the generation by the base rules of deep structures which cannot be developed into surface structures and cause the transformational part to 'block' (3.2.1);

  iii   to permit a clear separation of deviant from non-deviant sentences (3.2.2);

  iv   to select the verb before the other, nominal or prepositional, parts of the sentence (3.2.2; 3.3.2);

  v   to permit a selection of the nominal lexical items such that this selection does not depend on the structure of an already generated noun phrase (3.3.1), and, moreover, such that

    a   this selection can be made according to rules of selectional restrictions (3.2.2); or

    b   this selection can be made arbitrarily (3.2.2); or

    c   this selection can be made according to rules of selectional instruction (3.3.1);

  vi   to give, both in deep and in surface structure, an adequate and explicit expression of the relational constituents (3.3.3; 3.4.1);

  vii   to provide a syntactically motivated apparatus for semantic descriptions (3.4.2).

Since, in this study, we are more concerned with deep than with surface structure, requirement (55) *i* will receive less attention than the other requirements. In the fifth chapter an attempt will be made to sketch a descriptive model of deep structure which takes account of these requirements.

4 Deep structure and operators

4.0 Introduction

Before an attempt can be made to incorporate the suggestions made in the previous chapter into a new model of deep structure description, something must be said about the concept of deep structure. A new category in deep structure, to be called the category of operators, will be proposed.

The concept of deep structure will be enlarged upon mainly for methodological reasons. It is emphasized that deep structure embodies a hypothesis set up for an adequate description of a language, and that no other arguments than descriptive adequacy are taken into consideration. Deep structure is set up on the basis of syntactic evidence in accordance with the requirements of explicitness, grammaticalness, greatest simplicity and semantic adequacy (see 1.4.3).

Application of this hypothesis to some syntactic material taken from English leads to the positing of a new category of operators. This category provides a possible answer to a number of problems which have hitherto remained unsolved, including negation, quantification, modalities and certain adverbial adjuncts. Two main constituents are distinguished in deep structure, the operator constituent and the nucleus. It is shown that essentially the same distinction is drawn by some philosophers, sometimes for logical reasons, sometimes on purely speculative grounds.

4.1 Deep structure

In modern linguistics the concept of deep structure originates with Chomsky, apart from some suggestions made by Hockett ((1958) pp. 246–52). It is a direct consequence of his position in the development of linguistics. He envisages a formalized, or explicit, description of a language, an idea that had emerged in post-war structural linguistics. So-called 'traditional linguistics' (a collective label for what in itself represents a rich variety of approaches to language) had tried to describe languages, but without the requirement of maximum explicitness. The various developments of structural linguistics that intervened between traditional linguistics and Chomsky (with the possible exception of phonology) were concentrated more upon analytic procedures of individual sentences or of a corpus of collected material, than upon a description of the totality of a language, although the idea of a total description of a language was always regarded as the ultimate ideal.

Gradually, under the influence of formal logic, the desire was felt to improve the quality of scientific knowledge by formalizing scientific procedures. Harris, in fact, presented an attempt to formalize procedures of analysis. Whatever the value of his formalized analytic procedures, they have at least the merit of having brought linguistics back, under the pressure of the need for precision, to the task of giving organized descriptions of languages. This is the result clearly formulated at the end of his *magnum opus, Methods in Structural Linguistics* (1951), pp. 372–3: 'The work of analysis leads right up to the statements which enable anyone to synthesize or predict utterances in the language. These statements form a deductive system with axiomatically defined initial elements and with theorems concerning the relations among them. The final theorems would indicate the structure of the utterances of the language in terms of the preceding parts of the system.'

Chomsky undertook the task of actually constructing such a deductive system. He called it a generative grammar. He also made us see that in order to construct generative grammars it is not necessary to formalize also the preceding procedures of analysis. The discovery procedures need not be formalized to lead to a formalized description. Thus he returned to the main aim of pre-structuralistic, traditional, linguistics, namely the description of languages, but now with the extra requirement of formalization.

While actually undertaking the task of describing (i.e. of giving a structural characterization of) the infinite set of sentences of a language, Chomsky came to see that significant and important simplification could be obtained by describing the sentences of a language in two stages. A possible idea was to characterize first a relatively simple subset of the set of sentences, from which all remaining sentences were to be derived by means of transformations. But closer observation of sentences then reveals that this simplifying effect can only be guaranteed if the two stages of description are distinguished in a different way. That is, it proves not altogether satisfactory to distinguish in a language between

a restricted set of relatively simple sentences and the remaining transformed sentences. It is simpler to distinguish two stages in the syntactic
generative process of all sentences. The first stage, called the *base*, will
lead to the generation of abstract structures, called *deep structures*. The
second stage, the *transformational part*, will transform the deep structures
into *surface structures*. The transformations will thus not relate
sentences to sentences, but deep structures to surface structures.

The reasons for assuming an abstract level of deep structure underlying every sentence of a language, rather than separating a set of actual
sentences as input to the transformations, are mainly reasons of simplicity and economy of description. If, for example, we want to generate
the passive sentence:

(1) the animals are fed by John

by means of transformational derivation from another sentence, which
would have to be:

(2) John feeds the animals

then the rule of agreement between a third person singular subject and
the verb, securing the proper form *feeds* in (2), will have been applied
unnecessarily, since the subsequent transformation into (1) must anyhow
destroy the effect of this rule, and a different agreement must be
established between the subject of (1), *animals*, and the corresponding
verbal form *are*. It is preferable, therefore, to generate a non-terminated
structure, where the rules of agreement between subject and verb have
not yet been applied, to form the domain of the passive transformation.
But such a structure cannot be an actual sentence. It must be some
abstract, hypothetical, underlying structure. (This led Chomsky to
introduce the concept of *kernel* defined as ((1957) p. 45): 'the set of
sentences that are produced when we apply obligatory transformations
to the terminal strings of the [Σ, F] grammar' (i.e. the base grammar).
Later on this concept was dropped, when the distinction between
obligatory and optional transformations came to be applied in a very
different way.)[1]

The same conclusion can be drawn from:

(3) John is loved by himself

which would conceivably be derived from a sentence:

(4) John loves himself

---

[1] See Chomsky (1957) chapter 6, especially p. 56. The same view is expressed in 1.4.1.

But then the formulation of the passive transformation would be complicated by the statement that reflexive objects are not transformed into subjects in the passive sentence. This complication can be avoided by assuming an underlying structure such as:

(5)   John loves (the same) John

to which the passive transformation applies regularly. An extra transformational rule can then be added to the effect that repetitions of the same noun phrase are replaced by reflexive pronouns. Such a solution is simpler and more general. But it requires the assumption of an underlying structure such as (5), which is not a well-formed sentence in English.

Nominalization transformations also provide evidence in support of this argument. If we want to derive:

(6)   John's interest in animals

from a sentence:

(7)   John is interested in animals

then, clearly, the agreement between *John* and *is* in (7) is again established superfluously, since it is irrelevant for (6). The present tense, moreover, in (7) is also a superfluous element for the generation of (6), which has no tense. One wants a tenseless underlying structure. Chomsky does not envisage tenseless deep structures, but they must be considered desirable. They are also required for the description of sentences such as

(8)   I taught John to swim

or:

(9)   I heard John shouting

where the embedded structures *John to swim* and *John shouting* are also tenseless. More will be said about this in the section about operators, especially in 4.2.2 and 4.3.4. A possible descriptive solution in the form of a tenseless nucleus is proposed in chapter 5.

But apart from reasons of simplicity, reasons of semantic adequacy were also seen to be relevant for the establishment of deep structures. The semantic effect of grammatical rules must be predictable, or regular. This is not the case if we apply, e.g., the passive transformation to actual sentences. Chomsky has pointed out ((1957) pp. 100–1) that in many cases there is a relation of synonymy between active and passive sentences, but that this relation does not obtain in all cases. He gives the examples:

(10)   everyone in the room knows at least two languages

and:

(11)   at least two languages are known by everyone in the room

Similar examples are given in 1.4.3 above, (1*a*)–(2*d*). In order to formulate a passive transformation which is semantically regular, it is at least necessary to postulate an abstract structure underlying all passive sentences and to which the transformation applies without semantic irregularity. So far, the problem of setting up such a structure has not been solved in linguistic literature, but a solution will be proposed below with the help of operators (4.2.1), and in chapter 5 reasons will be advanced for not considering passives as transforms at all, but rather as a form of variation within deep structure.

The grammatical description of questions raises much the same problems and suggests also a refinement in the concept of deep structure. Leaving aside here the so-called *yes/no*-questions, we might envisage a transformational relationship between declarative deep structures and *wh*-questions. A declarative deep structure containing an element *some* might be said to fall under the domain of a *wh*-transformation, by which *some* would be transformed into the *wh*-element:[1]

(12)   you Past see someone
(13)   whom did you see?

or:

(14)   you Past see John somewhere
(15)   where did you see John?

But if a deep structure contains more than one occurrence of *some*, then, within this solution, the grammar obviously has the choice of determining which occurrence, or which occurrences of *some* will be transformed into *wh*-elements. Thus a deep structure such as:

(16)   someone Past see someone somewhere

may then be transformed into any of the following sentences:

(17)   who saw someone somewhere?
(18)   whom did someone see somewhere?

---

[1] Katz and Postal (1964) pp. 86 ff.; Klima (1964) p. 253.

(19)   where did someone see someone?
(20)   who saw whom somewhere?
(21)   where did who see someone?
(22)   where did someone see whom?
(23)   where did who see whom?

(17)–(23) all have different meanings, and it would be desirable to have the different semantic features reflected in the transformational processes leading from (16) to any of (17)–(23). But it is easily seen that these processes are quite complicated and are not directly related to the semantic differences of (17)–(23). It is clear, for instance, that if there is only one *wh*-element, this comes at the beginning of the resulting sentence. If there is more than one *wh*-element, the order of the original *some*-elements is preserved (with generally statable alterations in the verb form), but *where* always takes precedence over the others. Yet none of these transformational rules accounts for the semantic differences of (17)–(23). Katz and Postal ((1964) pp. 86–117) proposed to solve this problem of semantic inadequacy by letting the base generate the *wh*-elements, so that the base-terminal strings, which underlie the transformational part of the grammar, contain the *wh*-element attached to certain constituents. The transformations do nothing else, then, but assign obligatorily the proper positions and forms to the different elements in the surface structures, on the basis of the indications provided by the base-terminal strings. The semantic properties of the resulting *wh*-questions will thus be readable from the base-terminal strings, and the transformations will have no semantic function at all. This solution involves a modified, more abstract, conception of deep structure.

   Similarly, it was proposed by Chomsky ((1957) pp. 61–2) to establish a transformational relationship between positive and negative sentences. But is soon becomes clear that positives and negatives are not related in a simple and straightforward way. Consider, for example:

(24)   John often smokes cigars
(25)   John often does not smoke cigars
(26)   John does not often smoke cigars

The negation element (*not*) can occur in different positions in the sentence, and such differences in occurrence may correspond to differences in meaning. A grammatical description which is to be semantically adequate must, therefore, specify not only which positions can be occupied by the negation element, but also which positional variations are semantically relevant. That is, the 'scope of negation' must be defined for every possible position. An approach as proposed by Chomsky in (1957) would require a complex transformational treatment for the correct assignment of possible positions to the negation element. Apart from (25) and (26), the transformational part would have to provide for:

(27) not often does John smoke cigars
(28) often John does not smoke cigars
(29) John often smokes no cigars
etc.

But there would be no way of concluding, from either the rules or the transformational history of each individual sentence, that, for example, (26) and (27), or (25), (28) and (29), are synonymous.

The answer proposed by Lees, and also by Klima, is to let the negation element be generated in the base and let the transformations assign all kinds of possible positions to it in the surface structures. This, again, modifies the base and makes it more abstract. Yet Klima's solution, given in (1964), which is the most elaborate grammatical study in existence so far of negation in English sentences, does not provide a satisfactory answer to the present difficulty (see also chapter 1, p. 11, note 1). Some, but not sufficient account is taken of the scope of negation. Klima says (p. 316): 'The scope of negation varies according to the origin of the negative element in the sentence (over the whole, over subordinate complementary structures alone, or only over the word containing the negative element). A single independent negative element, whose simplest reflex is *not*, is found to account for sentence negation; its scope is the whole sentence, but because that element is mobile and capable of fusing with other elements (for example in *nobody*), its ultimate position and form have great latitude. When the negative element originates in other constituents (as for example in the extreme case of *doubt*), the scope of negation is restricted to structures subordinate to those constituents. However, granted the differences due to varying scope, it was found that the phenomena connected with negation could be described grammatically on the basis of a single negative element.' This solution accounts only for total sentence negation, negation of an embedded structure and negation of a single word or constituent (*unlikely*, *unpleasant*). But it does not account for partial sentence negation (without embedding), such as is found in (25), (28) and (29), as opposed to (26) and (27). The difference is accounted for simply by 'the great latitude' of the ultimate position and form of the negation element. His position-assigning transformations, therefore, still have irregular semantic effects.

One wants not only the negation element to be generated by the base, but also the scope of negation to be unambiguously defined by the base. Kraak (1966) attempted to solve this problem for the Dutch language, but, as is maintained in Seuren (1967), it has not been entirely successful, although it presents a considerable improvement of Klima's work. In the second part of this chapter, it will be suggested that a satisfactory answer can perhaps be found in the assumption of an operator of negation.

From this informal discussion it can be seen that a consistent application of the principle of semantic regularity in grammatical description leads to considerable modifications in the base. One was led to consider grammatical solutions in which the transformations have no semantic effect, and where all semantic information is contained in the deep structures. The function of the transformations is limited, in these cases, to the assignment of correct positions and forms in surface structures. The same holds for imperative sentences. These can be assumed to contain an underlying element 'imperative' to be generated in the base. This was proposed by Katz and Postal ((1964) pp. 74–9), and it is not necessary to reiterate their arguments here. We saw, furthermore, that the passive transformation should be formulated in such a way that no semantic irregularities are introduced. As far as embedding transformations (formerly called generalized transformations) are concerned, it has been made clear by Chomsky[1] that here, too, transformations do not affect meaning, and that the meaning of the total sentence is reflected in its deep structure. Considerations of this kind have led to the adoption of the general principle (accepted throughout this study—see 1.3) that transformations should *never* have any semantic effect: the meaning of every sentence must be reflected entirely in its deep structure. This principle finds further empirical support in the fact that so far it has invariably been found that descriptions based on it are simpler than those which are not.

The summary exposition given above of the genesis of the concept of deep structure serves mainly to illustrate on what grounds deep structure is postulated. It must embody the simplest possible hypothesis to account

[1] Chomsky (1966a) pp. 33–42; (1966b) pp. 13–17, 55–6.

formally for the infinite variety of the sentences of a language.[1] It is justified solely by the requirements that it should give a finite description of a language subject to the criteria of explicitness, grammaticalness, simplicity and semantic adequacy (1.4.3). These four criteria of adequacy provide the only arguments relevant to a discussion of the form of deep structure, or indeed of grammar. There is no point in postulating a particular deep structure on speculative grounds. Thus one is not justified in postulating, for instance, a deep structure 'the tower is high' for the sentence 'the tower is not low' for the sole reason that one takes the former to be a simpler paraphrase of the latter. Semantic considerations are relevant only to the extent that the same semantic features throughout the language are treated in the same way throughout the grammar. Paraphrase relations between sentences presuppose common elements in their deep structure, but these are only one factor in its precise formulation. The setting up of deep structure requires careful and systematic scrutiny of the sentences of a language and must lead to an adequate solution of descriptive problems within the totality of a grammatical framework.

Syntactic investigations aiming at a satisfying hypothesis of deep structure will lead to a consistent and explicit identification of semantic features, both lexical and grammatical. Such features have hitherto always been identified on an intuitive and *ad hoc* basis, and no attempt has been made as yet to give a language-wide and consistent account of those semantic features which are relevant in a language. Semantic features are relevant if they have a formal support in deep structure. A particular deep structure hypothesis is set up partly on the basis of intuitive semantic judgements of sameness or difference in meaning, and of non-deviance. The judgements given by native speakers and serving as evidence never involve breaking down meaning into semantic features: this is taken to be the linguist's task.

---

[1] A striking parallel with the linguistic concept of deep structure is found in the traditional metrical description of Greek and Latin verse forms. Here an underlying 'standard' form, which is only rarely realized as such, is distinguished from the finite set of all possible manifest realizations related to the standard form by means of a set of explicitly defined rules. A relatively simple instance is the standard form of the hexameter: $- \cup \cup \, / - \cup \cup \, / - \cup \cup \, / - \cup \cup \, / - \cup \cup \, / - \underset{\smile}{} $ ('$-$' standing for a long syllable, '$\cup$' for a short syllable, '$\underset{\smile}{}$' for a syllable which may be either long or short). The possible variations are mainly defined by the rule that two successive short syllables may be replaced by one long syllable. In the theory of Greek and Latin metre it would not be inappropriate to take the 'standard' form as the deep structure, the realizations as surface structures, and the rules of variation as transformations.

A few concrete examples will clarify this point. While setting up rules for non-deviant collocation of lexical items (selectional restrictions), one defines lexical subcategories on the basis of semantic features, which are then made part of the description of each lexical item and incorporated into the lexicon. Individual lexical meanings are thus to some extent analysed into semantic features, or, one might say, they are factorized. This analysis will only be complete when the selection restriction rules are known for all lexical items in the language in collocation with each other. Clearly, the total number of lexical items of a language is too large to be dealt with at once. A possible approach, therefore, is to select, more or less at random, a limited number of lexical items and to define the selectional restrictions of their collocations with each other. This approach is exemplified in chapter 5.

While delimiting for each verb in the limited vocabulary the corresponding class of possible non-deviant object-nouns, one finds that practically every verb has its own unique selection. On careful analysis, however, it appears to be possible to make subclassifications of nouns in such a way that every verb can be said to take as possible object a relatively small number of subcategories of nouns. The establishment of these subcategories is a question of trial and error: one tries to find the solution with the smallest number of subcategories for each verb. The result is an intricate network of subclassifications. In the limited vocabulary selected in chapter 5, the set of nouns that can fill the object-position with the verb *write* contains, among others, the subset *distance, age, length, name, change, wish, price*, etc. The same subset can be distinguished among the possible object-nouns for the verbs *read, see, hear, say, tell, ask, learn, teach*, and others, among the possible predicate nouns for, *inter alia*, the adjectives *clear, new, old*. But, apart from this specific subset of nouns, the verbs and adjectives mentioned also take other nouns as their object or predicate nominal, and these, in turn, recur as subsets in other positions for other verbs. Within the limits of this small vocabulary it proves useful, therefore, to assign specific features to the various nouns, so that they are classified in subcategories. On the basis of the common semantic property of each subcategory the relevant features can be given significant names, such as 'parameter' (*par*) for the subcategory *distance, age*, etc. mentioned above. Such features thus embody specific hypotheses about the deep structure of some lexical items in English. If in other limited vocabularies the same feature can be isolated so that it proves useful in the joint description of all limited vocabularies investigated in the same way, and ultimately in the description of the total lexicon of the language, then it is fairly safe to assert that this is a relevant semantic feature in the lexicon of the language.

It is clear that such an assertion can only be made on the basis of careful and detailed analysis. The assignment of semantic features for the purpose of defining selectional restrictions without such analysis can only be *ad hoc* and intuitive. The features assigned by Chomsky to the lexical items in his 'illustrative fragment of the base component' ((1965) p. 107; see 2.3) are not based on a detailed analysis of a limited vocabulary of any reasonable variety, and must, therefore, be taken as offering no more than a non-committal illustration of his notational formalism, with few pretensions to descriptive adequacy. Similarly, Katz and Postal (1964) give semantic feature analyses for a few isolated items (*bachelor*, on p. 14; *colourful* and *ball*, on p. 22), but they do not justify these analyses in the light of an over-all description of the lexicon of English. In 3.4.2 we have seen that the most likely assumption is that they draw upon philosophical preconceptions about the organization and contents of human knowledge in the mind. It is true that they do not present these analyses as a way of describing selection restriction features, which are bundled together under a general heading 'ω', but they give no details about these intended selection restriction features, and do not indicate why and how these are to be distinguished from the 'semantic markers'. Yet they recognize the need for a justification of analyses as given by them. On p. 14 they say: 'The meaning of a lexical item is not an undifferentiated whole. Rather, it is analysable into atomic conceptual elements related to each other in certain ways', to which they add a note (p. 28), where they mention the anthropologists as having been the first to carry out a 'componential analysis' of lexical meanings. They continue:

However, such studies have failed to recognize that the analyzability of meanings extends beyond certain limited lexical sets like kinship terms, body parts, etc. to include all lexical items. More importantly, work in componential analysis of individual lexical items or sets has not shown how the componential analysis of such items may be integrated in a full linguistic description which supplies semantic interpretations for each of the infinite set of well-formed sentences and their constituents. This gap is due largely to the failure to consider the need for projection rules and the failure to consider componential analysis within the context of explicit generative linguistic descriptions.

One wonders where Katz and Postal themselves provide information how the results of componential analysis can be made to form part of an adequate integrated linguistic description. They have in view, here, the integration of semantic and syntactic descriptions into full linguistic descriptions, but their argument extends as well to the componential analysis of lexical items itself: if this is to be integrated into a full semantic-syntactic description of a language, it will be subject to the general requirements for such descriptions, i.e. the requirements of descriptive adequacy.

An example of a grammatical, or syntactic, semantic feature identified on the basis of a particular deep structure hypothesis for English is provided by the analysis of such sentences as:

(30)   John sleeps on the sofa
(31)   John sleeps on Monday morning

On the face of it, one would establish underlying structures for these two sentences, where the predicate consists of an intransitive verb (*sleep*) plus a prepositional phrase of place (*on the sofa*) or time (*on Monday morning*). But closer analysis reveals that there are syntactic differences between (30) and (31), which make it necessary to establish different deep structures for them. Thus, for example, we can say:

(32)   this is the sofa John sleeps on

but rather not (depending on dialectal and idiolectal variations):

(33)   (*)this is the morning John sleeps on

or:

(34)   the sofa is slept on by John

but not (or hardly):

(35)   (*)Monday morning is slept on by John

The same difference is found in pairs of sentences like:

(36)   John works at this book
(37)   John works at Cambridge

or:

(38)   John decided on the dearer quality
(39)   John decided on my behalf

These observations lead to the postulation of a deep structure differentiation between (30), (36) and (38) on the one hand, and (31), (37) and (39) on the other. This is precisely what is done by Chomsky ((1965) pp. 101–6; see also (33)–(41) in 2.3). This difference in syntactic structure reveals itself as a semantic difference also, as appears from the fact that it is very easy to construct homonymous sentences whose different meanings are distinguished by this syntactic feature. (It is, actually, far more difficult to find unambiguous examples than ambiguous ones.) Thus we have Chomsky's example ((1965) p. 101):

(40)   he decided on the boat

which means something different according to whether it is paraphrased as:

(41)   the boat was decided on by him

or as:

(42)   on the boat he decided

Or else:

(43)   John works at this machine

which can be paraphrased as either:

(44)   this machine is worked at by John

or:

(45)   at this machine John works

One notices that the paraphrase as found in (42) and (45) is typical of the deep structure of (39), (37) and (31), since we have:

(46)   on my behalf John decided
(47)   at Cambridge John works
(48)   on Monday morning John sleeps

but not:

(49)   *on the dearer quality John decided
(50)   *at this book John works

We can have, however,

(51)   on the sofa John sleeps

which indicates that the apparently simple and unambiguous sentence (30) is, after all, homonymous: in the interpretation underlying (32) and (34) it has the same syntactic and semantic feature as (36) and (38), but its paraphrase (51) presupposes the syntactic and semantic interpretation of (31), (37) and (39).[1]

---

[1] Chomsky's statement that *John lived in England* is ambiguous ((1965) pp. 217–18, note 27; see also (41) in 2.3) finds support in the same arguments. This ambiguity is therefore not far-fetched or doubtful, as one might be inclined to think.

The semantic difference involved can be tentatively described as a difference of cohesion between the verb and the prepositional phrase (as is said by Chomsky (1965) p. 101). More specifically, one might say that the prepositional phrase in (36) and (38) is a verb complement and, therefore, directly dependent on the verb, whereas in (31), (37) and (39) it extends semantically over the whole rest of the sentence. (30), being homonymous, is open to both interpretations. This indication of the semantic quality of the feature under discussion is admittedly vague, but it would be premature to be too precise here, since much work both in syntax and in semantics still remains to be done, and it is quite possible that further distinctions and refinements will have to be made.

Here again, then, identification of the two semantic features was only possible after a careful analysis of the syntactic properties of at least some English sentences, and of subsequent statements about their deep structure. Intuitive or speculative judgements alone would not easily lead to the recognition of (30) as being ambiguous, in contrast to the unambiguous (31), or would, at any rate, not easily enable one to defend this statement against the possible criticism that the ambiguity of (30) would be too far-fetched (see p. 101, note 1). We are in a position now to supply convincing evidence in support of both syntactic and semantic analyses.

An adequate deep structure analysis will therefore contribute to at least a partial semantic description of the language, and thus to the establishment of a semantic descriptive language in which to describe the relevant semantic features of each sentence. So far linguistics has lacked an adequate semantic descriptive language and all semantic descriptions of lexical items as well as of grammatical patterns have been largely *ad hoc*, unsystematic and generally inadequate. In 1.4.4 it was said of this state of affairs that it complicated the description of the meanings of strange or deviant sentences. In 5.4.2 more will be said about the relation between deep structure and semantic description. Ideally, an adequate semantic descriptive language will be a one-to-one interpretation of the deep structures generated by the base: it will thus describe in semantic terms the relevant semantic features of a language and their combinations in larger idiosyncratic wholes or sentences, while at the same time excluding meaningless combinations or ungrammatical strings.

There is a general feeling among transformational linguists that deep structure somehow reflects universal features of human language, i.e.

features independent of any specific language. This feeling derives from the observation that the deep structure hypotheses set up so far for different languages are considerably closer to each other than the corresponding surface structures. It is strengthened by a certain amount of wishful thinking, inasmuch as a universal deep structure grammar underlying all languages would be a splendid asset to linguistic theory. If it were available, it would, among other things, provide important insights into the process of translation, and would help towards an objective evaluation of translations and also towards a formalization of translation procedures.

Chomsky expresses himself rather cautiously on this point (see chapter 1, p. 1, note 1). It should be kept in mind, at any rate, that there is, as yet, no convincing evidence of a deep structure underlying all languages. One must be careful in setting up hypotheses. We are in the process of developing a deep structure hypothesis of English, and it would certainly be rash on our part if we assumed, on the basis of very scanty evidence indeed, that our ultimate model for English deep structure would be the most adequate also for all other languages. It is theoretically possible that we shall have to devise a 'second degree' hypothesis applicable to deep structure models of every particular language. For the moment we must wait and see which deep structure hypothesis for, for instance, English is the most adequate, expecting that the best will emerge. Once we have similarly tested hypotheses for other languages, we shall be in a position to compare them.

It is, on the other hand, not unreasonable to keep an eye on the possibility of a universal deep structure. For it can hardly be denied that actual work in different languages has shown that they are at least more general than the surface structures corresponding to them. One obvious obstacle is the idiosyncratic character of lexical items in different languages: hardly ever is there an exact semantic equivalence of two items belonging to two different languages. Perhaps this obstacle could be overcome, eventually, by admitting only lexical semantic features in deep structure, so that the actual items would be introduced transformationally. But such considerations still have too weak a basis to be given any further attention here (see 5.4.2 for further discussion in the light of the description given in chapter 5).

4.2   Operators as a deep structure category

A number of English sentences will now be investigated in accordance with the method outlined in the preceding section, and a deep structure hypothesis will be framed for their description.

4.2.1 Some reasons for the assumption of some operators. Let us consider the sentence:

(52)   John ate the apple

and its passive counterpart:

(53)   the apple was eaten by John

Let us suppose that (53) was transformed from a deep structure similar to that of (52), but for the additional constituent *by + Passive*, according to the passive transformation (11) in chapter 2; and let us take (7) of chapter 2 as a fragment of the corresponding base grammar, the category of nouns being extended to include *apple* and *John*, and the category of verbs to include *eat*. The underlying base-terminal string of (53) would then be:

(54)   John Past eat the apple by Passive

Let us now gradually extend grammar (7) of chapter 2. We can, tentatively, reformulate rule *viii* as:

viii′ $\text{T} \to (\text{Neg}) \begin{Bmatrix} \text{Pres} \\ \text{Past} \end{Bmatrix}$

(assuming that the element *Neg* will be assigned its possible positions by means of a set of transformations). We can now form:

(55)   John Neg Past eat the apple by Passive

This is passivized into:

(56)   the apple Neg Past be en eat by John

Following a possible transformation by which *Neg* is not detached from *T*, from which it was developed by *viii′*, we arrive at:

(57)   the apple was not eaten by John

So far, there is complete semantic regularity. The meaning of (53) and (57) is not very different from that of the sentences based on similar deep structures but without the element *by + Passive*. That is, (53) means roughly the same as (52), and (57) means the same as:

(58) John did not eat the apple

Or, in other words, the constituent *by + Passive* in the deep structure is meaningless in these cases. It is an abstract marker bringing about the obligatory application of the passive transformation and ruling out—on the basis of restrictions of its occurrence specified by the base rules— ungrammatical passivizations of deep structures with verbs such as *have*, *be*, or *resemble*. (It is questionable whether such a treatment of the passive is compatible with the requirement of a semantically determined deep structure, but this complication may be overlooked here: the treatment of the passive given here is the one generally found in the literature on transformational grammar. See, however, what is said in 5.1 about the status of passive sentences.)

Let us now add a further element to our grammar by reformulating rule *vi*, again tentatively, as:

$$vi' \quad A \to \begin{Bmatrix} \text{Def} \\ \text{Indef} \end{Bmatrix}$$

(assuming that *Def* will be rewritten transformationally as *the*, and *Indef* as *a* before a singular count-noun beginning with a consonant, as *an* before all other singular count-nouns, and as null before a singular non-count noun and before all plurals). The base-terminal string:

(59) John Neg Past eat Indef apple by Passive

will now become:

(60) Indef apple Neg Past be en eat by John

Under the same *Neg*-transformation as above for (57) this becomes:

(61) an apple was not eaten by John

which, according to many speakers of English at least, is ungrammatical, and should be replaced by either *one apple was not eaten by John* or *there is (was) an apple which was not eaten by John*.

We see that here we have an irregularity, not only in form, but also in meaning. (61), or, if one wishes, its more correct versions, has a meaning different from the active sentence derived from the passiveless deep structure corresponding to (59), viz.:

(62) John did not eat an apple

This implies that, in this case at least, the addition of *by + Passive* has a semantic effect which in other cases it does not have. The blame for this might seem to lie with the introduction of the indefinite article into the grammar. It is easily seen, however, that it is not simply the introduction of the indefinite article which is responsible for this irregularity. For if we leave, for the moment, rule *viii* as it stands and introduce first rule *vi'*, the grammar permits us to generate a base-terminal string:

(63)   John Past eat Indef apple by Passive

with its transform:

(64)   Indef apple Past be en eat by John

where no irregularity occurs. If we replace *viii* by *viii'*, the grammar permits us again to generate (59) and (60), and the irregularity could be said to be due to the introduction of the negation element. The correct answer seems to be that it is the joint occurrence of the negation element and the indefinite article which is the root of this difficulty.

Before trying to formulate a descriptive solution at this point, let us consider some more examples. The semantically regular passive of (62) is:

(65)   no apple was eaten by John

It is also to be noticed that the same difficulty is found in sentences combining the occurrence of *Neg* with numerals not preceded by the definite article. We have, for example:

(66)   John did not eat two apples

with its semantically irregular passive:

(67)   two apples were not eaten by John

and the semantically regular:

(68)   no two apples were eaten by John

But

(69)   John did not eat the two apples

has the regular passive:

(70)   the two apples were not eaten by John

One might reply that here again it is the difference between under-lying definite and indefinite article which is at issue, so that we still have the joint occurrence of *Neg* and the indefinite article. But then we must observe that we also have:

(71)   everybody ate two apples

with its semantically irregular passive:

(72)   two apples were eaten by everybody

and the regular passive:

(73)   by everybody two apples were eaten

Similar instances (see also (10) and (11) in 4.1 and (1 *a*)–(2 *d*) in 1.4.3) are discussed by Katz and Postal (1964), who refer to Chomsky ((1957) pp. 100–1): '...we can describe circumstances in which a "quantificational" sentence such as

(74)   everyone in the room knows at least two languages

may be true, while the corresponding passive

(75)   at least two languages are known by everyone in the room

is false, under the normal interpretation of these sentences—e.g. if one person in the room knows only French and German, and another only Spanish and Italian. This indicates that not even the weakest semantic relation (factual equivalence) holds in general between active and passive.' Katz and Postal's answer (pp. 72–3) is partly correct in that they maintain that the grammar must be such that there is a relation of semantic regularity between active and passive sentences, but also partly incorrect when they deny a semantic difference between (74) and (75), both, as they say, being ambiguous in the same way. But Chomsky speaks of the 'normal interpretation of these sentences', which is quite a legitimate concept in this case, since it is accompanied by a normal intonation: under normal, or non-contrastive, sentence intonation (74) and (75) do mean something different. (It will be shown below that this difference can be attributed to a different order of operators in deep structure, reflected in the order of the representatives of these operators in surface structures. It is interesting to notice how, in English at least, intonational breaks and contrasts can make up for irregular surface orderings of operator representatives.)

Katz and Postal's argument breaks down, furthermore, if we take another example. Consider, e.g.:

(76)   nobody in the room knows two languages

and

(77)   two languages are known by nobody in the room

To maintain that (76) and (77) are ambiguous in the same way would hardly seem acceptable. One sees, moreover, that (77) is synonymous with:

(78)   two languages are not known by anybody in the room

but not, for example, with:

(79)   by nobody in the room are two languages known

which would rather be the semantically regular passive of (76). Similarly, rather than (75), the regular passive of (74) must be taken to be:

(80)   by everyone in the room at least two languages are known

We would wish our grammar to account for these observations.

   We remark, furthermore, that the active sentence corresponding to (67) is rather to be taken as:

(81)   two apples John did not eat

Similarly, the regular active for (72) would be:

(82)   two apples everybody ate

(no matter how nonsensical such a sentence would have to be). For (75) we would have:

(83)   at least two languages everyone in the room knows

and for (77):

(84)   two languages nobody in the room knows

But (81)–(84) sound somewhat forced in English, and we would rather say 'there are two apples which...' or 'there are (at least) two languages which...'. In fact, the expected regular active of (61), viz.:

(85)   *an apple John did not eat

is ungrammatical, and must be replaced by either:

(86)   one apple John did not eat

(if this is, indeed, equivalent to (61) and (85)), or, better, by:

(87)   there is (was) an apple which John did not eat

   A number of considerations readily arise out of this context, for example, that there seems to be a closer connection between the indefinite article and the numeral *one* than is perhaps thought at first glance, or that the deep structure of a sentence such as (87) is not adequately described by taking 'there is an apple S' as the embedding S with an embedded relative clause 'John did not eat the apple' (as is done by Katz and Postal (1964) p. 73). But let us reserve these considerations for future discussion and pause to notice that a relation of order between certain elements seems to be crucial to the semantic regularity between active and passive sentences. We see that in (62) and (65), which form a regular pair, the negation element precedes the indefinite article, whereas in (86) or (87) on the one hand, and (61) on the other, the order is reversed. Again, in the regular pair (66) and (68) *Neg* precedes *two*, but in (81) and (67) *two* precedes *Neg*. Likewise, the order of *everyone/body* and *two* is the same in (71), (73), (74) and (80), but reversed in (82), (72), (83) and (75). Finally, in (76) and (79) *nobody* precedes *two*, but in (84) and (77) *two* precedes *nobody*. This suggests that the order of at least these elements in relation to each other is a relevant feature of the meanings of the sentences in which more than one of them occur together.

A great many more examples confirm this impression. We have, e.g., Klima's examples ((1964) p. 271; see 4.1 for a critical summary of Klima's work on negation in English):

(88) they had not left much food
(89) not much food had been left by them

to which we may add:

(90) much food had not been left by them
(91) much food they had not left

Under normal sentence intonation (88) and (89) mean the same (apart from any possible semantic difference introduced by the passive), and also (90) and (91). The same order-bound semantic features are observed independently of the active–passive relation. Compare, for example:

(92) two spectators did not cheer
(93) no two spectators cheered

Or some other examples given by Klima ((1964) p. 284):

(94) many smokers do not chew gum
(95) not many smokers chew gum

The same alternation seems to occur between (25), (28) and (29) on the one hand, and (26) and (27) on the other, where *Neg* and *often* interchange their order. It occurs again between:

(96)   I do not know anybody

and

(97)   somebody I do not know

where it is assumed that *some* is, or can be, replaced by *any* when preceded by a non-contiguous negation element. Thus *Neg . . . + some* is rewritten transformationally as *Neg . . . + any-*. But *Neg + some* becomes *no-*. For *sometimes* let us suppose the additional rule that *any + times* becomes *ever*, and *no + times never*. This is essentially the description of *any* proposed by Lees (1960 *b*). It is adopted here as it is sufficient for the present purpose. But the discussion in 4.2.4 shows that it is insufficient for a full grammatical description.

   Moreover, if no other elements of the type of element we are discussing intervene between *Neg* and *some*, a synonymy relation can be said to hold between the contiguous and the non-contiguous position of *Neg* with regard to *some* in the surface structure. Thus:

(98)   I do not know anything

and

(99)   I know nothing

are largely synonymous. (Any possible regular semantic difference would have to be established by careful analysis of selected examples.) In the same sense (96) is synonymous with:

(100)   I know nobody

This explains, in principle, the degree of synonymy between (77) and (78). On the basis of these grammatical assumptions we say that in (96) and (100) *Neg* precedes *some*, but in (97) *some* precedes *Neg*.

   If we take three elements out of this gradually emerging class, and distribute them over sentences, the possible syntactic-semantic variations become more numerous. Let us consider a set of examples based on *Neg, something* and *sometimes* (cf. Klima (1964) p. 276):

(101)   nothing is ever right
(102)   never is anything right
(103)   something is never right

(104) something is sometimes not right
(105) sometimes nothing is right
(106) sometimes something is not right

(101) and (102) are synonymous, as well as (104) and (106). But there are no further synonyms. The synonymy of these two pairs is due, as it seems, to a general rule that two consecutive elements containing *some*, that is, without any other member of the class occurring between them, may interchange their position without a change of meaning. Thus, in (101) we have the order *Neg—something—sometimes*, whereas in (102) we find *Neg—sometimes—something*. A similar interchange of positions is easily recognized in (104) and (106).

Let us see now if we can formulate a hypothesis to incorporate these observations into a deep structure description of English. A possible solution for a description aiming at a regular association of deep structure with meaning is, perhaps, to single out those elements whose order partly determines the meaning of the sentences in which two or more of them occur together, and which disturb the regular effect of certain transformations. They can then be generated separately in some order and be associated with certain elements in the rest of the deep structure. The transformations will take care of the correct incorporation of the elements generated separately into the rest of the sentence, according to their position in the deep structure. The relevant semantic information will be read immediately from the deep structure, and the transformations will leave the meaning untouched.

To be more precise, we single out a class of elements containing:

(107) Neg   (negation element: 'it is not true that...')
       $E(x)$ ('there is/are a/some x such that...')
       $E(1x)$ ('there is one x such that...')
       $E(2x)$ ('there are two x such that...') etc. for all natural
                    numbers
       $E(Mult\ x)$ ('there is/are much/many x such that...')
       $A(x)$ ('for all x it is true that...')

Let us suppose that there are deep structure rules permitting the derivation of, for example:

(108) Neg: John Past eat the apple

as the base-terminal string underlying (58), and interpretable as 'it is not true that John ate the apple'. Generally, two main constituents are

distinguished in the deep structure of at least some sentences (we shall
see below that there are good reasons for considering every sentence as
consisting of these two constituents), namely the *operator constituent*
and the *nucleus*. The former contains elements from (107)—which
will have to be extended to include many more elements, as we
shall see below—; the latter does not contain any such element but con-
forms to a relatively simple pattern of *subject—verb—object—indirect
object—prepositional object*, or *subject—copula—predicate nominal*. The
colon indicates the boundary between these main constituents in the
base-terminal strings. Thus we want the base to generate also, for
example:

(109)   Neg E(apple) : John Past eat the apple

to be interpreted as 'it is not true that there is an apple such that John
ate the apple', and underlying (62). Or:

(110)   E(apple) Neg : John Past eat the apple

underlying (87) and meaning 'there is an apple such that it is not true
that John ate the apple'. (61) would correspond to:

(111)   E(apple) Neg : John Past eat the apple by Passive

(or else: $E(1\ apple)$ etc.) (67) would be derived from:

(112)   E(2 apples) Neg : John Past eat the apples by Passive

and (68) would have the same deep structure but for the reversed order
of the two operators.

   The solution to the difficulty of the semantically irregular passives
now becomes obvious: the transition to passive is a matter of the nucleus
alone, and the operators are incorporated transformationally after the
transition to the passive (whether this is a transformation or an operation
within the base, is immaterial here). Thus (11) of chapter 2 appears to
be correct, since its domain does not include QU of (7) i, which, as we
shall see, must be regarded as an operator.

   (71) would be reducible to:

(113)   A(individuals) E(2 apples) : the individuals Past eat the apples

(i.e. 'for all individuals it is true that there are two apples such that the
individuals ate the apples'). If the nucleus of (113) is passivized, the
surface structure becomes (73). The passivized nucleus with the two
operators interchanged results in (72).

(76) would have an underlying base structure:

(114)   Neg E(individual in the room) E(2 languages) : the individuals
        Pres know the languages

('it is not true that there is an individual in the room and that there are two languages such that the individual knows the languages').

(77) and (78) would correspond to:

(115)   E(2 languages) Neg E(individual in the room) : the individual
        Pres know the languages by Passive

(94) would be the result of an underlying:

(116)   E(*Mult* smokers) Neg : the smokers Pres chew gum

and (95) would have the same underlying structure, but with the two operators interchanged.

For (101) we would have:

(117)   Neg E(thing) E(moment) : the thing Pres be right at the moment

('it is not true that there is a thing and that there is a moment such that the thing is right at the moment'). And (102)–(106) would be analysable in the same way, but with different positions for the three operators.

It is not difficult to see that the distinction between operators and nucleus must be made at the very beginning of the base. Kraak's treatment of the negation element may serve as an example. He proposes ((1966) p. 150) the following rules at the beginning of the base:

(118)   *i*   Sent → (Neg)Nucleus
        ii Nucleus → NP + VP

He thus gives it the position of an operator, but treats it as a unique element and does not consider the possibility of its belonging to a larger class of operators. Yet he mentions the similarity of these rules to those proposed by Katz and Postal ((1964) p. 115) for *yes/no*-questions—see rules (7) *i* and (7) *ii* of chapter 2. If we take both Kraak's and Katz and Postal's proposals to be correct, the first rule of the grammar should be:

(119)   Sent → ($\left\{ \begin{matrix} Neg \\ QU \end{matrix} \right\}$)Nucleus

Extending the class containing *Neg* and *QU* to the whole category of operators, we may replace the right-hand side of (119) and (118) *i* by: (*OP*)*Nucleus*. Since, as we shall see below, every sentence has at least two operators, namely a sentence qualifier (or operator of

8   SON

entertainment),[1] such as *assertion, question, command,* and a tense operator, we shall have to write: $OP + Nucleus$.

Katz and Postal's arguments for separating QU from the Nucleus, and thus treating it in effect as an operator, are doubtless valid. This suggests that QU must be assumed in the category of sentence operators. But there are also other reasons for classifying QU as an operator. Consider, for example, the ambiguous sentence:

(120)   can I leave something for John?

the ambiguity of which can be naturally described by distinguishing:

(121)   E(thing) QU Poss : I Pres leave the thing for John
(122)   QU E(thing) Poss : I Pres leave the thing for John

to be interpreted as 'there is a thing such that I wish to know whether it is possible that I leave the thing for John' and 'I wish to know whether there is a thing such that it is possible that I leave the thing for John' respectively. QU is thus considered to mean 'I wish to know (whether)'.[2]

The assumption of *Poss* ('it is possible that') as an operator is justified by examples such as:

(123)   John may not come
(124)   John cannot come

interpretable as 'it is possible that it is not true that John comes/will come' and 'it is not true that it is possible that John comes/will come' (see also 4.3.4 and 4.3.6). But before adding more elements to our category of operators, let us consider some general questions.

One might be tempted to argue that a deep structure hypothesis such as (114) with its semantic interpretation is rather far-fetched for a sentence as simple as (76). But the answer is, obviously, that our analysis has precisely shown that (76) is not so simple as one might think without actual detailed observation. Objections to this deep structure description should show either that it is semantically inadequate, or that a simpler explanation can be given, or both.

The term 'operators' has been chosen for the elements of (107) because of their striking similarity with the operators of logic. One recognizes the existential and universal operators (also called quantifiers), which have the property of binding variables.

---

[1] This term is taken from Lewis (1946) p. 49; see 4.2.2.
[2] In view of the treatment of *wh*-questions in 4.3.5, the element 'whether' is bracketed here.

Among the operators investigated so far two subcategories can be distinguished, the one comprising *Neg*, *QU* and *Poss*, the other the various forms of the existential and the universal quantifiers. The latter group will be called 'quantifiers' here too, as in logic, since, analogously to their logical namesakes which bind variables, they operate on nominal elements in the nucleus. The former will be designated by the term 'qualifiers', since they have a bearing on the semantic 'quality' of their operand, which is never less than a nucleus.[1] We shall see in chapter 5 that the rules for qualifiers differ considerably from those relating to quantifiers.

4.2.2 Operators and logic. It seems quite reasonable to expect that the distinction of a deep structure category of operators will throw some new light on the relationship between logic and linguistics. That the two are found to be related should cause no surprise: both deal with products of the mind, thoughts, though from different points of view (see p. 12 above). A number of philosophers, who have undertaken an analysis of natural language, found that, for logical and semantic reasons, the sentences of natural language should be considered as consisting of two main constituents. It seems that we can now make the same distinction on syntactic grounds, thus bridging the gap from the other side.[2]

In his *Formal Logic* ((1955) p. 186) Prior mentions a question raised by Aristotle about the negation of sentences containing a modal auxiliary verb: 'Aristotle begins his discussion of modal statements in the *De Interpretatione* (Chs. 12, 13) by remarking that although we generally form the denial of a statement by attaching a "not" to its verb, "B may not be A" is not the denial of "B may be A". And the reason for this, he suggests, is that "may" is not the real "verb" here, for "B may be A" means "That B should be A is possible", while "B may not be A" means "That B should not-be-A is possible", the true contradictory of the former being not this, but rather "That B should be A is-not-possible", i.e. "B cannot be A".' (Compare (123) and (124) given above.)

---

[1] The terms *semantic quality* and *qualifier* are admittedly vague in this context, but there seems to be no more precise denomination available, the term *modality* being too restricted to necessity, possibility, and the like. The exposition which follows, however, will give a more precise meaning to the term *qualifier*, in so far as it succeeds in characterizing the class of qualifiers.

[2] I am most indebted to Prof. G. Nuchelmans of the University of Leyden for the references that follow. His article 'Taaldaden', *Forum der Letteren* VIII (1967) pp. 208–23, gives a much better account of the development of the distinction between operators and nucleus in the history of modal logic than I could possibly present. In fact, what follows is partly taken from his article and wholly due to it.

The text by Aristotle referred to here may be said to mark the beginning of a logic of modal statements, or modal logic, the development of which up to modern times made it possible for von Wright to state ((1951) Preface): 'There is an obvious formal analogy between so-called quantifiers on the one hand and a variety of concepts, including the traditional modalities, on the other hand.' Our hypothesis of operators as a deep structure category in grammar thus has a philosophical pedigree leading back to both the theory of quantifiers and the logic of modalities. A category of operators as distinct from a nucleus is found in both, but it is most clearly related with the sentences of natural language in modal logic. It is more than just a coincidence that the concept of modal operators, after an almost complete standstill of several centuries, was taken up again and further developed by the modern school of analytic philosophers.

Up to the end of the Middle Ages modal logic was developed mainly on the basis of three operators, possibility, necessity and contingency.[1] That is, deductive rules were established for the derivations of modal statements from other modal statements with the preservation of the same (modal) truth values. The operators were subsumed under the category of *modus*, the nucleus was called *dictum*. Then Pseudo-Scot proposed a considerable number of new modal operators,[2] including *per se, true, false, dubium* (doubtful), *scitum* (known), *opinatum* (thought), *apparens* (clear), *notum* (generally known), *volitum* (lawful), *dilectum* (preferred). He was followed in the eighteenth century by Isaac Watts, who proposed supplementing these operators with *certain, probable, improbable, agreed, granted, said by the Ancients, written* (i.e. in Holy Scripture).[3] In recent times it was even proposed that *de fide* (article of faith) and *heretical* should be added as theological operators.[4] This tendency of modal operators to proliferate is seen in an extreme form in the work of Kerner (1966), who maintains (p. 145) that the number of modal operators is infinite, and mentions not only questions and promises, already recognized by others,[5] but also 'challenging, protest-

---

[1] See Prior (1955) pp. 185–93; Kneale (1962) pp. 212–14. Sometimes also a fourth modal operator was acknowledged, namely *impossibility* (Bocheński (1962b) pp. 211–13), but this is easily seen to consist of *not + possibility*.

[2] See Bocheński (1962b) pp. 261–2; Kneale (1962) pp. 242–3.

[3] See Prior (1955) pp. 215–16.

[4] I. Thomas, 'Logic and Theology', *Dominican Studies Oct. 1948*, quoted by Prior (1955) p. 216.

[5] For questions see, for example, Lewis (1946) p. 49. Promises were distinguished as such by Austin in his 'Performative utterances' of 1956, published in Austin (1961) pp. 220–39.

ing, envisaging, favouring, approving, &c.' Although Kerner is un-doubtedly right in criticizing Hare ((1952) pp. 17–20) for admitting only the two operators ('neustics') indicative and imperative, one wonders whether Ockham's razor is not called for here.

There should at least be some criterion by which one can decide when an expression is to be regarded as an operator. For natural language a sensible deep structure hypothesis will provide such a criterion. In logic this necessity is felt by Lewis (1946),[1] who writes in a footnote on p. 49: 'Exact logic has not as yet much concerned itself with these various moods of entertaining propositions [the term commonly used in logic for what is called "nucleus" here; in 4.3.2 and 4.3.3, however, the two will be distinguished]. Assertion is recognized, and postulation—though postulation is usually dealt with inconsistently and confused with assertion. Also it begins to be understood that the imperative or hortatory mood has its own logical principles, and that the so-called modal statements, of possibility and necessity, demand separate con-sideration. If these matters were to be adequately treated, we should, of course, expect some attempt at economy; the reduction of some moods to expression in terms of others.' He himself proposes (p. 49): '"$\vdash p$" for assertion of "p", "Hp" for the postulation of it, "$!p$" for the mere greeting of it as a presentation of sense or imagination, "$?p$" for putting it in question, "Mp" for entertainment of it as consistently thinkable or possible, and so on', at which point he appends the footnote quoted above. It is, perhaps, not unreasonable to submit that, apart from the limitations imposed by the development of a maximally simple modal logic, a maximally simple hypothesis of grammatical deep structure will be of some help here.

Lewis wants his propositions to be separated from operators (p. 49): 'The proposition is something assert*able*; the *content* of the assertion; and this same content, signifying the same state of affairs, can also be questioned, denied, or merely supposed, and can be entertained in other moods as well. For example the statement, "Mary is making pies", asserts the state of affairs, Mary making pies now, as actual. "Is Mary making pies?" questions it; "Oh that Mary may be making pies", expresses it in the optative mood; and "Suppose that Mary is making pies", puts it forward as a postulate.' He includes the element 'now', indicating the present tense, in the proposition. Other logicians, however, go further, and consider tenseless propositions. Bocheński ((1962*b*)

---

[1] Also by Prior (1955) p. 217.

p. 212) separates the tenseless *Socratem currere* ('Socrates running') from the modal operators, while Quine ((1960) p. 165) separates it from quantifiers. In 4.1 mention was made, in connection with (6)–(9), of the desirability of tenseless underlying structures. We can now be more explicit on this point and say that it is desirable to let the grammar generate tenseless nuclei, the element 'tense' being relegated to the category of operators. (Grammatical evidence will be given below, in 4.3.4, in support of the hypothesis to regard 'tense' as a qualifier, and the deep structures given in (108)–(117) and (121)–(122) will have to be amended accordingly.) It is interesting to note that some logicians came to an analogous conclusion in logic.

It need hardly be said that in the present study no attempt is made at solving the problem of the number of operators in modal logic. Nor is it feasible to give an exhaustive grammatical description of the category of operators in the deep structure of English. Only a first start can be made here. But the conclusion at least emerges that grammar and logic are not as far apart as is commonly believed.

4.2.3 Scope. Operators provide a natural answer to the question of scope. In general terms, this question arises from the fact that, on the one hand, one clearly feels that certain elements in the sentences of a language extend semantically over other elements, but that, on the other hand, no descriptively adequate account of this feeling has so far been given. Thus it is intuitively felt that the scope of the negation element in (25) is different from that in (26). In fact, one would say that *often* in (25) does not come within its scope, but that in (26) it does. Klima (1964) is one of those grammarians who have treated the problem of scope, but, as we have seen, his attempt was not entirely successful. Seen in terms of our hypothesis, scope assigns a semantic property to operators, and the scope of an operator O is precisely that part of the deep structure which follows O. The scope may thus embrace one or more operators apart from the nucleus, which comes within the scope of any operator.

This way of defining scope coincides essentially with the device of bracketing, as it is usually found in logical formulae. A clear instance is provided by Carnap's use of parentheses for operators. In (1964), p. 21, he writes: 'If $\mathfrak{A}_1$ and $\mathfrak{A}_2$ are operators, then, instead of writing $\mathfrak{A}_1(\mathfrak{A}_2(\mathfrak{S}))$, we shall write simply $\mathfrak{A}_1 \mathfrak{A}_2(\mathfrak{S})$'—where '$\mathfrak{S}$' is equivalent to our nucleus. He refers for this abbreviated notation to p. 19: 'for the sake of brevity..., we shall (as is customary) leave out the brackets surrounding a partial expression $\mathfrak{A}_1$ (which may be either a sentence or the syntactical designation of a sentence) in the following cases:...5. When $\mathfrak{A}_1$ is an operand and itself begins with an operator'. The unabbreviated notation $\mathfrak{A}_1(\mathfrak{A}_2(\mathfrak{S}))$ is normally interpreted as: the scope of $\mathfrak{A}_1$ is $\mathfrak{A}_2(\mathfrak{S})$, and the scope of $\mathfrak{A}_2$ is $\mathfrak{S}$.

4.2.4 Any, some, every, all. In order to give an approximate idea of the complexity and variety of the category of operators, let us investigate some classes of grammatical phenomena to see if these can be adequately described by a system of operators.

A particularly agonizing problem in the category of quantifiers is presented by the word *any*. In recent literature the problem is discussed by Quine ((1951) pp. 70–1; (1960) pp. 138–41), Lees (1960), Bolinger (1960) and Klima ((1964) pp. 274, 279, 285). But none of their solutions seems satisfactory. The solution given by Lees was briefly mentioned in 4.2.1 in connection with (96)–(100). He proposed this description in his review of Bolinger's *Interrogative Structures of American English* (1957). Bolinger replied in his article (1960), which, apart from being a most sensible approach to grammatical problems in general, shows a great number of disturbing examples. He leaves the problem open and ends by quoting Jespersen ((1933) p. 181): '*Any* indicates one or more, no matter which; therefore *any* is very frequent in sentences implying negation or doubt (question, condition).' Klima's treatment of *any* suggests that he considers it an amalgam of *Neg + Indef* (i.e. the existential quantifier), but Klima is more concerned with the description of surface idiosyncrasies than with deep structure regularities.

Quine (1960) treats *any*, as opposed to *every*, as the universal quantifier with the largest of two possible scopes. In a section entitled 'Ambiguity of scope' he discusses the following examples:

(125) if any member contributes, he gets a poppy
(126) if every member contributes, I'll be surprised
(127) I do not know any poem
(128) I do not know every poem

He paraphrases them as, respectively:

(129) each member is such that if he contributes he gets a poppy
(130) if each member (is such that he) contributes, I'll be surprised
(131) each poem is such that I do not know it
(132) not each poem is such that I know it

The scope of *any* and *every*, to which he limits his analysis, is thus defined by the length of the 'such that' clause, which, unlike 'which' clauses, occurs also in predicative position: 'And we now see that such use of them is not idle after all; for it is precisely the means of making scopes explicit' (p. 141).

Quine does not consider the possibility of taking *any* in (125) and (127) as the existential operator, but simply gives the following solution ((1960) p. 139): 'Sentences (125) and (126) were unambiguous for three instructive reasons. One is that (125) has "he" in its second clause, with "any member" as grammatical antecedent; we cannot take the scope of "any member" as just the first clause of (125), on pain of leaving "he" high and dry. A second reason is that "every", by a simple and irreducible trait of English usage, always calls for the shortest possible scope. A third reason is that "any", by a simple and irreducible trait of English usage, always calls for the longest of two possible scopes. This third reason is supernumerary for (125), on the account of the "he"; but it asserts itself in:

(133)   if any member contributes, I'll be surprised.'

Let us see whether his simple explanation is satisfactory. As far as the first reason is concerned, there is, in fact, nothing to prevent us from taking 'the scope of "any member" as just the first clause of (125)', without 'leaving "he" high and dry'. If we paraphrase (125) as:

(134)   if there is a member such that he contributes, he gets a
        poppy

then *any member* equals 'there is a member such that he' and does not extend beyond the 'if' clause of (125). Generally, pronouns tend to refer to elements in other clauses or sentences, without any obligation to remain within the scope of an operator.

It appears, furthermore, that *every* and *any* do not correspond to such 'simple and irreducible traits of English usage' as are mentioned by Quine. Compare, for example:

(135)   since any member will contribute, I shall do so too
(136)   since every member will contribute, I shall do so too

In Quine's terms, both should be paraphrased as:

(137)   since each member is such that he will contribute, I shall do
        so too

Or else we have, for example:

(138)   John won't be here any minute

which denies:

(139)   John will be here any minute

so that *any* falls under the scope of *not*, and not *vice versa*.

(139) also shows that *any* is not simply a scope-determined but semantically equivalent alternative for *each* or *every*. For replacement of *any* by either of these yields a different meaning, although the scope remains constant. A paraphrase with the help of the universal quantifier seems to require the addition of *Poss*:

(140)   for each minute it is possible that John will be here in that minute

so that (139) is roughly synonymous with:

(141)   John may be here any minute[1]

Quine is also criticized by Kraak ((1966) p. 172). Kraak directs his criticism at Quine ((1951) pp. 70–1) and shows likewise that *any* is not semantically equivalent to the universal quantifier manifested by *every*. He contrasts:

(142)   I should like to make an appointment with every man on the team

with:

(143)   I should like to make an appointment with any man on the team

The latter two examples are instructive in that they also show the difference between *every* and *all*. Replacement of *every man* by *all men* in (142) results in a sentence with a different meaning. In:

(144)   I should like to make an appointment with all men on the team

mention is made of only one appointment, whereas (142) refers to as many appointments as there are men on the team. In (143) again one

---

[1] In Dutch, this sentence would run: *Jan kan elk ogenblik hier zijn*, and in Italian: *Giovanni può essere qui ogni momento*, both literally 'John can be here every moment'. *John will be here each minute* is equivalent to *John will be here all the time/every single minute*, whereas *John will be here every minute* can also mean 'John will be here at regular intervals of one minute'. Little can be said here about the distinction between *each* and *every*, since their quantificational implications are only poorly understood at present. Cf. Vendler (1962).

appointment is mentioned, but not with all men together, as in (144), but with one arbitrary man out of all the men on the team.

There is reason, therefore, to differentiate the simple universal quantifier $A(x)$, as mentioned in (107), from other universal quantifiers. Perhaps, the existential quantifier provides an analogy: we might assume, beside $A(x)$, also $A(1x)$, $A(2x)$, etc. to be interpreted as 'for every one x it is true that', 'for every two x it is true that', etc. and to be rewritten transformationally as *every* (or as *each* in the case of 'for every one x'; see note 16). (140) would thus correspond to a deep structure containing the two operators $A(1 \ minute)$—*Poss*.

Not only can *any* in (139) not be commuted into *every* or *each* without a noticeable change in meaning, but also not into *some*. Substitution of *some* for *any* would lead to a sentence meaning 'there is a minute such that John will be there in that minute'. This is much more of an affirmation of the existence of such a minute than (139), which rather stresses the arbitrariness of the minute of John's arrival. The same is true for, e.g.:

(145)   can I leave anything here for John?

where replacement of *any* by *some* or *every* results in different meanings (see also (120) above).

A further argument against equating *any* with *each* or *every* is found in questions such as:

(146)   do you know any poem?

meaning 'is there at least one arbitrary poem of all poems, such that you know the poem?' The universal quantifier can also be used for paraphrasing *any* here, although the intonation of the sentence will then change: 'do you know all poems, no matter which?', so that we are led to assume that there is more than just one *any* in English.

It thus appears that Quine may well have underestimated the complications of English usage as far as *any* is concerned. His observations even are not completely correct: (125) is, in fact, not unambiguous, as Quine has it, since it not only means 'if there is an arbitrary member who contributes, he gets a poppy', but also 'if every arbitrary member is such that he contributes, he gets a poppy', the same ambiguity we found in (146). In the same way, sentences such as (127) are, apart from intonational differences, ambiguous. Take, for instance:

(147)   we don't sell to anybody

which, according to different intonational patterns, is equivalent to either 'we don't sell to just anybody' or 'we don't sell to anybody at all' (cf. Palmer (1922) p. 1).

From a grammatical point of view Bolinger is more realistic, but he remains puzzled and, as was said above, ends by falling back on Jespersen's 'no matter which'. Jespersen's remark, however, may prove to be a good starting point for further analysis. For it is a remarkable fact that in practically all cases of its occurrence *any* can be replaced by 'no matter who/which/what/how much', let us say, by 'no matter wh-'. In order not to complicate the picture unduly, let us collect some simple examples. Beside (125), (127), (135), (138), (139), (141), (143), (145), (146) and (147), we have, for instance:

(148)   John helps anybody
(149)   bring me anything
(150)   don't bring me anything
(151)   anybody may know that
(152)   anybody may not know that
(153)   anything won't do

In all these sentences *any* can be replaced by 'no matter wh-' without a change in meaning, although some reordering is sometimes necessary. Thus, for (125) we have either 'for no matter which member, if he contributes he gets a poppy' or 'if no matter which member contributes, he gets a poppy'. And for (127) we distinguish 'for no matter which poem, I don't know it' from 'I don't know no matter which poem'. One might, therefore, be inclined to reckon with only one single *any*. Yet most dictionaries and handbooks of grammar tend to distinguish two different *any*'s, one equivalent to *some*, the other to *all* or *every*. The problem presented by *any* is precisely the problem of giving a consistent quantificational description of it: it seems to be both one and many.

We have seen that at least in some cases ((139), (143) and (145)) *any* cannot be equated with either *some* or *every*. But in other cases it seems to be quite natural to take *any* as a form of either the existential or the universal quantifier. Thus there is hardly any appreciable difference between, for example, (127) and:

(154)   I know no poem

(compare also (96) and (100), (98) and (99)).[1]

---

[1] We shall not consider cases such as *I don't know a (some) poem*, as their interpretation is often uncertain and their grammaticalness doubtful.

The sentences with *any* may be said to be slightly more emphatic, but apart from that a difference can hardly be detected. There is thus, in this class of examples, an almost complete semantic equivalence between *not* attached to the verbal form followed by *any* in the rest of the sentence, and *no* dissociated from the verb and occurring in the position of *any*. This suggests that the rules given in 4.2.1 for (96)–(100) are not in conflict with the facts of the English language. On the other hand, one might also consider the possibility of interpreting *any* here as an instance of the universal quantifier, as Quine does. In the latter solution the synonymy relation between (96) and (100), (98) and (99), (127) and (154) would be explained by the well-known logical equivalence of the universal quantifier followed by the negative operator and the negative operator followed by the existential quantifier. A description in these terms, however, would probably lead to transformational complications, and it will be made clear below that there are other reasons for not adopting this solution.

Apart from the sentences with a preceding *not* there seems to be no other class of cases with general semantic equivalence between *any* and either the universal or the existential quantifier. One might be tempted to consider (146) equivalent to:

(155)   do you know a (some) poem?

but then one stumbles over the interpretation of:

(156)   do you know anybody on the board?

and

(157)   do you know a person (somebody) on the board?

where the former refers to an arbitrary person, and the latter to a specific person. In the same way, the apparent equivalence of (148) with:

(158)   John helps everybody

is misleading because of the differences noted in (142) and (143).

In short, as appears from the generally possible paraphrase by 'no matter wh-', there is a common semantic element of 'arbitrariness' in all instances of *any*. But this element does not make for quantification. Jespersen sums up this situation most succinctly, when he says: '*Any* indicates one or more, no matter which.'

The above considerations suggest a description of *any* in terms of two different quantifiers, the one a form of the universal, the other of the existential quantifier. Let us add, therefore, as further tentative sub-categories to the universal and existential quantifiers:

$A(arb \text{ x})$ ('for every arbitrary x it is true that...')
and $E(arb \text{ x})$ ('there is at least one arbitrary x such that...')

both being transformationally rewritten as *any* (although often with a different intonation). The semantic differences signalled above between *any* and *every* on the one hand and *some* on the other, are now accounted for by the additional element 'arb' in both the universal and the existential quantifiers.

However, there remains an anomaly, illustrated, for example, by (148). Assuming that the proposed solution is correct, it still remains to be explained that (148) can only have $A(arb \text{ x})$ in its underlying structure, and that it can never be derived from:

(159) $E(arb \text{ individual})$: John Pres help the individual

Indeed, (159) does not have any surface structure corresponding to it, and must therefore be considered ungrammatical at the deep structure level. This difficulty can be surmounted by adding a rule to the grammar effecting that $E(arb \text{ x})$ is prevented from occurring in the leftmost position or some other positions to be specified. Such a rule can be motivated by a closer description of the meaning of the element 'arb' in the existential *any*.

The existential *any* never refers to a specific existing individual or property or lump of material, let us say, a specific existing piece of reality. It never occurs in a context where the existence of a specific piece of reality is asserted or implied. The context is always such that no existing piece of reality can be singled out as referred to specifically. Thus in (125) *any member* does not refer to some member in particular, but to every member whosoever fulfilling the condition of contributing. In (127) *any poem* does not refer to a particular poem known by the speaker. In fact, the existence of any such particular poem is denied. In (145), (146), (147) and (149) the same applies. We take it to be a principle, therefore, that the existential *any* never refers to one specific piece of reality whose actual existence is asserted or implied.

In order to make this principle explicit in a formal syntactic description of deep structure it is necessary to anticipate the results of 4.3.2. It is assumed there that assertions have a qualifier ASS ('I assert that...'); suggestive, or conducive, questions (which expect either *yes* or *no*) have a qualifier SUGG ('I suggest that...'); questions have *QU* ('I wish to know whether...'). These belong to the class of sentence qualifiers, which tend to occur in leftmost position, although this is not compulsory (see (121)). The existence of one or more pieces of reality is asserted or suggested by an operator string with *ASS* or *SUGG* preceding an existential quantifier without an intervening *Neg*, or with an existential quantifier preceding a sentence qualifier. The semantic property of the existential *any* never to refer to an actually existing piece of reality precludes the position of *E(arb x)* after *ASS* of *SUGG* (unless preceded by *Neg*), or before a sentence qualifier. It can occur, however, after *Neg* or *QU*, which deny or question the existence of *x*. This seems to account for the existential *any* in (127), (145), (146), (147) and (150).

We still have, however, the existential *any* in one of the two interpretations of (125), (133) and (149). In (125) and (133) *any* occurs in an *if*-clause; in (149) in an imperative. *If*-clauses contrast with, for instance, *since*-clauses, as it is seen that (135) does not allow for the existential *any*. In semantic terms it is clear why this difference must exist: *since* is assertive, but *if* casts doubt or questions. In terms of formal syntactic description this complication can be dealt with, in principle, by postulating the qualifier:

Hyp ('under condition of the truth of...')[1]

transformationally rewritten as *if*, and for which it must be specified that it can only be generated in an embedded clause (see 4.3.4). We then add *Hyp* to the list of qualifiers after which *E(arb x)* is permitted. Whether *since* is also to be described as an operator—if so, it must ban a following *E(arb x)*—is a question that will be considered briefly in 4.3.4.

It appears from the interesting observations by Vendler (1962) that an underlying *if* may be assumed to be present in at least some occurrences of *any*: *Any doctor will tell you that Stopsneeze helps* is equivalent to: *if you ask any doctor, he will tell you that Stopsneeze helps* (p. 153). A deep structure *if*-element of *any* would help to account for *the students who had done anything at all, passed*, reducible, perhaps, to something like *for all students, if they had done anything at all, they passed*. Note that the universal quantifier is necessary here, so that **this is the student who has done anything at all* is ungrammatical. This opens very interesting per-

---

[1] We have seen (4.2.2) that Lewis ((1946) p. 49) proposed the operator *H* for the postulation of a proposition.

spectives for further investigations into the deep structure of *any* and of *if*-clauses. But we cannot go into these questions here.

Sentence (149) approximates to 'bring me something, no matter what'. Here, consistently with the other cases, no reference is made to one particular piece of reality the existence of which is asserted or implied. The deep structure of (149) cannot contain *ASS* or *SUGG*, since it is an imperative. The idea of postulating a sentence qualifier:

IMP   ('I request that...')

readily presents itself and is intuitively appealing (see, for instance, Lewis (1946) p. 49, footnote, quoted in 4.2.2). It can be motivated on syntactic grounds (see Katz and Postal (1964) pp. 74–9; p. 149, note 9). This qualifier imposes the restriction on the nucleus that it be in the second person singular or plural, unless it is embedded. (149) can now be described as:

(160)   IMP E(*arb* thing): you Pres bring the thing to me

('I request that there be an arbitrary thing such that you bring the thing to me.')

(161)   bring me a letter of his
(162)   bring me some letter of his

or:

(163)   bring me one of his letters

which have the deep structure:

(164)   IMP E(letter of his) : you Pres bring the letter to me

come close to:

(165)   bring me any letter of his

which, in our hypothesis, will have the deep structure:

(166)   IMP E(*arb* letter of his) : you Pres bring the letter to me

This analysis also accounts for the almost complete semantic equivalence between (96) and (100), (98) and (99), (127) and (154): if the statement 'it is not true that there is an x such that...' holds for a class of x's, then this statement covers the whole class of x's, due to the logical equivalence of $Neg + E(x)$ and $A(x) + Neg$. The addition of 'no matter which' can only reinforce the statement, which is precisely the difference we detected. The transformational rules for English will even have to neutralize this difference in emphasis in sentences where $Neg + E(arb\ x)$ needs to be incorporated into the surface structure in a position preceding the finite verb form: *nothing* in (101) and (105) is the only possible form, and cannot be replaced by *not anything* (although additional emphasis can be given by adding *at all*).

The distinction drawn between the universal and the existential *any*, together with the deep structure regularities signalled above, make it unnecessary to adopt Quine's suggestion that one treat *any* in these cases as a universal quantifier. It would present awkward problems if one were to account for the fact that this universal *any* must be prevented from occurring when it is to be transformationally incorporated before the finite verb form. Moreover, it appears that the addition of *at all* is regularly possible after the existential *any*. This regularity would be disturbed if we interpreted *any* in (96), (98) and (127) as a universal quantifier.

In the quotation from Jespersen given at the beginning of this section, the word *therefore* is not immediately self-evident. The hypothesis for the description of *any* put forward here, with the principle of *any* never referring to an actually existing piece of reality, will have brought to light some of the reasons why *any* is particularly 'frequent in sentences implying negation or doubt (question, condition)'.

This description of *any* as two different quantifiers but with a common semantic element of 'arbitrariness' is as far as we can go here. It may be claimed that it solves some descriptive problems, but one is also quite justified in saying that the solution does not look entirely satisfactory, and that one must look for further, deeper, regularities accounting for the occurrences of this extraordinary word. For some of the seemingly more complicated occurrences, however (which we have deliberately excluded from the discussion so far), it can be shown without much difficulty that they fit into the description given. Although, apparently, they do not yield to our solution, they are, in fact, naturally explained by it. Thus, for example:

(167)   John is taller than anybody in his class

Comparative constructions are notoriously troublesome in transformational descriptions.[1] But with the help of the existential operator $E(x)$ and the negation element (which Jespersen ((1917) p. 80), Ross and Joly

---

[1] See Lees (1961); Smith (1961); Pilch (1965); Ross (unpublished); Huddleston (1967); Joly (1967); Doherty and Schwartz (1967).

postulate for comparatives), a natural description can be formulated. Let us take, for example:

(168)   John is taller than Mary

This can be described as resulting from an underlying:

(169)   E(degree) : John Pres be tall to that degree
        and Neg : Mary Pres be tall to that degree

Without going into too much detail, one observes that the semantic feature 'gradability', which is necessary for adjectives to enter into a comparative construction, is accounted for in a simple way by the introduction of the notion of *degree* under the existential quantifier. The occurrence of the operator *E(degree)* will have to be made dependent on selection restriction rules. The negation element is brought out in the synonymous sentence:

(170)   Mary is not so tall as John[1]

A second existential quantifier, in the second sentence of the conjunction, is introduced in:

(171)   John is taller than someone in his class

which is analysable as:

(172)   E(degree) : John Pres be tall to that degree
        and E(individual in his class) Neg : the individual Pres be tall
        to that degree

The universal quantifier is present in:

(173)   John is taller than everybody in his class

to be analysed as:

(174)   E(degree) : John Pres be tall to that degree
        and A(1 individual in his class) Neg : the individual Pres be
        tall to that degree

In the same way the universal *any* can be said to be present in (167), which is now analysed as:

(175)   E(degree) : John Pres be tall to that degree
        and Neg E(*arb* individual in his class) : the individual Pres be
        tall to that degree

---

[1] Remarkably, in French, a negative remnant *ne* (the so-called 'ne explétif') is obligatory in comparative sentences with a second verbal form: *Jean était plus grand que je ne pensais* ('John was taller than I thought'). The same goes for Italian, where this sentence would be: *Giovanni era più alto che non pensassi*. The transformational rules for French and Italian thus seem not, or in the case of French only partially, to delete the underlying negation element when there is a second verb.

where the occurrence of the existential *any* is explained by the preceding *Neg*.

Another complication seems to arise in, for example:

(176)   it is too hot to do anything

Here also a negation element is concealed. (176) can be analysed as:

(177)   E(degree) : it Pres be hot to that degree
        and Neg Poss E(*arb* thing) : one Pres do the thing

where E(*arb thing*) is in a regular position for the existential *any*, after *Neg*. The elements *Poss* and *Neg* are brought out in the synonymous:

(178)   it is so hot that it is not possible to do anything[1]

If this analysis is correct, the deep structure of (176) shows some resemblance with that of (167) and the other comparatives. That the two constructions are somehow semantically related appears, for example, from the fact that in classical Greek (176) is naturally translated into, for instance, πλέον κάεται ἢ ὥστε ποιῆσαί τι, i.e. literally 'it burns more than that one could do anything'. (There are, of course, other ways of rendering (176) in classical Greek, but it is remarkable to note that in those cases the negation element is always present in some form or other.) Further investigation would take us too far afield, but there seems, at least, to be no reason for undue alarm about (167) and (176).

A similar solution can probably be given for cases like:

(179)   John is the tallest of anybody in his class

which can be treated as a transformational variant of (167).[2]

The negation element can also be expected to underlie the preposition *without*, as in:

(180)   John arrived without any luggage

In point of fact, if there are other, independent, indications that *without* might conceal a hidden *Neg*, the fact that it occurs with the existential

---

[1] It is remarkable to note that in Latin (176) cannot be translated into a syntactically analogous surface structure. Its equivalent must roughly conform to (178): *aestus talis est ut nihil facere possis*, or the like ('the heat is such that nothing can be done'), or it must contain a comparative: *maior est aestus quam ut quicquam fieri possit* ('the heat is greater than that anything can be done').

[2] It is to be noted that (179) is not accepted as fully grammatical in English by some authorities; see Fowler (1965) sub *any*.2.

any can be used as corroborative evidence. The same goes for *prevent from* in, for example:

(181)   this prevented John from doing anything

where *from* seems to represent 'so that not' or the like.[1]

The quantifying word *few* also allows for the existential *any*:

(182)   few students did anything

Perhaps, *few* is to be considered a composite of $Neg + E(Mult\ x)$, so that it is equivalent to 'not many'.

Only, as in:

(183)   only John did anything

seems a contraction of 'and nobody else' in (183), so that there would be two underlying subjects, and two underlying sentences:

(184)   John did something and nobody else did anything

to be collapsed transformationally into *John and nobody else did anything*, and further into (183).

A negative element must likewise be detected in *hardly, scarcely, seldom, rarely, little*. Hornby ((1966) p. 5) calls attention to the fact that 'inversion of the subject and finite verb...occurs after a front-position negative (including such semi-negatives as *hardly, scarcely, little*)'. Kruisinga ((1932) p. 532) remarks: 'The negative meaning of *hardly, scarcely, only*, and *little* is the explanation of the inverted word-order when these words open a sentence.' Klima ((1964) pp. 262–3) regards *seldom* and *rarely* as negative pre-verbs, because of the possibility of their replacing the first occurrence of *not* in: *the writer will not accept suggestions, not even reasonable ones*, whereas *often, commonly, always*, are excluded here. The negative element thus accounts, in principle, for the existential *any* in:

(185)   John hardly/scarcely/seldom/rarely did anything

or:

(186)   little did anybody realize how great the dangers were

Little would thus be 'not much'; *seldom* and *rarely* would stand for 'not often', and *hardly* and *scarcely*, perhaps, for $almost + Neg$ (Kruisinga (1932) p. 531), or for 'and nothing more than that' (although this, in

---

[1] In Latin, verbs with a semantic feature of prohibition require a negative subordinate clause.

itself, would require further analysis). This may throw some distant light upon the negative element presumably present in *as soon as*-clauses, witness cases like: *as soon as you see anything, please tell me*; or upon the equivalence of: *no sooner had he arrived than he fell asleep* with: *as soon as he had arrived, he fell asleep*. It is worth noting, in this connection, that the Italian for *as soon as* is: *non appena*, i.e. literally, 'not hardly'. A complete account of these cases will no doubt reveal an intricate system of negations and quantifiers. Let it be sufficient here to remark that there is good reason for assuming a deep structure also in vocabulary items.[1]

Embeddings of sentences give rise to certain complications. But these are due to the general problem of embedding rather than to the particular problem of *any*. The solution proposed here for *any* seems to be applicable to sentences containing embedded sentences. Let us consider one set of examples:

(187)   I don't force Andrew to eat anything
(188)   I don't force Andrew to eat something
(189)   I force Andrew not to eat anything
(190)   I force Andrew not to eat something

The following deep structure analyses may be proposed. For (187), which is ambiguous:

(191)   Neg E(*arb* thing) : I Pres force Andrew so that he Pres eat the
        thing
or:

(192)   Neg A(*arb* thing) : I Pres force Andrew so that he Pres eat the
        thing

For (188):

(193)   Neg E(thing) : I Pres force Andrew so that he Pres eat the
        thing

For the ambiguous (189) the following pair can be given:

(194)   I Pres force Andrew so that Neg E(*arb* thing) : he Pres eat the
        thing
or:

(195)   I Pres force Andrew so that Neg A(*arb* thing) : he Pres eat the
        thing

---

[1] This was mentioned in 3.4.1, especially notes 13 and 14 of chapter 3. Compare also Bolinger's example ((1960) p. 383) *having to hurt anyone is contrary to his nature*, which suggests that there is a semantic feature of negation in the lexical item *contrary*.

And for (190):

(196)   I Pres force Andrew so that E(thing) Neg : he Pres eat the
        thing[1]

Finally, there remain some instances of *any* which are not immediately transparent:

(197)   this was the first time she paid any attention to Robert
(198)   it has been a week since she paid any attention to Robert

In both cases the existential *any* is involved, and in both cases it is preceded by a restrictive phrase implying that she had never before, or not for a week, paid any attention to Robert. Perhaps a hidden *Neg* must be postulated for these sentences, but grammatical evidence for such an assumption has not been provided so far. Perhaps they will have to be accounted for differently. It is clear, at any rate, that these first explorations in the field of operators call for much further work to be done in the future.

Much of what has been said above may seem uncertain. It must be stressed, therefore, once again, that nothing more is involved here than the tentative setting up of deep structure hypotheses. Inevitably, some of the hypotheses put forward are better motivated than others. On the whole, the greatest possible regularity and simplicity have been striven for, in both operators and the nuclei. The transformational consequences of the deep structures postulated here were mentioned only incidentally and not in great detail. Often the transformations preserve the order of the operators in the surface structures. But sometimes other means than order, such as intonation, are used in surface structures to distinguish different orders of operators, as in (123) and (124), or in (147). Or else transformations may merge different deep structures into identical surface structures, thus giving rise to ambiguities. It must be borne in mind, however, that unambiguous and semantically regular deep structures are a necessary prerequisite for any transformational component, and that so far no deep structure hypothesis has been formulated

---

[1] In fact, the situation is more complicated, as appears from the ambiguity of *I force Andrew to eat something*, which is either 'E(thing) : I Pres force Andrew so that he Pres eat the thing', or 'I Pres force Andrew so that E(thing) : he Pres eat the thing'. (193) is the negation of the former, and 'Neg : I Pres force Andrew so that E(thing) : he Pres eat the thing' denies the latter. Both negations, however, result in (188), which is therefore also ambiguous. But these questions cannot be answered within the limits of the present discussion.

which meets this requirement. The important question presenting itself here is whether a hypothesis can be formulated which suits the facts better than that presented here.

4.3 Some more operators

So far we have identified, on various grounds, a set of quantifiers comprising: $E(x)$, $E(1, 2 \ldots x)$, $E(arb\ x)$, $E(Mult\ x)$, $A(x)$, $A(1, 2 \ldots x)$, $A(arb\ x)$, and a set of qualifiers: Neg, QU, IMP, Poss, Hyp. Without aiming at a complete characterization of the category of operators, we may try to gain some idea of its variety by going into some further, provisional, explorations.

4.3.1 Suggestion. Bolinger ((1960) p. 378) raises the problem of 'conducive' questions, i.e. of questions calling for either an affirmative or a negative answer: 'The question

(199)   didn't you publish some poetry back in 1916?

is commutable with

(200)   isn't it true that you published some poetry back in 1916?

and expects an affirmative answer. The question

(201)   didn't you publish any poetry back in 1916?

is commutable with

(202)   is it true that you didn't publish any poetry back in 1916?

and is non-conducive, i.e. anticipates yes and no equally.'

In terms of the operators available, (201) and (202) can be analysed as:

(203)   QU Neg E(*arb* poetry) : you Past publish the poetry back in 1916

But in (199) and (200) *not* is apparently not the normal negation element, since nothing is denied. The sentence *you published some poetry back in 1916* is called in question but with the expectation of the answer *yes*. They are equivalent to the 'polar' tag-question (i.e. a negative tag for a sentence without negation, and *vice versa*):

(204)   you published some poetry back in 1916, didn't you?

For (201) and (202) there is no such tag-question.

Let us assume a sentence qualifier

SUGG ('I suggest that...')

accounting for tag-questions. (199), (200) and (204) will then be reduced to:

(205)   SUGG E(poetry) : you Past publish the poetry back in 1916

In point of fact, tag-questions are a more general form for conducive questions than (199), since only *yes*-expecting questions can have the form of (199), and *no*-expecting questions are necessarily formulated as tag-questions:

(206)   you didn't publish any poetry back in 1916, did you?

where the real negation element is found, and which amounts to:

(207)   SUGG Neg E(*arb* poetry) : you Past publish the poetry back
       in 1916

Here, *E(poetry)* may replace *E(arb poetry)* without much change in meaning:

(208)   you published no poetry back in 1916, did you?

The deep structure:

(209)   SUGG E(poetry) Neg : you Past publish the poetry back in
       1916

(where *E(arb poetry)* is excluded—see 4.2.4) corresponds to a variety of synonymous sentences:

(210)   some poetry you didn't publish back in 1916, did you?
(211)   there is some poetry which you didn't publish back in 1916,
       isn't there?
(212)   isn't there some poetry which you didn't publish back in 1916?

Noticeably, (210) does not have a conducive question as an alternative, but (211) does, as appears from (212). This again confirms the conclusion that tag-questions are more general than conducive questions of the type (199), which are only allowed for *yes*-expecting questions. (210) expects *no*, whereas (211) and (212), although meaning the same, anticipate *yes*. A conducive question transformation can be formulated operating on tag-questions with a negative tag and placing the finite verb form of the tag, with its negation, in first position, changing the rest of the sentence accordingly. The regular transformational treatment for *SUGG* will consist of a transformation into a polar tag-question.

The assumption of a sentence qualifier *SUGG* thus leads to a fairly straightforward and regular treatment of a group of apparently irregular cases. It yields analyses in which the partial similarity of the sentences of this group is expressed in their identical nucleus. As there is no more adequate analysis available at present to account for the deep structure of these sentences, we shall adopt the solution outlined above, and accept *SUGG* as a sentence qualifier.

4.3.2 Assertion. The deep structures of (201) and (206) are identical, in our analysis, except for the first operator, which is *QU* for (201) and *SUGG* for (206). (201) is to be read as 'I wish to know whether you did not publish any poetry back in 1916'; (206) as 'I suggest that you did not publish any poetry back in 1916'. One wonders whether another sentence qualifier is not required, or desirable, for:

(213)   you didn't publish any poetry back in 1916

Such a qualifier would give explicit expression to the fact that the proposition 'you not publishing in the past any poetry back in 1916', which is called in question in (201) and suggested to be true in (206), is asserted to be true in (213). Although in English assertions do not usually have overt surface features to distinguish them from propositions such as occur in subordinate clauses (unless one takes the declarative sentence intonation as such a feature), there are reasons for adopting a separate sentence qualifier

ASS   ('I assert that...')

First, the qualifier *ASS* will simplify the transformational treatment of assertions. An assertion transformation is needed in any case to transform assertive deep structures into assertive surface structures. The presence of *ASS* will be a sufficient deep structure marker to let this transformation operate.

Secondly, there seem to be grounds for distinguishing between $ASS + E(x)$ and $E(x) + ASS$, in much the same way as was done in (120) for the qualifier *QU*. Take, for example:

(214)   John has eaten something

When this is said as a statement of fact, after a period of John's complete fasting, the following analysis is suitable:

(215)   ASS E(thing) : John Perf eat the thing

But when this is said in answer to a question such as 'why is John ill'? a better analysis would be:

(216)   E(thing) ASS : John Perf eat the thing

In the latter case *something* in (214) may be specified by, for instance, *bad* or *poisonous*. But a specification of *something* in interpretation (215), with its context, would be less appropriate. There, further specifications are better given in separate sentences, such as: *John has eaten something, but is was poisonous*, or: *John has eaten something, and it was delicious*. That is, the specifications tend to be of a non-restrictive kind here.

Admittedly, the ambiguity of (214) is less clear than that of (120), and it is not immediately evident that the different analyses as given in (215) and (216) do, in fact, account for it. Perhaps what we have here is a difference in order of the existential qualifier on the one hand and the qualifier of tense (which will be identified as such in 4.3.4) on the other. It may also be argued that what is involved is not so much a difference of structure and meaning as of application in specific contexts. This would then touch upon a fundamental problem in linguistic description, namely, the problem of what is available evidence for establishing difference or sameness of meaning. The general answer to this is that we start considering clear cases of semantic sameness or difference, and leave the unclear cases to be decided by the descriptive results based on the clear ones. (214) would then be an unclear case, and the viability of a particular description, justified by other, independent, motivations, would provide grounds for considering (214) ambiguous or not. It seems that the present analysis does provide the terms for distinguishing two different meanings for (214).

Another example is:

(217)   somebody has stolen my money

which, as a statement of fact after the discovery that the money is missing, is:

(218)   ASS E(individual) : the individual Perf steal my money

and is equivalent to:

(219)   my money has been stolen (by somebody)

with the main stress on *stolen* and an optional on *somebody*. But if the speaker wants to suggest that he knows, or has an idea, who stole it (*somebody has stolen my money; I will report him to the police*), the analysis is more likely to be:

(220)   E(individual) ASS : the individual Perf steal my money

and its equivalent passive is:

(221)   my money has been stolen by somebody

with the main stress on the obligatory *somebody*.[1]

The introduction of *ASS* also establishes a distinction between assertions and propositions. In 4.2.2 propositions were considered to be roughly equivalent to nuclei. In the light of our more detailed analysis of operators this does not seem to be appropriate. It is more adequate to take as a proposition a sentence without its sentence qualifier. Usually, but not always, a proposition is the scope of the sentence qualifier, i.e. that part of the deep structure which follows it (4.2.3). $E(x)$ in (121) and (162) are thus part of a proposition, not of an assertion. More will be said about the distinction between sentences, propositions and nuclei in 4.3.4, where the operators of tense are discussed. A proposition will then be said to consist minimally of a tense operator plus a nucleus. The nucleus will be described as purely relational.

The decision to distinguish between sentences, propositions and nuclei has considerable semantic and syntactic advantages, which provide another reason for the assumption of *ASS* as a sentence qualifier. Every sentence now has one and only one sentence qualifier. Embedded clauses consist of only a proposition, introduced by a clause qualifier. A description based on this principle is more adequate than one which is not, since it allows for a simpler and more regular syntactic specification of embedded clauses and tenseless structures, and at the same time identifies syntactically the semantic elements that make a sentence a sentence, a clause a clause, and tenseless structure a tenseless structure.

It is a noticeable feature of those syntactic-semantic elements which make a sentence a sentence, namely the sentence qualifiers, that their semantic interpretation is formulated as a phrase beginning with the first person singular 'I', followed by a 'performative' verb in the present tense: *assert, wish to know, request, suggest.* This semantic feature of sentence qualifiers not only accounts for the speaker, and with him the expressive quality of speech, as a necessary factor in all linguistic communication. It also throws into relief the property of every actually

---

[1] In Latin, the *somebody* of (218) would be *aliquis*, but the *somebody* of (220) would be rendered by *quidam* ('somebody, a certain person whom I don't mention').

uttered sentence of being implicitly 'performative'. Austin ((1961) pp. 220–39) distinguished explicit performative utterances, characterized by such phrases as 'I promise', 'I undertake', 'I declare'. It is a deeper and more general property of language that all sentences are sentences because of a performative semantic feature of entertainment.

This naturally raises the question how to describe those sentences characterized by Austin as performative. They are characterized by the fact that they cannot be false: *I promise to pay my debt at the end of the year* cannot be false, because by the very fact that one says *I promise* one does make a promise. This is no longer so if the sentence is not an assertion, if the person is not 'I' or 'we', or if the tense is not *present*. An answer is, perhaps, to disregard Austin's category of performative sentences for the purposes of grammar. Every performative sentence will then be described as a normal assertive sentence. But then one must also accept: *do I promise that...?*, or: *I promise that...*, *don't I?*, although many speakers will regard these as ungrammatical. Another answer would be to take account of this category of sentences in grammar, and treat them as transformational variants of the same sentences that do not have the sentence qualifier expressed explicitly. In this solution the number of sentence qualifiers must be increased considerably. But it seems to have several attractive aspects. Not only do we rule out questions and suggestions of performatives, but also, for example, *I question whether I promise that...*, or *I undertake that I question whether...*, etc., that is, impermissible combinations of sentence qualifiers, one of which is only permitted for each sentence. It also makes for a straightforward way of stating that certain sentence qualifiers require certain tenses (*future*). Furthermore, it provides us with a simple grammatical means of distinguishing between two meanings of the sentence: *I will pay my debt at the end of the year*, which is either a promise or a prediction about the future. One wonders, however, if it is true (which would be expected) that it can only be a promise if it occurs in the first person, and in an assertive sentence in the present tense. But, as in so many other cases, further research must be done before we can hope to have a conclusive answer to this problem.

Several linguists have been aware of the general sentence qualifying feature of entertainment. Jespersen (1924) distinguishes *nexus* and *junction* (p. 97): 'If now we compare the combination *a furiously barking dog* (*a dog barking furiously*), in which *dog* is primary, *barking* secondary, and *furiously* tertiary, with *the dog barks furiously*, it is evident that the same subordination obtains in the latter as in the former combination. Yet there is a fundamental difference between them, which calls for separate terms for the two kinds of combination: we shall call the former *junction*, and the latter *nexus*.' And on p. 115: 'The former is a lifeless, stiff combination, the latter has life in it. This is generally ascribed to the presence of a finite verb (the rose *is* red; the dog *barks*), and there is certainly much truth in the name given to a verb by Chinese grammarians, "the living word" as opposed to a noun which is lifeless.' Unfortunately, however, he does not exploit his image of 'the living sentence' to the full. He goes on to identify this sentence-characteristic with the combinations of subject and predicate, thus confounding sentences with propositions and nuclei: 'But exactly the same relation between a primary and a secondary word that is found in such complete sentences is also found in a great many other combinations which are not so rounded off and complete in themselves as to form real sentences. We need not look beyond ordinary subordinate clauses to see this, e.g. in (I see) *that the rose is red*, or (she is alarmed) *when the dog barks*. Further, the relation between the last two words in *he painted the door red* is evidently parallel to that in *the door is red* and different from that in *the red door*.' The evident nature of this difference, however, is not made very clear. Jespersen argues (pp. 115–16) that *the red door* forms 'one denomination, a composite name for what conceivably might just as well have been called by a single name. As a matter of fact, instead of *new-born dog* we often say *puppy*, instead of *silly person* we may say *fool*.' But then it should also be mentioned that there are in the lexicon single denominations for expressions analogous to 'to paint the door red', or, more generally, for expressions consisting of verb plus object. Thus we have 'to make up' for 'to make the face ready for show', or 'to brew' for 'to make beer', etc. When Jespersen comes to defining the sentence, he says (p. 306): 'only an *independent* nexus forms a sentence', and does not enlarge upon the characteristics of this independence.

De Groot (1964) follows in Jespersen's footsteps. His terms for the semantic analogue to junction and nexus are *referential meaning* and *attitudinal meaning* respectively (p. 65): 'The referential semantic features concern a relation intended by the speaker to obtain between the thing or the things referred to by the one and the other constituent of the construction: *red tulips*, *three tulips*, *very beautiful*, *to eat fish*, and the like. With the attitudinal semantic features the speaker expresses a personal attitude; this can be a belief in the real existence of the relation, an "assertion" (*Mary is sleeping.*), it can be a desire on the part of the speaker to hear an assertion about the existence of the relation (*Is Mary sleeping?*), it can be a degree of certainty or uncertainty of his belief (*Perhaps—Mary is sleeping.*), etc.'[1] The 'etc.' with which this quotation ends is then seen to apply to words and expressions which are regarded here as representatives of qualifiers, like *perhaps, probably* (see 4.3.7), to embedded clauses, and even to words with an element of what is often called 'emotive' meaning (p. 231), like *crook* for a dishonest person, or *fiddle* for a violin, or, for that matter, for the dishonest keeping of accounts or records. Just as Jespersen made independent nexus the distinguishing property of sentences, they are said by de Groot to have attitudinal meaning and to be capable of occurring in isolation. The original, promising, idea of 'attitude' has here been diluted and is made to cover as divergent a collection of things as sentence and other qualifiers, predication, and even emotive meanings. The capability of sentences to occur in isolation receives no further semantic elucidation.

It is the same concept of 'speaker's attitude' which underlies Lewis's term 'entertainment', understood in the sense of entertaining an idea, a proposition: the entertainment operator governing a proposition gives expression to the speaker's decision how to assess the truth of a proposed statement.

Jespersen's and de Groot's distinction between nexus and junction is correct in its starting-point, but is worked out in a fragmentary and not always consistent way. A deep structure hypothesis incorporating a category of operators enables us to give a more precise and systematic account of features only vaguely perceived by these authors. In such an account *ASS* will have its proper place as one of the sentence qualifiers, which make a sentence a sentence and distinguish it from propositions and nuclei.

4.3.3 Some adverbial operators. Adverbs and adverbial constructions are known as a notoriously heterogeneous category. They are, therefore, difficult to describe grammatically. We shall not attempt to provide an

---

[1] The translation is mine. The text of the original is: 'De referentiële [betekenis-momenten] betreffen een betrekking die de spreker bedoelt tussen de zaak of zaken die hij met het ene lid en die hij met het andere lid van de constructie bedoelt: *rode tulpen, drie tulpen, erg mooi, vis eten,* e.d. Met de attitudinele drukt de spreker een houding van hemzelf uit; deze kan een geloof zijn in het bestaan van de betrekking, een "bewering" (*Marie slaapt.*), het kan een wens zijn van de spreker een bewering te vernemen ten opzichte van het bestaan van de betrekking (*Slaapt Marie?*), het kan een graad van zekerheid of onzekerheid van zijn geloof zijn (*Marie slaapt— misschien.*), etc.' (See also de Groot (1965) p. 95.)

exhaustive description here: it seems a better procedure to single out some groups of adverbial expressions and indicate the lines along which these can be accounted for.

In 2.3 it was pointed out that Chomsky distinguishes different 'degrees of cohesion' between the verb phrase and some adverbial expressions. He accounted for this difference by introducing them either as part of the predicate phrase or as part of the verb phrase (see (33) in 2.3). The same point returned in 4.1 in connection with (30)–(51).

A simpler and more general description than that proposed by Chomsky can be given by taking some adverbial expressions out of the nucleus and introducing them as operators. The passive transformation (or at least the transition to the passive), which was already seen in 4.2.1 to be limited to the nucleus, will then be automatically applicable to (34), (41) and (44), where the adverbial phrase is part of the nucleus. In (31) and (39) the adverbial phrase will be interpreted as an operator, so that the noun cannot be taken as the subject of a passive sentence. *At Cambridge* in (37) is probably best regarded as an adverbial adjunct, result of an embedded structure attached to the verb. As such it is also excluded from subjectivization in the passive voice.

In restrictive relative clauses, likewise, the relative pronoun (when not in subject position) can be said to be transformationally deletable only if the noun from which it is derived is not part of a qualifying operator. (It is assumed here that descriptive relative clauses are derived from a conjunction of two sentences—see 5.1—, and restrictive relative clauses from an embedded proposition, here to be called *P*.) (32) is thus derivable from an underlying (simplified):

(222)   this is the sofa P
|
John sleeps on the sofa

but

(223)   this is the morning P
|
on this morning : John sleeps

where *on this morning* is taken as an operator, is transformed into:

(224)   this is the morning on which John sleeps

and preferably not into (33), the grammaticalness of which is doubtful.

Transposition of this class of adverbial expressions to front position is only possible if the adverbial expression is an operator, as appears from (42), (45), (46), (47), (48) and (51).

Further evidence for regarding some of these expressions as operators is derived from the fact that their scope varies according to their position, as appears from:

(225) John did not decide on my behalf

and:

(226) on my behalf John did not decide

Adverbial phrases of place often lead to ambiguous sentences:

(227) I can't sleep in that hotel

which is roughly equivalent to either 'there is no place for me to sleep in that hotel' or 'I can't sleep when I am in that hotel'. In the former interpretation the adverbial phrase is probably best described as an adverbial adjunct attached to the verb. In the latter it can be regarded as a shortened form of a subordinate clause. Only in the latter interpretation can it be shifted to front position:

(228) in that hotel I can't sleep

To treat adverbial phrases of place always as operators would probably lead to complications elsewhere in the grammar: embedded nuclei allow for adverbial phrases of place (see chapter 5).

Clearly, an adequate account of all data of this kind will require an elaborate set of rules, which cannot be given here. Language being an enormously complicated phenomenon, any adequate grammar must reflect this. But if the operator hypothesis is correct, it must be expected that it will reduce at least some of this complexity to fairly simple general statements.

Let us consider further those adverbial expressions which delimit the time of the predication referred to by the verb, that is, which are somehow connected with the tense of the verb: *today, at this moment, now, yesterday, last year, in 1250, tomorrow*, etc. The expression *at this moment* is similar to the phrases discussed above because of its being a prepositional phrase. In:

(229) Richard is not sleeping at this moment

it is not part of the nucleus, as appears from, for example:

(230) *this moment is not being slept at by Richard

or:

(231) *this is the moment Richard is not sleeping at

We can only regard it as an operator. Yet its scope does not seem to vary with its position with regard to *Neg*, as there is no semantic difference between (229) and:

(232)   at this moment John is not sleeping.

Whatever difference there is, must be regarded as stylistic.

The same is true for the semantically closely related *now, at the moment, at present, today,* etc. which may replace *at this moment* and can be transposed to front position without a change in meaning. Of these expressions only *at the moment* can be subjected to the passive and relative clause test in order to establish whether it is part of the nucleus. The results show unambiguously that it is not. Although the other expressions do not lend themselves to these tests, it is only reasonable to assume that they follow their synonyms: it would be very disturbing, semantically and syntactically, if they did not (see 5.4). In point of fact, there is some evidence that adverbial expressions of time play their part in the system of operators. Consider, for example:

(233)   John may have promised that last year

and:

(234)   John could promise that last year (he can't promise it any more
          now)

The difference between these two is expressible in terms of order of operators. (233) corresponds to 'it is possible that it was last year that John promised that'; (234) is analysable as 'it was last year that it was possible that John promised that'.

Regarding adverbial expressions of time as qualifying operators, we can analyse (229) and (232) as:

(235)   ASS Neg at this moment : John Pres be sleeping[1]

(233) will be:

(236)   ASS Poss last year : John Past promise that

and for (234) we assume an underlying:

(237)   ASS last year Poss : John Past promise that

(although it becomes clear in 4.3.4 that this analysis is incomplete).

---

[1] Perhaps, for (232) an analysis could be given where *at this moment* precedes *Neg* in the string of operators. Semantically, however, this would be less satisfactory, since the negation applies to the truth of the following proposition, including the specific time in which it is said to occur or to be true. A preceding *Neg*, moreover, has the advantage of providing a simple definition for negative sentences, i.e. sentences paraphrasable with 'it is not true that...', apart from the sentence qualifier. We assume, therefore, that adverbials of time are not immediately followed by *Neg* (see 4.3.6).

4.3.4 Tense. In 4.1 we saw that in deep structure it is desirable to distinguish a predicative construction without an element of tense. In 4.2.2 it was pointed out that some logicians let the modal and other operators operate on tenseless structures. It is, therefore, not unreasonable to enquire whether there is grammatical evidence in support of the assumption of operators of tense.

In the preceding section it was said that there is a connection between adverbials of time and the tense of the verb. Shifting our interest now from adverbials of time to the tense of the verb, we may again consider (233) and (234). Let us leave out *last year* in both sentences and try to describe the difference between them with the help of an operator of tense, *Past*. (233) would then be describable as:

(238)   ASS Poss Past : John promise that

and (234) as:

(239)   ASS Past Poss : John promise that

interpretable as 'it is possible that in the past John promised that' and 'in the past it was possible that John promised that', respectively. One notices that the assumed operator *Past* fulfils much the same function in (238) and (239) as the operator *last year* in (236) and (237). The question now naturally presents itself how one is to combine the two assumptions in a single description. This can be done by postulating a past tense operator *Past(x)*, where '*x*' stands for an optional adverbial expression of past time. Now (233) can be analysed as:

(240)   ASS Poss Past (last year) : John promise that

and (234) as:

(241)   ASS Past (last year) Poss : John promise that

Remarkably, the position of *Poss* preceding *Past* in (238) and (240) is brought out in the surface structure (233) by the fact that *may* is followed by a past infinitive: *have promised*. But there is no priority of *Poss* with respect to *Past* to be found in the surface structure (234).

In the same way a present tense operator can be postulated: *Pres(x)*. The difference, however, between:

(242)   John may come now

and:

(243)   John can come now

is not accounted for adequately by:

(244) ASS Poss Pres(now) : John come

and:

(245) ASS Pres(now) Poss : John come

analogously with (240) and (241). For (245) corresponds rather to a surface structure:

(246) John can now come

where *now* relates to *can*: 'now it is possible '. In (243) *now* is rather connected with *come*: 'it is possible for John to come now'. We may even have:

(247) John can now come now

('now it is possible for John to come now'). This implies that we must assume two occurrences of tense qualifiers in (243), (246) and (247), so that they are better analysed as:

(248) ASS Pres Poss Pres(now) : John come
(249) ASS Pres(now) Poss Pres : John come
(250) ASS Pres(now) Poss Pres(now) : John come

Replacing *Pres* in the different positions of (248)–(250) by *Past* will give us (*now* being left out):

(251) John could come (Past—Poss—Pres)
(252) John can have come (Pres—Poss—Past)
(253) John could have come (Past—Poss—Past)

(241) is thus seen to be insufficient: the qualifier *Pres* is required after Poss.

One might be inclined to treat (240) and (244) in the same way, that is, to insert *Pres* between *ASS* and *Poss* in both cases, in order to account for a supposed present tense of *may*. But it must be noted that there are no past, future, or perfect tense forms of *may*, as there are for *can* (*could*, *will be able*, *have been able*). The form *might* (when representing *Poss*) is either a subjunctive ('it is perhaps possible' or 'it would be possible if...') or, when referring to the past, can only be used in an embedded object clause preceded by a main clause in the past tense, as in:

(254) it seemed that this might be true

Subjunctives, either in main sentences or in embedded clauses, are not dealt with at all in this study. The phenomenon of 'sequence of tenses' will be discussed below.

May can thus be described as being of indeterminate tense. How this can be accounted for in a grammatical description is not a simple matter. Two possibilities come to mind.

First, one may think that the possibility expressed in *may* is taken to be true for the time expressed in the preceding operator. It would then not differ, in this respect, from *Neg* or from the quantifiers, which are all said to be true for the time expressed in the preceding operator. If the preceding operator is a sentence qualifier, such as *ASS*, then the time referred to by *Neg* and the quantifiers is the time referred to by the sentence qualifier, which, being a performative expression of the speaker's attitude as to the truth value of the proposition following, always refers to the present time. *May* would thus represent a tenseless *Poss*.

There is, however, reason to assume an indeterminate, or universal tense, to be found in universal statements such as *snow is white, whales are mammals, people do not live to be two hundred years*. From a semantic point of view, such sentences cannot properly be said to be in the present tense. We posit, therefore, a universal tense qualifier *U*. It may be argued that *may* contains this universal tense operator, which would explain the lack of forms in other tenses. It is not clear, given the present state of enquiry, which solution is the best. In this study, we shall, tentatively, adopt the latter. For reasons of descriptive regularity modals will thus always occur with a preceding tense qualifier. It must be clear, however, that this is only a provisional decision, which, admittedly, leaves many problems unsolved: again, more detailed analysis will probably reveal a simpler and more general system.[1]

We thus distinguish between *time* and *tense*, and state that the modals, *Neg* and the quantifiers are always placed in the time determined either by their preceding sentence qualifier, which always refers to the present time, or by an intervening tense qualifier. But they are themselves without tense. It thus seems appropriate to describe, generally, *may* as $U + Poss$, but the forms of *can* as one of the specific tenses followed by *Poss*. A sentence such as:

(255)   John may have known something

[1] A rather different, but at first sight promising, line of investigation would be to incorporate somehow the leftmost occurrence of *Neg* and the modals of indeterminate tense into the sentence qualifier (except *IMP*), so that they would not be part of the proposition, but would modify the sentence qualifier. *He may be wrong* would then be interpreted as something like: 'I assert that it is possibly true that at present he is wrong.'

is now analysable as:

(256)   ASS U Poss Past E(thing) : John know the thing

('I assert that, generally, it is possible that at a previous time there was a thing such that John knew the thing.')

Further investigations into the nature of *Poss* would divert us too much from our present argument (in 4.3.6 the modal operators will be more fully discussed). But observations such as these strongly suggest that tense qualifiers are a useful instrument for the description of deep structure. We shall not go now into a detailed description of the system of tenses in the English verb forms (it would then be necessary to take into account also a concept of 'aspect'). We shall, tentatively, simply envisage five operators of tense: *Present* (*Pres*), *Past*, *Future* (*Fut*), *Perfect* (*Perf*) and the *universal tense* (*U*).

As far as can be seen in this limited discussion, the simplest description of tense qualifiers is given by ascribing to them a semantic property of being placed in time. The five different tenses are then distinguished by their relation to the time of the preceding operator or operators, as determined either by a preceding sentence qualifier or by an intervening other tense qualifier. *Pres* is then semantically defined as simultaneous with its time; *Past* as previous to its time; *Fut* as subsequent to its time; *Perf* as a present statement of an event which took place in the period previous to its time;[1] and *U* as independent of its time. Thus we present the following tense qualifiers with their meanings:

> Pres   ('at this time')
> Past   ('at a previous time')
> Fut   ('at a future time')
> Perf   ('it is a present fact that at a previous time')
> U   ('generally', 'at any time')

This treatment of tense qualifiers enables us to limit their number. The pluperfect, for example, can now be described as *Past* followed by *Past*. If the two *Past*'s are separated from each other either by other operators or even by a nucleus, there is still a notion of pluperfect 'time' in the sentence. A sentence such as:

(257)   it seemed that John had been away

---

[1] It seems likely that *Perf* represents a composite notion of tense and aspect. But since aspects are not considered here, we shall content ourselves with this semantic interpretation of *Perf*. On the whole, tense phenomena in language are so complicated that anything more than a very rough approximation cannot be attempted here.

can be analysed as:

(258)   ASS Past : it seem that Proposition
                        |
                   Past : John be away

Accordingly,

(259)   it seemed that this was true

is described as having the deep structure:

(260)   ASS Past : it seem that Proposition
                        |
                   Pres : this be true

The transformational component of English seems to operate on *time* instead of *tense* in *that*-clauses. It will convert *Pres* in (260) into a surface, or 'morphological' past tense *was*. Notably, in some languages, such as German or Modern Greek, the present tense is found in surface structures analogous to (259):

(261)   er sagte dass es wahr *sei* (he said that it was true)
(262)   φαινόταν πού εἶναι ἀλήθεια αὐτό (it seemcd that this was true)

Perf, however, has the peculiarity of not entailing a past time to the operators following it:

(263)   I have heard that this is true

is described as:

(264)   ASS Perf : I hear that Proposition
                       |
                  Pres : this be true

Accordingly, *Pres* is rewritten as *is* in English.

This account of tense qualifiers also enables us to describe *may* as $U + Poss$. (254) is describable as having the deep structure:

(265)   ASS Past : it seem that Proposition
                       |
              U Poss Pres : this be true

A transformational rule will specify that *U*, when in the past *time*, due to *Past* in the main clause, is transformationally rewritten as *might*. *Pres* in the *that*-clause accounts for the present tense surface infinitive *be true* in (254).

It emerges that the analysis given above opens the way to a simple description with a high degree of semantic adequacy. Generally, in this chapter, it is not implied that there are no other operators than those discussed, nor is it maintained that the analyses given here will prove to be the correct ones. The point is rather that the correctness or incorrectness of any proposal made at this stage can only be proved or disproved if more evidence is made available. We are doing no more than proposing a descriptive framework which seems more promising than any other proposed so far.

As was pointed out in 4.3.2, the adoption of tense qualifiers permits us to distinguish between *nucleus, proposition,* and *sentence.* The nucleus is that part of the deep structure which contains just lexical items in certain definable relational constituents. A sentence is a deep structure including at least one sentence qualifier, which characterizes the sentence as a performative act and is the bearer of this specific sentence meaning. A proposition consists of a nucleus plus at least an operator of tense, but never a sentence qualifier. This distinction is useful in syntax as embedding of constructions sometimes involves tense (clauses) and sometimes not (nominalizations, infinitive or participle constructions); it sometimes also involves a sentence qualifier (descriptive relative clauses; see 5.1). We can now allow for embeddings of nuclei, propositions or sentences. Semantically, this distinction is useful, as it provides a regular formal means of distinguishing semantically between different types of sentences (assertions, questions, etc.), between independent sentences and dependent clauses, and between these and tenseless nuclei.

The nucleus is now purely relational: it does nothing more than define grammatical relations (subject, verb, object, etc.) among lexical items. This is exactly what takes place, for example, in *Mary playing Bach* in:

(266)   I heard Mary playing Bach

We state that *Mary playing Bach* is an embedded nucleus: it can have no tense (**I heard Mary having played Bach*), nor a modal auxiliary (**I heard Mary having to play Bach*). Yet, quantifiers occur freely in embedded nuclei: *I heard Mary playing some sonatas.* This difficulty is solved in chapter 5, where the quantifiers are generated in the nucleus first, contingent upon any noun occurring, and then transposed into the string of operators. If no qualifiers are allowed to occur, as in the case of embedded nuclei, the quantifiers are transposed all the same, but will then be the only operators (see chapter 5, under (62) *vii*). The same procedure applies to those nominalizations that can be described as derived from nuclei and are, roughly, characterized by the occurrence of the preposition *of*, as opposed to those which are derived from propositions.

It will probably be necessary to distinguish between sentence qualifiers and clause qualifiers. With the exception of *Hyp*, briefly discussed in 4.2.4, we have only dealt with independent sentence qualifiers. If clause-introducing conjunctions like *since, although, when,* are to be treated as clause qualifiers along with *Hyp*, then they will probably be best regarded as forms of sentence qualifiers in subordinate position: the former three imply an assertion, but *Hyp* is more closely related with questions, since it requires the answer to the question expressed in it, for the main clause to be stated as true or untrue. Hence the interpretation of *Hyp* in 4.2.4 was formulated as 'under condition of the truth of...'. (The interpretation of hypothetical, or conditional, clauses as a form of subordinate questions, would make it clear why so many languages use the same conjunction for such clauses and embedded questions. In English, *if* is used in both cases, in French *si*, in Italian *se*, etc. In Dutch, different conjunctions are used: *als* for conditional clauses, but *of* for dependent questions. Yet it is a remarkable fact that Dutch children and dialect speakers often use the conditional *als* to introduce dependent questions. Since, obviously, this cannot be explained by assuming interference from another language, it is only reasonable to suppose that they possess a correct deep structure grammar for these cases, but that they have not yet internalized a correct transformational treatment—see 1.4.2 for a discussion of the psychological relevance of grammatical descriptions.) Within the framework of this general exposition the question of clause qualifiers cannot be discussed in great detail. Let us, however, by way of example, probe into the problem of embedded questions.

4.3.5 Embedded questions, *wh*-questions. It was stated in the preceding section that embedded clauses never contain a sentence qualifier. This naturally raises the question of embedded questions: do they or do they not contain a question element? We must distinguish between *yes/no*-questions and *wh*-questions. We have an embedded *yes/no*-question in, for example:

(267)   I wonder if John arrived in time

which cannot be reduced to:

(268)   ASS Pres : I wonder if Sentence
$$|$$
QU Past : John arrive in time

to be interpreted as 'I assert that at present I wonder if I wish to know whether in the past John arrived in time', since this is not the meaning of (267). It might seem preferable to let a proposition follow after *I wonder if*, so that (267) would be analysed as:

(269)   ASS pres : I wonder if Proposition
$$|$$
Past : John arrive in time

Although, semantically, this seems adequate (the synonymy relation is preserved), a number of difficulties arise. For one thing, we are no longer in a position to account for the existential *any* in, for example:

(270)   I wonder if John did anything

which we would naturally like to account for by a preceding question element, so as to remain within the regularities described in 4.2.4. This can be done if we stipulate that the element *if* is not to be generated in the nucleus, but is to be transformationally rewritten from a dependent question operator (clause qualifier): *Qu* ('the truth about the proposition...'). Now *any* can be said to occur after *Qu*, as it does after *Hyp*. *Qu* and *Hyp* are followed by propositions. The embedded question can be regarded as derived from a nucleus constituent *Object*. (How the question element common to *Hyp* and *Qu* is to be accounted for in deep structure, is a matter still to be clarified.) (267) can now be analysed as:

(271)   ASS Pres : I wonder Object
$$|$$
Qu Past : John arrive in time

('I wonder about the truth about the proposition: "John arrived in time"'). (270) as:

(272)   ASS Pres : I wonder Object
$$|$$
Qu Past E(*arb* thing) : John do the thing

('I wonder about the truth about the proposition: "John did something, no matter what"').

The clause qualifier *Qu* is also useful for distinguishing in deep structure between the embedded clause in:

(273)   do you know that John arrived in time?

where *John arrived in time* is probably best regarded as an embedded assertion, and:

(274)   do you know whether John arrived in time?

where it is qualified by *Qu.*

Wh-questions call for a special treatment. Let us first consider how to describe independent *wh*-questions. The solution briefly mentioned and rejected in 4.1 for general reasons of semantic adequacy, must also be rejected, for the same reasons, in the framework of operators. For if (13), *whom did you see?*, were transformationally derived from (12), *you saw someone*, preceded by a question operator, there would be no deep structure difference between (13) and:

(275)   did you see someone?

Katz and Postal's proposal ((1964) pp. 89–90), however, can perhaps be adapted to fit into our system of operators. They propose the generation by the base of the question marker *QU* and *wh*-elements in the positions of noun phrases. These elements are then transformationally rewritten into surface *wh*-forms in the proper positions. This solution avoids ambiguity in the base, but it does not give a maximally straightforward semantic interpretation of the deep structure of *wh*-questions. In particular, it does not bring out the remarkable fact that in *wh*-questions there is no proposition directly dependent on the question operator: what is questioned is not a proposition, but the identity of the thing or person said to be in subject, object, or other relation to the verb in the nucleus. We have here an exception to the general rule that a sentence or clause qualifier governs a proposition. This is even more clearly seen in the case of embedded *wh*-questions. In:

(276)   I wonder what David has eaten

the part *what David has eaten* cannot be provided with labels like 'true', 'false' or 'possible', as could be done with *John arrived in time* of (267). It calls for an answer consisting of the identity of what David has eaten.

In Katz and Postal's solution, the deep structure of a question such as:

(277)   what has David eaten?

can be rendered (partially) as:

(278)   QU + David + Pres + have + en + eat + wh-thing

(where QU is introduced by a rule like (7) *i* in chapter 2). Their general interpretation of *wh*-questions (p. 90), applied to (278), will give:

(279)   'I request that you give an answer, i.e. produce a true sentence one of whose readings is identical with the reading of (278) except that the content of QU is not present and the reading associated with X in (278) is supplemented by further semantic material, i.e. semantic markers.'

Apart from minor details, such as the consideration that the element 'you give an answer' is less appropriate in the interpretation of QU, since not all questions call for an answer given by the listener, it is to be noted that their semantic interpretation does not consist of a left-to-right 'reading' of a synonymous deep structure, automatically yielding an interpretive text in a semantic descriptive language, but necessitates a rather complicated set of rules for the establishment of such a text. Nor does it make explicit that the information required is not the assignment of a truth-value, but the identity of the thing or things said to be in object relation to *David has eaten*.

The semantic component can be simplified and made more explicit by the assumption of an operator $\imath(x)$ ('the identity of the specific x such that...'). The deep structure of (277) will now be:

(280)   QU $\imath$(thing) Perf : David eat the thing

('I wish to know the identity of the thing such that it is a present fact that at a previous time David has eaten the thing').

The interpretation of QU followed by $\imath(x)$ is defined as 'I wish to know', leaving out the element 'whether', which is a function of a following proposition (see p. 114, note 2). Likewise, the element 'the proposition' is left out in the interpretation of Qu followed by $\imath(x)$, so that the deep structure of (276) will be:

(281)   ASS Pres : I wonder Object
$$\mid$$
Qu $\imath$(thing) Perf : David eat the thing

('I assert that at the present time I wonder about the truth about the identity of the thing such that it is a present fact that at a previous time David ate the thing').

As far as can be seen now, the occurrence of $\imath(x)$ should be limited to the position after QU or Qu.

The presence of Qu in embedded *wh*-questions is required, at least, by the occurrence of the existential *any* in embedded *wh*-questions:

(282)   I wonder who did anything

to be derived from:

(283)   ASS Pres : I wonder Object
                            |
              Qu $\imath$(individual) Past E(*arb* thing) :
                                  the individual do the thing[1]

Since the specific question operator, $\imath(x)$, is connected with nouns in the nucleus, this solution would not apply to questions such as: *how tall is David?* Here the element questioned is not simply a noun in the nucleus, but the degree of David's tallness. If we compare this with the analysis proposed for comparative constructions in 4.2.4, it seems that we can assume an element 'degree' in the deep structure of some sentences containing a gradable adjective. How this can be done, is a matter that cannot be gone into here. Likewise, this analysis of *wh*-questions would not seem to account for cases such as: *how many apples did David eat?* Perhaps we can solve this problem by refining our notion of quantifiers. We may, perhaps, treat elements such as *arb*, or *Mult* in quantifiers as embedded relative clauses attached to the quantified noun: 'there is a thing, which is arbitrary', or: 'there are apples, which are many'. (This suggestion will be made again in 5.1.) In principle, a sentence such as: *how many apples did David eat?* would then be set on a par with *how tall is David?* Again, however, it would take us too far to pursue this suggestion any further here.

The operator $\imath(x)$ cannot be regarded as a quantifier, although it operates on a noun phrase in the nucleus or an embedded relative clause. It is distinguished from the quantifiers in that it must immediately follow QU or Qu and does not introduce a proposition but a specific noun phrase. It is not surprising, therefore, that a single noun phrase is sufficient answer to a *wh*-question containing one occurrence of this operator. It shares the feature of being a denominative, or descriptional, operator with its namesake in logic, '$\imath$', which, as Quine says ((1960) p. 164), has 'figured prominently among the basic operators of mathematical logic

[1] A deep structure like 'QU $\imath$(individual) E(individual) Past: the individual see the individual' will be ambiguous, since it may lead to either *who saw someone?* or *whom did someone see?* This difficulty is easily overcome by the introduction of variables (x and y), so that this deep structure will now read, for example, 'QU $\imath$(individual x) E(individual y) Past : the individual x see the individual y'.

from Frege and Peano onward'. Carnap ((1964) pp. 22–3) calls it the *K-operator*: 'The K-operator, $(K_3)\,\beta$, is not a sentential operator, but a descriptional operator.'

4.3.6 Modal operators. We had occasion above (4.2.1; 4.3.4) to distinguish a qualifier *Poss*, manifested by *can* (*could*, etc.) if preceded by a non-universal tense qualifier, and by *may* if preceded by the universal tense qualifier. We shall see below that these and other distributional features of *Poss* are shared with an operator of necessity *Nec* ('it is necessary that...'), and one of permission *Perm* ('it is permitted that...'). In conformity with traditional logical usage we shall call these *modal operators* (*qualifiers*). It is not maintained that there are no modal operators other than those mentioned and discussed here, but only that there is reason for positing a class of modal operators including at least *Poss*, *Nec*, and *Perm*.

On the basis of 4.3.4 we distinguish the following combination of *Tense* and *Modal*:

(284)   Tense-Modal-Tense

That is, we find two expressions of tense, one in the modal auxiliary, and one in the infinitive following.

If the pre-modal tense is not the universal tense, *Poss*, *Nec* and *Perm* have the following forms for the four different tenses:

	Poss	Nec	Perm
Pres	can	have to	be allowed to
Past	could	had to	was/were allowed to
Fut	will be able to	will have to	will be allowed to
Perf	have been able to	have had to	have been allowed to

Poss, *Nec* and *Perm* are transformationally rewritten as *may*, *must* and *may* respectively, if they are preceded by the universal tense operator. It is to be noted, however, that not all instances of *must* are describable with the operator *Nec*. It will be seen below that *mustn't* is derived from Perm preceded by the negation element. In other cases *must* seems to be best described as representing the sentence qualifier *IMP*. More will be said about this in 4.3.7.

In the tense expressed in the infinitive following the modal auxiliary, *Past* and *Perf* merge transformationally into one past infinitive, consisting of *have + past participle of main verb* for active nuclei, and *have + been + past participle of main verb* for passive nuclei. *Fut* and *Pres*, when following *Modal*, merge transformationally into the present infinitive, consisting of the verb simple for actives and *be + past participle of main verb* for passives.

Taking *Poss* for *Modal*, we thus have, for example:

(285)   John may be at home now
            (from: ASS U Poss Pres(now) : John be at home)

(286)   John may be at home tomorrow
            (from: ASS U Poss Fut(tomorrow) : John be at home)

(287)   John may have eaten now
            (from: ASS U Poss Perf(now) : John eat)

(288)   John may have eaten yesterday
            (from: ASS U Poss Past(yesterday) : John eat)

(289)   John can be at home tomorrow
            (from: ASS Pres Poss Fut(tomorrow) : John be at home)

(290)   John will be able to be at home tomorrow
            (from: ASS Fut(tomorrow) Poss Pres : John be at home)[1]

Analogous examples can easily be construed with *Nec* and *Perm*. If *Nec* takes the place of *Poss* in (285)–(290), then *may* is replaced by *must* in (285)–(288); *can* in (289) by *has to*; and *will be able to* in (290) by *will have to*. If *Perm* is used instead of *Poss*, (285)–(288) remain the same; (289) becomes: *John is allowed to be at home tomorrow*, and in (290) *able* is replaced by *allowed*.

One may wonder whether any structure of the form *Fut-Modal-Past* is possible at all. Often such a construction will sound 'unnatural', but not always. With *Nec* for *Modal* the result will sound quite natural:

(291)   from next year onward all teachers will have to have passed
            this exam

With *Perm* the result is less natural:

(292)   from next year onward no teacher will be allowed to have had
            less than five years' university training

With *Poss* examples are also difficult to find:

(293)   from next year onward no teacher will be able to have had less
            than five years' university training

---

[1] But 'ASS Fut Poss Pres(now) : John be at home' would lead to **John will be able to be at home now*, which is ungrammatical unless *now* is taken to refer to the whole sentence, which would then be equivalent to *now John will be able to be at home*. *Pres* is not present *time* here, but future *time*, although it is present *tense* (see 4.3.4). Apparently, however, adverbials of time refer to time and not to tense in English, so that in this case *now*, which refers to present *time*, cannot be combined with the present tense, which refers to future *time* here.

Generally, the naturalness of such sentences depends on context, and it seems that we are not yet in a position to give a systematic account of the rôle of context in grammar.

The distinction between modals preceded by U and those preceded by the other tense operators is also reflected in an interpretive difference. Thus, (286) can be paraphrased as 'it is possible that John will be at home tomorrow', and (289) as 'it is possible for John to be at home tomorrow'. This difference in interpretation is generally applicable to all occurrences of *can* as opposed to *may*. In the same way the difference between:

(294)   John must be at home now
            (from: ASS U Nec Pres(now) : John be at home)
and:

(295)   John has to be at home now
            (from: ASS Pres Nec Pres(now) : John be at home)

is expressible as 'it is necessary that John is at home now' and 'it is necessary for John to be at home now' respectively. And:

(296)   you may go home now
            (from: ASS U Perm Pres(now) : you go home)

can be paraphrased as 'it is permitted that you go home now', whereas:

(297)   you are allowed to go home now
            (from: ASS Pres Perm Pres(now) : you go home)

is rather 'it is permitted for you to go home now'.

We can thus formulate an interpretive rule for partial strings of operators of the form *non-universal tense + modal*, which states that in such strings *Poss* is interpreted as 'it is (was, etc.) possible for subject to...', *Nec* as 'it is (was, etc.) necessary for subject to...', and *Perm* as 'it is (was, etc.) permitted for subject to...'. The full interpretive reading of (289) is now 'I assert that at this time it is possible for John at a subsequent time, tomorrow, to be at home'. (295) is read as 'I assert that at this time it is necessary for John at this time, now, to be at home'. And for (297) we can give the reading 'I assert that at this time it is permitted for you at this time, now, to go home'.

Assuming for the moment that there are further modal operators, such as 'probability' (*Prob*), to be interpreted as 'it is likely that...', we see that the same interpretive rule is applicable: when preceded by a non-universal tense qualifier it is interpretable as 'it is (was, etc.) likely for subject to...' (or 'subject is (was, etc.) likely to...'). The deep structure:

(298)   ASS U Prob Past : Plato write this letter
        ('I assert that it is likely that at a previous time Plato wrote this letter')

can be said to be transformable into:

(299)   probably Plato wrote this letter

But:

(300)   ASS Pres Prob Past : Plato write this letter
        ('I assert that at this time it is likely for Plato at a previous time to have written this letter')

becomes:

(301)   Plato is likely to have written this letter

We have not considered, so far, the occurrence of *Neg* in conjunction with qualifiers of tense and mood. In 4.3.3 it was said in passing (p. 144, note 1) that adverbials of time are not immediately followed by *Neg*. Since in 4.3.4 time adverbials were subsumed under the tense qualifiers, this implies that *Neg* should not be allowed to be generated immediately after a tense qualifier. The order *Neg-Tense* is preferable to *Tense-Neg*.

A preceding *Neg* enables us to give a simple formal and semantic definition of negative sentences.[1] A negative sentence is a sentence whose proposition immediately following the sentence qualifier is the denial of another proposition. Or, in logical terms, a negative proposition is the contradiction of another proposition: the falsity of the one entails the truth of the other, and *vice versa*. This means that a negative proposition can always be paraphrased as 'it is not true that...' In grammatical terms we define a sentence as negative if and only if in its deep structure *Neg* is the leftmost propositional qualifier.

The order *Neg-Tense* is satisfactory also when an operator of mood occurs. The sentence:

(302)   Plato may not have written this letter

which is not a negative sentence,[2] is analysed as:

(303)   ASS U Poss Neg Past : Plato write this letter

---

[1] For a first attempt at defining negative sentences in terms of operators, see Seuren (1967).

[2] See the quotation from Prior (1955) at the beginning of 4.2.2.

where *Neg* is not the leftmost propositional qualifier, but precedes the second occurrence of the tense qualifier. On the other hand,

(304)   ASS Neg U Poss Past : Plato write this letter

one expects to be, in English:

(305)   it is not possible that Plato wrote this letter[1]

The negative sentence:

(306)   Plato can't have written this letter

can be analysed as:

(307)   ASS Neg Pres Poss Past : Plato write this letter

But the non-negative:

(308)   Plato can *not* have written this letter

has *Neg* after *Poss* but before *Past* in its deep structure.

For the negation of *Nec* under the universal tense qualifier English has a more compact transformational product than for *Poss* (305). Whereas *U-Nec* is rewritten as *must*, *Neg-U-Nec* is rewritten as *need not* or *needn't*, as in:

(309)   John needn't go now
            (from: ASS Neg U Nec Pres(now) : John go)

Perm preceded by *U* is rewritten as *may*, as we have seen. *Neg-U-Perm* becomes *must not* or *mustn't*, and in more formal or old-fashioned usage *may not* or *mayn't*:

(310)   John mustn't go now
            (from: Ass Neg U Perm Pres(now) : John go)

The form *mustn't* can thus only represent *Neg-U-Perm*, and never *Neg-U-Nec*, which is transformed into *needn't*.

From the above discussion it follows that we consider the following to be the only admissible sequences of *Tense, Modal* and *Neg*:

(311)   *i*   Tense
            ii   Neg-Tense
            iii   Tense-Modal-Tense

---

[1] There is a difficulty here to which no immediate solution can be given. One might suggest that the deep structure of (305) should be 'ASS Neg Pres : it be possible that S'. Perhaps, sentences containing *be + Adjective + that + S* without a subject (i.e., with the impersonal *it*), must be accounted for, generally, by means of modal or other operators.

    iv   Neg-Tense-Modal-Tense
    v   Tense-Modal-Neg-Tense
    vi   Neg-Tense-Modal-Neg-Tense

(The sequences *v* and *vi* are exemplified, by, for example, *this can also not be true* and *this can't not be true*, respectively.)

At this point we can, as a corollary, state the conditions for a transformation converting *Neg* into *n't*. This transformation will, under certain conditions, be an optional alternative to that rewriting *Neg* as *not* (assigning it its proper position in the sentence). In non-formalized terms, the *n't*-transformation can be formulated as follows:

> If *Neg* does not immediately precede a second tense qualifier and if there is no quantifier incorporated into the nucleus before the finite verb form so that it would attract *Neg* (as in: *not all Swedes are blond*), then *Neg* can be rewritten as *n't*, attached to the finite verb form.

This accounts for the fact that *not* in, for example, (302) cannot be replaced by *n't*, but that in (306) both *not* and *n't* are allowed. (In the *not*-transformation it must be specified that *Neg-Pres-Poss* becomes *cannot*, and that *Pres-Poss-Neg* becomes *can not*.) This transformation also accounts for the fact that in:

(312)   (in order to avoid the rush hour) you must not leave at five
          (from: ASS U Nec Neg Fut(at five) : you leave)

mustn't would be inappropriate, but that it is correct in (310).

Although the above analysis of the modal operators *Poss*, *Nec* and *Perm* is nothing more than a tentative exploration and will certainly have to be amended, it seems that a deep structure hypothesis in terms of operators offers an adequate descriptive apparatus for the peculiarities of the English modal auxiliary verbs.

4.3.7 Adverbial modal operators.

In the preceding section we saw that an infinitive following a modal auxiliary verb is ambiguous, since it represents either an original *Pres*, *Fut* or *U*, or an original *Past* or *Perf*. This ambiguity can be eliminated in those sentences which contain *may* representing *Poss* by the use of the adverb *possibly*. A transformational rule can be set up specifying that if *Poss* is preceded by the tense qualifier *U*, without *Neg*, it can be rewritten not only as *may* but also as *possibly*. We thus have both:

(313)   *i*   Plato may have written this letter
and:
    ii possibly Plato wrote this letter

This transformation does not apply when *U* is preceded by *Neg*, as in (304):

(314)   *impossibly Plato wrote this letter

Nor does it apply when *Poss* is preceded by a tense qualifier other than *U*: the tense expressed in a sentence introduced by *possibly* must always be described as following after *Poss*. (234) and (290), for example, have no alternative form beginning with *possibly*. Accordingly, we state that this is also true for sentences containing *Pres-Poss* in their deep structure, such as (289). The sentence:

(315)   possibly John will be at home tomorrow

is equivalent to (286) and not to (289).

We do not consider here cases like:

(316)   John can't possibly be at home now

which can, perhaps, be described by a double occurrence of *Poss*: *Neg-Pres-Poss-Poss-Pres*.

For the qualifier *Nec* there is an analogous alternative *necessarily*, for cases where *Nec* is preceded by *U*. Thus (294) has an alternative:

(317)   necessarily John is at home now

But, unlike *possibly*, *necessarily* is also allowed when *U* is preceded by *Neg*:

(318)   big men are not necessarily strong men
        (from: ASS Neg U Nec U A(big men) : the big men are
        strong men)[1]

which is equivalent to:

(319)   big men needn't be strong men

It must also be noted that not all sentences containing the auxiliary *must* are paraphrasable with *necessarily*:

(320)   you must go home now

has no such alternative and seems to be best described as:

(321)   IMP Pres(now) : you go home
        ('I request that at this time, now, you go home')

so that it is an alternative form of:

(322)   go home now

---

[1] We disregard here the process whereby adjectives are embedded.

Transformational rewriting of *IMP* as *must* is necessary in some embedded imperatives, such as:

(323) I say that you must go home now

or

(324) then I said to John that he must go home

(Here an imperative clause qualifier must be assumed, distinct from, but in some definable way analogous to, the sentence qualifier *IMP*. This imperative clause qualifier can be called *Imp*.) We state, generally, that only if *must* or *needn't* is derived from *Nec* can it be rewritten as *necessarily*.

For *Perm* there is no adverbial alternative in English. But if we accept a modal operator *Prob* (see 4.3.6), we can state that it is transformable into *probably* if preceded by *U* without *Neg*, as in (299).

It is not impossible that adverbs like *apparently, justifiably, notoriously, foolishly, cleverly, gallantly, unmistakably, unexpectedly*, when occurring in a surface structure position roughly defined as immediately following the subject, or in front position, can also be accounted for by regarding them as, possibly modal, operators. Some of these adverbs also occur as verbal modifiers in other positions in the sentence. Thus we have, for example:

(325) John unexpectedly spoke very cleverly

But a detailed discussion of these possible operators would go beyond the scope of the present discussion.

4.4 Conclusion

The results set out in this chapter are, of course, provisional and much further research will have to be done to correct and supplement them. But the main purpose of this chapter was to illustrate the viability of the concept of operators as a deep structure category. The operators discussed here seem to present a descriptive apparatus that enables us to account for a large number of grammatical phenomena in an adequate way.

A deep structure grammar of operators will certainly be complex. But there is no way of circumventing the fact that language in general, and every separate language in particular, is a complex whole of data. An adequate description of any complex set of data must necessarily reflect this complexity. The ideal of simplicity in grammatical descriptions is perhaps better characterized as the ideal of least complexity. The category of operators in deep structure grammar seems to enable us to reduce substantially the complexity of the data provided by the sentences of natural languages.

The requirement of semantic adequacy seems to be better fulfilled than was hitherto possible in transformational grammar. An analysis in terms of operators permits us not only to define the sentences of a language syntactically, but also to present a motivated and precise account of some of their semantic characteristics. The underlying structure of every sentence can be read linearly[1] from left to right by simply concatenating the interpretations of the operators and reading the nucleus. These readings lead to 'texts' in an empirically established semantic descriptive language. There are good grounds for suggesting, therefore, that the category of operators may well open the way to the establishment of an adequate semantic descriptive language, which, as we saw in 1.4.4, is still lacking in linguistics. We shall return to this problem in 5.4.2.

---

[1] A possible exception consists in the reading of the modal operators discussed in 4.3.6, when they are preceded by a non-universal tense qualifier. We saw that in these cases the subject of the nucleus is incorporated into the modal operators. Such exceptions must be statable in general rules of semantic interpretation.

5 *A specimen of description*

5.0 Introduction

Given the considerations of the previous chapters one naturally wonders what form a grammatical description might possibly take. In the present chapter a tentative description will be given of a particular deep structure hypothesis of English in so far as this has been developed. This hypothesis takes into account both the category of operators as described in chapter 4, and the requirements for grammatical description formulated at the end of chapter 3. That is, no deep structures will be generated that make the transformational component 'block' because they cannot be developed into surface structures; deviant sentences will be clearly separable from non-deviant ones; the main verb of the sentence in generation will be selected before the noun or nouns occurring in noun phrases; the development of noun phrases will be dependent on a selected noun; it will be possible to select nouns according to rules of selectional restriction, rules of selectional instruction, or arbitrarily; relational constituents will be marked as such throughout the generative process. And finally, it will become clear that the grammar itself will provide relevant clues for the description of meanings.

The deep structure grammar presented here will be based on a limited vocabulary of ordinary English words. Nouns, verbs, and adjectives will be specified in terms of semantic selectional features, which are taken into account in the rules of lexical selection in such a way that no deviant sentences are generated when the feature specification is observed.

The specification in terms of features will be given in a 'static' form, which might give the impression that the rules for deviance and non-deviance are fixed, or can be fixed, once and for all, for the whole language. It is, however, becoming increasingly apparent that deviance is too flexible and dynamic a phenomenon to be completely dealt with in such a way. The intuition of deviance seems to depend a great deal on the previous 'history' of the speaker and, in particular, on previous context. Generally speaking, for every grammatically well-formed sentence a context can be thought up, into which this sentence fits quite naturally, so that it loses its deviant character. In a fairy tale trees may whisper without deviance. And a sentence such as *this mathematical paper is very Californian*[1] will sound deviant to most speakers of English, but perfectly normal to those who are acquainted with Californian mathematical publications. It is not at all clear how this variable property of deviance can be adequately described. It may be necessary to set up a device for the generation of lexical meanings such that semantic features can be added or deleted under specifiable conditions in certain contexts. But such a procedure would clearly exceed the bounds of the present study, or indeed, of what can be considered feasible at present. It can, in fact, only be carried out in the light of a comprehensive theory of meaning and context, which, needless to say, is still lacking. In the circumstances we can only exclude context from consideration. For the present study we posit as a principle that a sentence is only said to be deviant outside any specific context, that is, in the general cultural context of mid-twentieth century Western civilization, with all its necessary indeterminacies.

The deep structure description presented here must, of necessity, be tentative. For one thing, the English language has not been investigated thoroughly enough to allow for a deep structure hypothesis which would cover the whole of it: we can only hope to cover as wide a range of phenomena as is possible with the analytic data available. For another, the relation between deep structure and meaning is by no means clear. We may expect that an adequate deep structure description will provide some of the semantic descriptive language which is still lacking in linguistics. This may be a possible starting-point for a wider theory of meaning, the need for which is strongly felt in all linguistic quarters. More will be said about the semantic implications of our deep structure hypothesis at the end of this chapter, in 5.4.2. If, in fact, deep structure rules provide adequate expressions of a semantically explanatory nature, it may well appear more appropriate to regard a deep structure description as a device generating meaningful structures, as a 'semantic generator', rather than as a generator of meaningless strings which are the input to a separate device of semantic interpretation. The semantic component of the grammar would then no longer be an interpretive component operating upon the products of the base, but would be the base itself. It would be premature, however, to indulge here in any further speculation as to what deep structure description, and, indeed,

[1] I owe this example to Dr Mary Hesse of the University of Cambridge.

grammars, might look like in the light of a sound semantic theory. For the present discussion we shall content ourselves with the concept of grammar as it is current nowadays in the theory of transformational grammar: the base will generate deep structures to which, presumably, a semantic interpretation can be applied.

It will be necessary, however, to disregard the restrictions imposed by present-day theory of transformational grammar on base rules. These rules will no longer be exclusively phrase-structure rules containing the instruction to rewrite given individual symbols as strings of other symbols in such a way that successive rewritings unambiguously permit the construction of a P-marker for any generated structure. We shall allow for rules requiring more 'intelligence' on the part of the reader, or reading device, than is required for simple PS-rules. Variables will be permitted, and, in general, information obtainable from previous generative stages will be employed. But no more intelligence will be required than is necessary for the reading of Chomskian transformations.

On the whole, there seems to be no compelling reason why the base should be limited to PS-rules. The distinction between the base and the transformational component can now be made on other grounds than the form of their rules. The limitation of the base to PS-rules seems to be largely due to historical reasons: the transformational model was born out of the inadequacy of a pure PS-model, and a combination of a PS-component with transformational rules seemed a viable solution. Experience shows, however, that such a combination is not, in fact, viable, and that more powerful rules must be allowed in the base. One remembers that in (1965) Chomsky allows for transformation-type rules including variables in the base, when he introduces the subcategorization rules. The recent discovery of the principle of semantically interpretable deep structure has lent independent support to a distinction between deep and surface structure, and has made the old limitations on the form of the rules quite unnecessary. It seems unwise to impose too many restrictions on the form of rules, as long as so little is known about deep structure and, generally, the complications of linguistic description.

The model of the base presented in this chapter looks in many ways like a tagmemic grammar. This is not mere coincidence, since, undeniably, modern concepts of grammar rest largely upon Bloomfield's work. Particularly, IC-analysis and tagmemics are direct offshoots of Bloomfield's *Language*. Whilst Chomsky's model of the base can be said to be a formalization of IC-analysis in generative terms, after Harris's unsuccessful attempt at a formalized analytic procedure, our criticism of Chomsky's work led to a base model which can be looked upon as, broadly speaking, a formalization of the tagmemic way of description associated with Pike and his school. Both IC-analysis and tagmemics are seen to be insufficient for an adequate description of a language: they need transformational complementation. In tagmemic circles this has been recognized, as is witnessed by Longacre's *Grammar Discovery Procedures* (1964) (see also Seuren's review of this book (1966)) and by Cook's *On Tagmemes and Transforms* (1964). The proposals made by both these authors, however, lack sufficient explicitness and do not seem to stand comparison with Chomskian transformational grammar.

5.1   Some deep structure rules

Assuming that the generation of deep structures can be adequately considered to start from an initial symbol, say *Sent*, we can formulate the following rules:

(1)   *i*   Sent → SQL + Prop

   ii   SQL → $\begin{Bmatrix} \text{ASS} \\ \text{QU} \\ \text{IMP} \\ \text{SUGG} \end{Bmatrix}$

   iii   Prop → QL + Nucleus[V]

where *SQL* stands for 'sentence qualifier', *Prop* for 'proposition', *ASS* for 'assertion', *QU* for 'question', *IMP* for 'imperative', *SUGG* for 'suggestion', *QL* for 'qualifier', and *V* for 'verb'. The symbol '+' is a concatenation symbol; $X \rightarrow Y$ means 'rewrite X as Y'; the braces indicate alternative choices, as in Chomskian grammar. The square brackets enclose the value of a parameter (see below).

We now develop *QL*. Since the number of quantifiers depends on the number of nouns in the nucleus, we develop, for the moment, only qualifiers. The analysis of qualifiers given in the previous chapter being admittedly incomplete, the rules generating them can only be provisional. They are meant to represent an instance of partial description, and there is no claim to final adequacy.

The rules for generating strings of qualifiers as given below ensure the occurrence of the negative, tense and modal qualifiers in the order required for them in the previous chapter.

We thus have:

(1) *iv* QL → (NEG) Tense

 v Tense → $\begin{cases} \text{T} \\ \text{T(Modal)} \end{cases}$ env IMP(NEG)—$\big\}$

 vi Modal → M (Neg) Tense

where the brackets indicate optional choice. The recursion of *Tense* from (1) *vi* to (1) *v* makes it possible to have a succession of modalities in the same sentence, as in: *you must have been able to be here at five*, or: *he may have had to work*, or: *it may have been necessary for him to work*. Possibly, these rules are too crude, and would allow for successions of modals leading to ungrammatical strings. Further refinements will then have to be added.

T (tense) is expanded in the following way:

(1) *vii* T → $\left\{ \begin{array}{l} \left\{ \begin{array}{l} \text{Pres} \\ \text{Fut} \\ \text{Perf} \end{array} \right\} \text{ env IMP (NEG)—} \\ \text{Pres} \\ \text{Fut} \\ \text{Perf} \\ \text{Past} \\ \text{U} \end{array} \right\}$

where *U* stands for the universal tense qualifier, discussed in the previous chapter. Rules (1) *xvii* and (1) *xx* below will ensure that a universal quantifier is selected where there is no modal operator.

The treatment of tenses, in these rules, is admittedly oversimplified. Thus, for example, a double occurrence of Past, leading to a pluperfect (as mentioned in 4.3.4), is not accounted for. A special monograph, however, would be required to deal with all problems connected with tense and, for that matter, with aspect.

The environmental restriction given in (1) *vii* seems necessary in view of the fact that the past tense does not occur in imperatives (for *U* this is less certain).

(1) *viii* NEG → Neg (Neg) (Neg)

The point of this rule is that it seems desirable to allow for double or treble sentence negation. In some languages repeated negation simply leads to two or three consecutive occurrences of the negative surface representative. It can be argued that double negation is rendered in

English by emphatic *do*-support: *the emperor* did *go to Canossa* (viz.: it is not true that it is not true that the emperor went to Canossa). There remain, of course, many problems and complications. Thus, the existential *any* would have to be excluded after two consecutive occurrences of *Neg*. But the expression *can help* (i.e. can do so that not), which only occurs after negation, would not be excluded after double *Neg*: *but you* can *help it*. Treble negation may be said to be rendered by a regular negation with heavy stress on *not*: *the emperor did* not *go to Canossa*;[1] not *many emperors are willing to humiliate themselves* (it is not true that it is not true that it is not true that...).

M (modal) will now be expanded into the three modalities discussed in chapter 4:

(1)   *ix* $M \rightarrow \begin{Bmatrix} \text{Poss} \\ \text{Nec} \\ \text{Perm} \end{Bmatrix}$

The way is now clear for the development of the nucleus. The nucleus is that part of the deep structure of every sentence, which contains lexical items and relational constituents, that is, lexical items in relation to each other. (Whether or not we can posit that all lexical items are restricted to the nucleus, is still an open question, since we have not yet found a way of dealing with certain categories of adverbs and prepositional phrases.)

According to rule (1) *iii* the nucleus is *Nucleus[V]*, where *V* stands for 'verb'. The square brackets indicate the slot filled by the symbol or symbols enclosed. *Nucleus* is the name of the slot, or of the relational constituent. Or, more adequately, we say that symbol groups of the form *X[Y]* consist of the parameter *X* and its value *Y*. The relational constituents of the nucleus are thus introduced as parameters, rather than as slots. These parameters are retained throughout the deep structure development, so that the transformations can operate upon them. From a formal point of view this is not only a natural notation, but it will also simplify transformational treatment, in that the parameter character of the terms they operate on has now become tangible in the form of symbols and is not obscured, as it is in Chomskian grammar, where one has to rely on

---

[1] Presumably, *the emperor* didn't *go to Canossa* can be accounted for by an operator of emphasis which can be attached to specific nucleus elements or to the whole sentence (i.e. to the sentence qualifier), as here. Emphasis is not considered in this study, although it is felt that it should be made to form part of deep structure.

statements of context, which are unnecessarily elaborate and, moreover, impose undue restrictions on the form of deep structure rules (see 3.3.3).

Symbol groups such as *Nucleus*[*V*] form one constituent, but two different symbols, which can be rewritten separately.

The next step is the selection of the main verb from the lexicon by means of the following rule:

(1) x $[V] \overset{L}{\to} v$

A rule of the type $[X] \overset{L}{\to} x$ means: 'go to lexicon; select an arbitrary x from the category X; write x for X.'

Under V the lexicon will contain all verbs, plus for each verb a specification of what subcategory or subcategories of nouns can figure as a non-deviant subject, object, indirect object, or prepositional object (if any), and/or what kind of embedded clause is allowed or required. In general, all syntactic and selectional idiosyncrasies correlated with individual verbs must be stated in the lexicon. It has not been possible, as yet, to set up such complete specifications, but we can present a viable system of a more restricted kind, which gives consistent specifications for the subject, object, indirect object and prepositional object that are compatible with a specific verb. Thus, the verb *drink* will be accompanied in the lexicon by at least the following specifications:

(2)   *drink* $S[n_{an}]$

$$*O[n_{lq}], [n_{c,vol,cont}]$$

$$*PO[Relator[p(\textit{from})]+Axis\,[n_{c,vol,cont}]]$$

Here the connecting lines indicate which relational constituents occur, or can occur, with the given verb. This verb must have a subject (which seems to be generally true for all except impersonal verbs), which must be filled by an animate noun. It may have an object (hence the asterisk). If there is an object, this must be a noun characterized by the feature 'liquid' (*lq*), or a noun with the features 'concrete', 'voluminous' and 'contentful' (*c, vol,* and *cont,* respectively). This verb may or may not have a prepositional object (*PO*) dominated by the relator *from*. This *PO* may occur whether there is an object or not: hence the line connecting S and *PO*. The noun in axis-position must be of the subcategory $n_{c,vol,cont}$.

Thus we have, according to this specification, for instance:

(3)   *i*   the man drinks
      ii the man drinks water
      iii the man drinks a cup[1]
      iv the man drinks from a cup
      v   the man drinks water from a cup
      vi the man drinks the cream from the milk
      vii the man drinks a cup from the bucket

Under the category of nouns the lexicon will contain all nouns, each followed by an enumeration of its selectional semantic features, such as:

(4)   *water*   c   m   vol   nsol   lq
              (concrete, mass, voluminous, non-solid, liquid)

These features are not given in matrix form, but are added as subscripts elsewhere in the grammar, and during the process of generation. The decision what features to assign to what nouns depends largely on laborious checking of an informant's intuition of deviance, and on considerations of descriptive economy.

The prepositional phrases beginning with *from* followed by a noun specified as concrete, voluminous, contentful are considered prepositional objects, because their nouns can be the subject of a corresponding passive sentence provided there is no object. In general, it can be stated for English that some prepositional phrases can become the subject of a corresponding passive, but only if there is no object or indirect object (see, however, p. 176, note 1). Such prepositional phrases are called prepositional objects here. Those prepositional phrases which are not *PO*'s probably belong to different classes: some function as operators, others as adverbial adjuncts to the verb (see (30)–(51) in chapter 4). In this study only *PO*'s are taken into account; in 5.2.4 below some general remarks will be made on prepositions and some examples given.

---

[1] It will have to be specified somehow that the object, if consisting of $n_{c, vol, cont}$, as in (3)*iii*, tends to be indefinite; we have: *the man drank two cups*, but rather not: *the man drank his cup*. Yet, *the man drank his cup of tea every day at four o'clock* is quite normal again. Perhaps we should assume a feature 'unit of measure', which, together with 'liquid', would characterize a possible class of object-nouns for the verb *drink*. On the whole, the specifications proposed here and elsewhere cannot be claimed to be even remotely complete, and further elaboration may well lead to drastic changes in the system itself.

Prepositional phrases which are not *PO*'s share their syntactic and selectional regularities with other adverbial expressions. Adverbial expressions of time, and many adverbial expressions of place, are to be regarded as operators (see 4.3.3). This does not mean, however, that they are to be generated along with the qualifiers in the *QL*-constituent. In fact, they seem to be too intimately connected with nucleus elements to be excluded from the nucleus, as appears, for example, from their occurrence in derived nominals, such as *the destruction of the city in 1940*, which are clearly derived from nuclei (see below). In this respect they are similar to quantifiers, which are generated in the nucleus and subsequently transferred to the string of operators (rules (1) *xvii*–(1) *xx*). They are more complicated than quantifiers, however, since, for one thing, selection of adverbials of time is dependent on the tense qualifiers (**he will come yesterday*), and, for another, we probably need a subcategorization system of verbs in terms of their intrinsic features (process verbs, stative verbs, etc.) in much the same way as is done for nouns, in order to determine which adverbials of place, if any, are allowed to occur. Such a subcategorization of verbs is left out of account here.

By rule (1) x V in the nucleus is replaced by a particular v, say *drink*. The syntactic and selectional specifications associated with *drink* in the lexicon are kept at hand (are kept in the short-term memory recording the generative process of each sentence), until the grammar delivers its product.

Now the following rule applies:

(1)   xi   Nucleus[v] →
      *S[N] + MV[v] + *O[N] + *IO[N] + *PO[Relator[P] + Axis[N]]

where *MV* stands for 'main verb', and *X means: 'select X if v requires X; select or do not select X if v allows for X; do not select X if X is not specified for v'.

The ' + '-sign implies a fixed order for the concatenated elements. In order to account for languages with relatively free word order, Staal (1967b) (see also Chomsky (1965) p. 124) proposes a deep structure grammar where the order of the constituents is not bound. He gives rules of the type S →{NP, VP}, where the right-hand part, enclosed by braces, represents an unordered set. Such a procedure may well prove justified for nucleus expansion, where the order of the constituents is, indeed, irrelevant, and can be determined by transformations. We have seen, however, that for the operators order in deep structure representations is of prime importance, so that Staal's proposals would not apply to the grammar of operators. It has not appeared so far, however, that an unordered nucleus expansion of the type proposed by Staal is useful or necessary for English as opposed to languages with free word order. And since we prefer to set up deep structure hypotheses for separate languages before allowing ourselves to go into problems of universality of deep structure, we feel reluctant to adopt Staal's suggestions here.

Thus, after the selection of the verb *drink*, a possible string would be:

(5) $S[N] + MV[drink] + O[N] + PO[Relator[P] + Axis[N]]$

The next step is to select a proper (i.e. non-deviant) preposition for the *PO*, if any, and proper nouns for the object, indirect object and/or axis. (The preposition is selected first, for reasons given in 5.2.4 below.) For this purpose we introduce rules of a type similar to (1) *x*, but with some extra elements:

(1)   *xii* $[P^{Relator}] \xrightarrow{L} p_s$

    xiii $\begin{Bmatrix} [N^O] \\ [N^{IO}] \\ [N^{Axis}] \end{Bmatrix} \xrightarrow{L} n_s$

A rule of the type $[X^Q] \xrightarrow{L} x_s$ means: 'go to the lexicon; select an x_s from the category X such that the string of features s attached to x in the lexicon comprises the string of subscripts attached to the slotfiller of Q as specified for the selected v in the lexicon; or select the specific x if any specific x is given as the slotfiller of Q in the lexical specification of the selected v; or select any member of the class X in the lexicon if no subscripts are attached to the slotfiller of Q as specified for the selected v in the lexicon; write the x_s (i.e. with the whole series of features as given in the lexicon for x) for X in slot Q.'

We must retain the whole series of subscripts as given in the lexicon, in view of later (transformational) stages of generation.

If the lexicon contains, under *Noun*, the nouns *water* as in (4) and *cup* as in:

(6)   *cup*   c   i   vol   cont
             (concrete, individual, voluminous, contentful)

then (5) can be rewritten, according to (1) *xii* and (1) *xiii*, as:

(7) $S[N] + MV[drink] + O[water_{c, m, vol, nsol, lq}] +$
                            $PO[Relator[from] + Axis[cup_{c, i, vol, cont}]]$

If the condition imposed on the value of the subscript s in rules of the type $[X^Q] \xrightarrow{L} x_s$ is neglected, the grammar will generate, apart from the non-deviant sentences, the deviant ones as well, but will not generate ungrammatical sentences. Care has been taken to ensure that for the generation of deviant but grammatical sentences to be possible it is necessary and sufficient to disregard the condition imposed on the subscript *s* in rules of this type. This can be done by interpreting rules of this type simply as: 'go to the lexicon; select any *x* from the class *X* in the lexicon; or, if any specific *x* is given as the slotfiller of Q in the lexical specification of the selected *v*, select this *x*; write the x_s (i.e. with all the features as given in the lexicon for *x*) for *X* in slot Q'.

In order to ensure grammaticalness it is still necessary to introduce the item, now randomly or specifically selected from its 'rough' category, with its associated features. It is also necessary to maintain the instruction of specific selection. For instance, the selection of any other preposition than *from* in (7) would lead, if not to an ungrammatical sentence, to the assignment of an incorrect structure, which would open the way to grammatical processes resulting in ungrammatical sentences. Thus, for example, if *towards* is selected, instead of *from*, the grammar would generate the ungrammatical: **this cup has been drunk towards*.

So far, the subject-slot has not yet been filled with a lexical item. The subject, in fact, requires special treatment because it can be filled either by a noun fulfilling the selective conditions stated by the verb for the subject, or by an already selected noun in the position of (*a*) object, (*b*) indirect object, or (*c*), if there is neither an object nor an indirect object, in the axis-position of the *PO*. If an already selected noun in non-subject position becomes the subject-noun, the verb becomes passive. Then the original slot of *O*, *IO*, or *Axis*, from which the subject has been taken, is either deleted or rewritten as an agent phrase (*AgPhr*), consisting of the relator *by* plus in the axis-slot again N^S. This process can be described formally in the following way:

(1) *xiv* $[N^S] \overset{L}{\rightarrow} n_s$

$[N^S] \rightarrow \begin{bmatrix} n_s^O \\ n_s^{IO} \\ n_s^{Axis} \text{ env } X - MV[v] + PO[Relator[p] + Axis- \end{bmatrix} \rightarrow$

(*a*) $\begin{bmatrix} O[n_s] \\ IO[n_s] \\ Axis[n_s] \end{bmatrix} \rightarrow \begin{Bmatrix} \varnothing \\ AgPhr[Relator[p(by)] + Axis[N^S]] \end{Bmatrix}$

(*b*) $[N^S] \overset{L}{\rightarrow} n_s$

(*c*) $MV[v] \rightarrow Pass + MV'[v]$

According to this rule the subject-noun can either be selected from the lexicon in the normal way as defined for (1) *xii* and (1) *xiii*, or *N* in the subject-slot can be rewritten as the noun (plus features) already selected in the positions of *O*, *IO*, or *Axis* of *PO* immediately preceded by the main verb.[1] Only if the second alternative is chosen, do rules (*a*), (*b*) and (*c*) become operative. The double-pointed arrow is the 'traffic sign' indicating the dependence of the separate block of rules (*a*), (*b*) and (*c*) on the second alternative. It is, in fact, a logical implication: if the second alternative is chosen, then (*a*), (*b*) and (*c*) become operative. Rule (*a*) states that the slot from which the subject-noun is taken is either deleted (∅ being the zero-element), or rewritten as an agent phrase consisting of *by* plus a noun to be selected according to the subject restrictions given with the verb. The square brackets over more than one line are used in the Chomskian manner: they indicate alternative choices, but only among the sets of elements arranged on one line. The N^S of the *by*-phrase is now selected by application of rule (*b*). It must be stated that there is no recursion from rules belonging to an isolated block to the 'main' rules, so that N^S cannot this time be taken as input to rule (1) *xiv*, Finally, the main verb is passivized by rule (*c*). The priming of *MV* serves to prevent recursion. The exact syntactic and morphophonemic treatment of the passivized verb is left to the transformations.

Rule (1) *xiv*, as it stands, does not allow for embedded object-clauses and nuclei to become the subject of a passive sentence. In a fuller

---

[1] Generally, in English, the axis-noun of a *PO* can only occur as the subject of a passive sentence if there is no object or indirect object: **the paper was written a letter on by me; *the paper was written him on by me; *Fido was thrown stones at by Archibald.* Hence the context restriction for the axis-noun in (1) *xiv*. There are some counter-examples to this rule, such as *he was taken care of*, or *she was paid attention to*, or *this was taken account of*. These must be taken account of in a fuller description. It was pointed out to me, moreover, by our student Paul Meara, that we do have *Fido had stones thrown at him by Archibald*. This construction can only be used if there is an object and a preposition to take up the subject again. It is also possible for sentences with object and indirect object: *I had a letter written to me*, which comes close to *I was written a letter*. It does not seem certain, however, that we should consider these sentences with *have*+past participle as a deep structure variant form of the passive. First, they tend to be limited to animate subjects. Secondly, they are not in perfect complementary distribution with the normal *be*+past participle passives: there is overlapping, and sentences without an object do not allow for this form: *he wrote to me on parchment* has no corresponding **I had written to me on parchment*, or **parchment had written on it to me*. Thirdly, it is not clear how these *have*-passives are related to derived nominals (see below). If, however, we do not take the passive as belonging to deep structure, but rather as a transformational manifestation of an underlying topic–comment distinction, then, perhaps, these *have*-passives can be regarded as another surface manifestation of the same underlying distinction.

description this possibility must be incorporated. Transformationally, these embedded structures may undergo various treatments, when passivized. The most straightforward process is that whereby the embedded structure simply becomes the surface subject: *that this is true is believed by most people*. Often, however, the 'empty' subject *it* may or must be employed: *it is believed by most people that this is true*; *it has been asked whether this is true*; *it has been said that you must go*. Sometimes also the subject of the embedded structure may or must become the surface subject: *this is believed to be true by most people*; *Mary has been heard playing Bach*; *Picasso is said to be the greatest living artist*; *Jim has been told to go home* (in this case it is impossible to see whether the indirect object *Jim* or the embedded imperative *that Jim must go home* has been taken as the subject of the passive sentence—see under (62) *x*).

There are various reasons for dealing with passives in this way. First, by letting passivization take place in the deep structure component we avoid the difficulty, arising in previous, transformational, treatments, of a deep structure object, etc., becoming surface structure subject, which complicates the relationship between relational constituents in deep and surface structure. The subject of a passive sentence is now also its deep structure subject, and its 'object-character' is accounted for by the fact that it is selected according to the selectional restrictions for the object, as stated for the selected verb in the lexicon. That is, it is accounted for by the lexicon. The same is true of the indirect object and the prepositional object. Similarly, the 'subject-character' of the agent in the *by*-phrase is accounted for by its selection according to the subject instructions entailed by the selected verb.

A second reason is that, since it is not necessary to select any N^S at all, it is no longer necessary to generate *by*-phrases with dummy elements for sentences without a *by*-phrase. This dummy representation is not only awkward, but also sometimes semantically undesirable, as in *his ability is generally recognized*, where something like 'by unspecified agent' is an inappropriate addition.

Another advantage of letting the base generate both actives and passives is that derived nominals[1] can now be generated simply as trans-

---

[1] The term *derived nominals* is taken from Chomsky, *Remarks on Nominalization*, 1967 *a*, unpublished, where he distinguishes between gerundive nominals of the form *John's eating the cake*, with the internal structure of a predicate phrase, and derived nominals of the form *John's proof of the theorem*, with the internal structure of a noun phrase. Chomsky accounts for the latter solely on the basis of lexical selectional features associated with a lexical item *proof/prove*. This account, which he calls the lexicalistic

forms of base-terminal nuclei. The tenseless character of derived nominals is now accounted for by their being derived from tenseless nuclei. *Archibald's eating of the pudding, the eating of the pudding by Archibald, their destruction of the city, the city's destruction by them* are now direct transforms from base nuclei, active or passive.

Generally, if the base-terminal nucleus is of the form *subject + verb* (irrespective of a possible *IO* and/or *PO*), then the derived nominal has the form *subject's + verb-ing* or *verb-ing of-subject*. Verbs that do not take a subject do not allow for a derived nominal: **the seeming to me that this is true* (see under (62) *xi* below). If there is an object in the nucleus, the derived nominal becomes *subject's + verb-ing + of-object*. The element *verb-ing* is later rewritten as the regular *ing*-form of the verb (*eating*), or as a special, irregular, form if this is available (*proof, destruction, explanation*). The prepositional object and agent phrase (for the passive) remain unaltered. The indirect object is preceded by an obligatory *to*. This applies equally to actives and passives (where the element *Pass* is deleted), except that if the subject of a passive base-terminal nucleus is a noun from an original indirect or prepositional object, this is placed back in its original position and the derived nominal is left without a subject. Thus, we can have *the writing on walls by the student*, but not **the walls' writing on by the student*, or **the writing of walls on by the student*. Or also: *the paying of compliments to Mary by Bill*, but not **Mary's paying of compliments to by Bill*. Similarly, embedded object-clauses are shifted back to their original position, without *of*, as in *the proof by Newton that the earth is flattened at the poles*.

This description accounts automatically for the fact that we do not

position, excludes the transformational derivation of derived nominals from deep structure sentences. Something similar was already suggested by him in (1965) pp. 219–20. This tallies very well with the derivation of derived nominals from nuclei, as proposed here, since the nucleus is a direct reflection of the lexicon. His argument, however, that derived nominals are largely irregular, which would justify their lexical treatment (cf. Chomsky (1965) p. 142) needs some qualification. Derived nominals are a normally productive category, but the regular form is not a noun such as *proof, refusal, destruction, doubt, criticism*, but an *-ing*-form of the type *John's eating of the pudding* or *the eating of the pudding by John*. Only for certain verbs is there a more or less idiosyncratic noun replacing the *-ing*-form. This appears most clearly from the fact that this *-ing*-nominalization is ungrammatical for those cases where there is an idiosyncratic noun: **John's proving of the theorem*. The idiosyncratic forms must, of course, be specified in the lexicon. The distinction drawn by Chomsky between the lexicalistic and the transformationalist position does not imply that lexicon and transformations are mutually exclusive. It rather means that the lexicon is more relevant than had been thought for the solution of certain grammatical problems, which is very true.

have, for instance, **John's paying of compliments to Mary by Bill*, since we cannot have two subjects in one nucleus. We do have, however, *the destruction (by the enemy)*, *the proof (by Newton)*, *the shouting (by students)*, which must be derived from a nucleus with zero subject, and with or without a *by*-phrase. This kind of nucleus cannot be derived from the rules given above. Noticeably, these subjectless derived nominals occur only with certain verbs, roughly 'process'-verbs: we do not find **the sleeping by the child*, **the waiting by clients*. A possible solution for these cases can be given by adding the following rule to (1) *xiv*, which will only apply to structures containing process verbs:

(1) *xiv a* $[\text{N}^\text{S}] \to \emptyset$ env—$\text{MV}[\text{v}_\text{pr}] \emptyset$ (where $\emptyset$ is the null string)

$\twoheadrightarrow (a)$ $\text{MV}[\text{v}_\text{pr}] \to \text{Pass} + \text{MV}'[\text{v}_\text{pr}]$

$(\text{AgPhr}[\text{Relator}[\text{p}(by)] + \text{Axis}[\text{N}^\text{S}]])$

(b) $[\text{N}^\text{S}] \overset{\text{L}}{\to} \text{n}_\text{s}$

For this rule to apply it is necessary that there be no direct, indirect or prepositional object. The subject is deleted, the main verb is passivized, and there may be a *by*-phrase containing the noun which would otherwise have been the subject. Such 'impersonal' passives take the form of *there was shouting (by the students)* in non-nominalized surface structures.

Cases such as *the story by Boccaccio*, *the painting by Giotto*, *the speech by Cicero*, if nominalizations at all, must belong to a different category. We do not have **the painting by Giotto in 1295*, but we do have *the city's destruction by the enemy in 1940* (see above, where adverbials of time were commented upon). This shows at least that these noun phrases are not derived from *the story written by Boccaccio*, *the painting made by Giotto*, etc. Probably their immediate source is *the story that is by Boccaccio*, *the painting that is by Giotto*, so that they are similar to, for example, *the house in Regent Street*, which is derivable from *the house that is in Regent Street*. This explains why we do have *the story by Boccaccio in the Decamerone*, *the painting by Giotto in Padua*, etc., but not **the rumour by the press*, **the opinion by the expert*, since we do not have **the rumour that is by the press*, **the opinion that is by the expert*. The origin of these relative *that*-clauses is a matter still to be clarified, but this does not concern us directly here. On the whole, we must admit that many problems remain unsolved, but it seems at least that we have provided the basis of a general solution for derived nominals.

Further reasons can be given to justify this treatment of the passive.

12-2

To mention just one, it accounts directly for the impossibility of the passive for impersonal verbs with embedded object-clauses, such as *seem, appear*. We have, for instance, *that this is true is believed by most people*, but not **that this is true is seemed*. The verb *seem* is specified in 5.2 as (62) *xi*. It does not take a subject, so that there is no domain for rule (1) *xiv* to apply to, which automatically rules out the passive for this verb. It is generally true for English, that passivization is dependent upon the presence of a subject-slot $S[N]$. The sentence *it rained manna* has no passive, but *he rained gifts upon my friends* has the passive *gifts were rained upon my friends by him*. (*This coat has been rained on* is doubtful.)

There is also, however, an argument against this treatment of the passive. Rule (1) *xiv* is specially tailored to English, and does not seem applicable to any other language. This would suggest that it ought to have its place in the transformations, rather than in the deep structure grammar, which one would wish to be less bound to a particular language. It might, perhaps, be suggested that the passive is just one form of a more general procedure of topicalization (see 3.3.3 above). One would then establish a selective subject, object, etc. (i.e. the subject, etc. of a verb according to the selective restrictions stated for that verb in the lexicon) and introduce a topicalization rule, specifying which constituent is to be taken as the topic, the semantic focus of interest. The topic could then coincide with the selective subject, but might also be another constituent, such as object or indirect object. In the latter case the topic could sometimes be made the grammatical subject so that the sentence became passive, or else the grammar would have to provide means for marking the topic as distinct from the subject (word order, particles, prosodic features such as stress). The whole question, however, of topic and comment is still too problematic for this suggestion to be pursued any further here.[1] And any claim to universality would have to be substantiated with many examples from many languages.

The time has come now for further specification of the selected nouns. It must be specified whether they are going to be singular or plural, whether or not, and if so how, they are going to be quantified or questioned. We therefore give the following rules:

(1)   *xv* $n_1 \rightarrow n_i' \begin{Bmatrix} sg \\ pl \end{Bmatrix}$

     xvi $n \rightarrow n' + sg$

---

[1] See also Chomsky (1965) pp. 220–1, note 32; and Staal (1967a) pp. 75–87, already mentioned in 3.3.3.

$$xvii \quad n' \rightarrow \left\{ \begin{array}{ll} QN+n & \text{env } X-U-Y-\\ (\imath)n & \text{env } \left\{ \begin{array}{l} QU \\ Qu \end{array} \right\} Z-\\ (QN)n & \end{array} \right\}$$

where U is the universal tense operator, n and n' are variables ranging over any selected noun, n_i and n'_i are variables ranging over any selected noun with the feature i (individual), $\imath$ is the specific question operator (see 4.3.5), X and Y stand for any string not derived from *Modal*, Z for any string, QN for 'quantifier'. The priming and depriming of n serve to prevent recursion.

The obligatory introduction of QN in structures under the universal tense operator without a modal is the first step to ensure that such structures will be universal statements.

The operator Qu, introducing embedded questions (see 4.3.5), is not to be found in the rules, but will be the result of the selection of certain verbs, such as *ask*, which, in the lexicon, have embedded questions as a possible object.

We now want to insert the $\imath$-operator into the string of operators immediately after QU or Qu. This we can do by means of a rule replacing a whole string by a new string:

$$(\text{1}) \quad xviii \quad \left\{ \begin{array}{l} QU \\ Qu \end{array} \right\} -X-\imath+n \left\{ \begin{array}{l} sg \\ pl \end{array} \right\} -Y \rightarrow$$

$$\left\{ \begin{array}{l} QU \\ Qu \end{array} \right\} \imath+n \left\{ \begin{array}{l} sg \\ pl \end{array} \right\} -X-n \left\{ \begin{array}{l} sg \\ pl \end{array} \right\} -Y$$

where X and Y stand for any string of symbols, including null.

The effect of this rule is that the specific question operator plus the singular or plural noun is placed immediately after the question operator, and the noun without its operator is retained in its original position.

Little attention has been paid, so far, to the setting up of tree diagrams in the manner of Chomskian deep structure grammar. This is mainly because tree diagrams have lost much of their relevance: most of the structure is now reflected in the strings themselves. Yet up to this point it has been possible to set up tree diagrams in the familiar manner. For the operators there is no difference at all with what is known from Chomskian rules. The nucleus is amenable to the same treatment if the slots plus their fillers are regarded as constituents, although consisting of two symbols. In fact, tree-diagram information has been used: in rule (1) *xvii* Y is a variable ranging over any string not derived from *Modal*.

In order to maintain tree structure we must define for rule (1) *xviii* to which constituent in the operator part of the structure the transposed specific question operator plus its noun is to be attached. Let us state, therefore, as a general principle for transposition rules ((1) *xviii* and (1) *xix*) that the transposed element will be attached to the node immediately dominating the element to the right of which it is placed. Thus, the specific question operator plus its noun is attached to the node *SQL*, which now dominates both *QU* and the transposed group.

A similar operation must be carried out to insert *QN* into the string of operators. For some cases it seems best to let quantifiers be placed after the tense operator: they are then interpreted in the time (not the tense—see 4.3.4) prevailing at the moment. Thus:

(8)   the Greeks kept many slaves

will be read as:

(9)   I assert that in the past there *were* many slaves such that the Greeks kept the slaves

and not as:

(10)   I assert that there *are* many slaves such that in the past the Greeks kept the slaves

In other cases, however, we would rather place the quantifier before the operator of tense.

(11)   Euclid proved many theorems

is best read as:

(12)   I assert that there *are* many theorems such that in the past Euclid proved the theorems

The double occurrence of tense with modal auxiliaries makes for the occurrence of quantifiers both before and after the modal. In the deep structure description of:

(13)   Archibald was allowed to drink one pint of beer

we are inclined to place the existential quantifier after the second occurrence of tense:

(14)   ASS Past Perm Pres E(1 pint of beer) : Archibald drink the pint of beer
       (I assert that in the past it was permitted for Archibald that at this time there was one pint of beer such that Archibald drank the pint of beer)

But:

(15)   Archibald was allowed to drink one sort of beer

is better analysed as either:

(16)   *i*   ASS Past E(1 sort of beer) Perm Pres : Archibald drink the
sort of beer
(I assert that in the past there was one sort of beer such that
it was permitted for Archibald at this time to drink the
sort of beer)

or as:

(16)   *ii*   ASS E(1 sort of beer) Past Perm Pres : Archibald drink the
sort of beer
(I assert that there is one sort of beer such that in the past it
was permitted for Archibald at this time to drink the sort
of beer)

There will often be a certain amount of ambiguity, such as in:

(17)   Benedict may have written one letter

which is analysed in one of the following ways:

(18)   *i*   ASS U Poss Past E(1 letter) : Benedict write the letter
(I assert that it is possible that there *was* a letter such that
Benedict wrote the letter)

     ii   ASS U Poss E(1 letter) Past : Benedict write the letter
(I assert that it is possible that there *is* a letter such that
Benedict wrote the letter)

    iii   ASS U E(1 letter) Poss Past : Benedict write the letter
(I assert that, regardless of time, there is a letter such that it
is possible that Benedict wrote it)

    iv   ASS E(1 letter) U Poss Past : Benedict write the letter
(I assert that there is a letter such that, regardless of time, it
is possible that Benedict wrote it)

where there seems to be very little, if any, difference in meaning between
iii and *iv*.

Or, to take another example:

(19)   everybody may be wrong

can be analysed in at least the following ways:

(20)   *i*   ASS U A(ind) Poss Pres : the individual be wrong
(I assert that, regardless of time, for everybody it is possible
to be wrong)

   ii   ASS A(ind) U Poss Pres : the individual be wrong
       (I assert that for everybody, regardless of time, it is possible
        to be wrong)
   iii ASS U Poss A(ind) Pres : the individual be wrong
       (I assert that it is possible that everybody is wrong at present)
   iv ASS U Poss Pres A(ind) : the individual be wrong
       (I assert that it is possible that at present everybody is
       wrong)

where *i* and *ii* on the one hand, and *iii* and *iv* on the other, seem to differ semantically only in the emphasis put on the operator of tense. *i* and *ii* reflect a universal statement about every living individual, whereas *iii* and *iv* represent occasion statements about a group of people.[1]

If there is more than one quantifier together with a modal auxiliary, then, of course, the number of possible underlying structures will be relatively large, although some will not differ in meaning from others If we take, e.g.:

(21)   someone may want some medicine

there are at least sixteen structural analyses according to the position of the quantifiers, such as, for instance:

(22) *i*   ASS U Poss E(ind) E(med) Fut : the individual want the
        medicine
    ii ASS U Poss E(ind) Fut E(med) : the individual want the
        medicine
    iii ASS E(ind) U Poss Fut E(med) : the individual want the
        medicine
    iv ASS E(med) U E(ind) Poss Fut : the individual want the
        medicine

And if we take the second occurrence of tense to be *Pres* instead of *Fut* (i.e. someone may be wanting some medicine), then the number of analyses is doubled.

---

[1] It is interesting to note that the future tense auxiliaries *will* and *shall* do not allow for ambiguities of this kind. This, together with the fact that there is no parallel with alternative negations, as in *he isn't allowed to drink* and *he is allowed not to drink* (see 4.3.6), strongly suggests that *shall* and *will* are not modals but rather tense auxiliaries. On the whole, however, the relationship between tense and quantifiers is in need of further clarification. Rescher's remark ((1966) p. 96): 'although the relationship between *time and modality* is unquestionably of substantial interest and importance, that between *time and quantification* may be even more interesting from a logico-philosophical standpoint,' is certainly also true for grammar.

In order to ensure that quantifiers are inserted in any of the desired positions we need only one rule:

(1) *xix* $X - \overline{T} - Y - QN + n \begin{Bmatrix} sg \\ pl \end{Bmatrix} - Z \rightarrow$

$$\begin{Bmatrix} X - QN + n \begin{Bmatrix} sg \\ pl \end{Bmatrix} - \overline{T} - Y - n \begin{Bmatrix} sg \\ pl \end{Bmatrix} - Z \\ X - \overline{T} - QN + n \begin{Bmatrix} sg \\ pl \end{Bmatrix} - Y - n \begin{Bmatrix} sg \\ pl \end{Bmatrix} - Z \end{Bmatrix}$$

where X, Y and Z stand for any string of symbols including null, and $\overline{T}$ stands for any symbol directly dominated by T.

According to the convention introduced for rule (1) *xviii* the transposed quantifier plus its following noun will be attached to the node immediately dominating its preceding symbol.

QN must now be developed further into any of the available quantifiers. We give the following rules:

(1) *xx* $QN + n \rightarrow \begin{Bmatrix} A & env \ X - U - Y - \\ A \\ E \end{Bmatrix} n' \ (Neg)$

  xxi $A + n'_i \rightarrow \begin{Bmatrix} A(arb) \ (num)n_i & env -sg \\ A((arb)num)n_i & env -pl \end{Bmatrix}$

  xxii $A + n'_m \rightarrow A(arb)n_m$

  xxiii $E + n'_i \rightarrow \begin{Bmatrix} E(mult)n_i & env -pl \\ E(arb(num))n_i & env \begin{pmatrix} QU \\ Qu \\ IMP \\ Imp \\ Neg \end{pmatrix} Z- \\ E(num)n_i \end{Bmatrix}$

  xxiv $E + n'_m \rightarrow \begin{Bmatrix} E(arb)n_m & env \begin{pmatrix} QU \\ Qu \\ IMP \\ Imp \\ Neg \end{pmatrix} Z- \\ E(mult)n_m \end{Bmatrix}$

where E stands for the existential, A for the universal quantifier, *arb* for the 'arbitrary' quantifiers represented by *any* (see 4.2.4), *num* for numerals (*one* for singular count nouns, *two*, *three*, etc., for plural nouns), *mult* for *much* with mass nouns, *many* with plurals, X and Y stand for any string not derived from *Modal*,[1] Z stands for any string.

Rule (1) *xx* ensures the selection of the universal quantifier in universal statements, allowing at the same time for the universal or the existential quantifier in all other sentences. Rule (1) *xxi* allows for *every man, all men, any man, every one man, any one man, every two, etc., men, any two, etc., men*, but not **any men*. Rule (1) *xxii* yields *all milk* and *any milk*. Rule (1) *xxiii* gives *a man, one man, two, etc., men, many men, (not) any man/men, (not) any two, etc., men*. Rule (1) *xxiv* gives *milk, much milk, (not) any milk*. Of course, these are only rough descriptions of the ultimate output of the rules; they are only intended as a guide in reading the rules. It is understood, for instance, that a sentence such as *a gentleman does not sneeze when taking snuff* contains a universal quantifier. The transformations are assumed to cater for this kind of surface representation.

The quantifier rules given here are still insufficient. They do not distinguish between, for instance, *each* and *every* for count nouns. Nor do they allow for numerals in definite noun phrases (*the one man, the two men*, etc.). Probably, the elements *arb, num, mult*, and possibly some others as well, can be adequately introduced in the form of relative clauses (see below, especially rule (1) *xix'*, for suggestions with regard to the treatment of relative clauses). Such a procedure was suggested, for different reasons, in 4.3.5. It would enable us to cover a wider range of data, but we would also have to state detailed restrictions and instructions for these relative clauses, involving more analysis than could possibly be carried out in the present context. Numerals would then be allowed to occur with both quantified and non-quantified nouns. *Two men are repairing the car* would then be analysed as: 'I assert that at present there are men, whose number is two, such that the men repair the car.' *The two men are repairing the car* would be: 'I assert that at present the men, whose number is two, repair the car.' The environment restrictions for the existential *any* would have to be stated only once. We would also formulate the rules in such a way that they generate *the many men, this much milk, much of the milk, many of the men, all the men, all the milk*, etc. In short, such a treatment would appear more profitable than the rules (1) *xx*–(1) *xxiv* given above. But given the lack of adequate information we shall content ourselves for the moment with the rules as they stand.

---

[1] In order to make the final products of the rules conform to the notational convention followed in chapter 4 we must introduce a few rules by which quantified nouns are placed between brackets and the nucleus is preceded by a colon. As this is nothing more than a notational detail, it requires no further attention.

As appears from (1) *xx*, a quantifier can be followed by a negation, which allows for sentences such as:

(23)   many citizens do not believe the president

to be analysed as:

(24)   ASS Pres E(mult citizens) Neg : the citizens believe the president

We also want to be able to generate deep structures such as:

(25)   ASS U Poss Perf E(book) Neg : Sebastian read the book

which becomes:

(26)   there may have been a book Sebastian hasn't read

A different order of *Perf* and the quantifier (plus negation) results in a different sentence with a different meaning:

(27)   ASS U Poss E(book) Neg Perf : Sebastian read the book

becomes, in English:

(28)   Sebastian may not have read some book

or rather:

(29)   there may be a book Sebastian hasn't read

It is interesting to note that in German and Dutch, for example, no equivalent of a *there*-phrase is required in this case:

(30)   der Sebastian hat vielleicht ein Buch nicht gelesen
(31)   Bas kan een boek niet gelezen hebben

The most natural French translation of these sentences is:

(32)   il se peut qu'il y ait un livre que Sébastien n'a pas lu

where both the modal qualifier and the existential quantifier are represented by a separate clause. From this point of view it can be maintained with reason that French is more analytic, or even, more logical than many other languages; that German and Dutch are more synthetic; and that English occupies an intermediate position between French on the one hand and German and Dutch on the other.

It is a noticeable feature of all the sentences (29)–(32) that the order of the modal, the quantifier and the negation in deep structure is preserved in the surface structure. One is inclined to think that it is because of the semantic relevance of the order of these operators in deep structure that a natural translation in Latin is:

(33)   forsitan librum aliquem non lēgerit Sebastianus

with the operators in the same order.

The periphrastic *there*-phrase is not necessary in English, when *Neg* follows immediately after *Poss*:

(34)   ASS U Poss Neg Perf E(book) : Sebastian read the book

which becomes:

(35)   Sebastian may not have read a book

or

(36)   Sebastian may have read no book

But if a second *Neg* occurs after the existential quantifier, as in:

(37)   ASS U Poss Neg Perf E(book) Neg : Sebastian read the book

the periphrastic phrase must be used:

(38)   there may be no book Sebastian hasn't read
       (or: there may not be a book Sebastian hasn't read)

or

(39)   possibly, there is no book Sebastian hasn't read

We shall not be concerned here with the precise formulation of the way deep structures are to be transformed into English surface structures. Let it be sufficient, for the moment, to see that there are clear regularities in the relations between deep and surface structures, so that we are justified in assuming that, in principle, rules can be formulated to describe these relations.

But even without a fully developed transformational component it seems clear that, for instance, relative clauses are not all extensions, descriptive or restrictive, of deep structure nouns. Some relative clauses, such as *Sebastian hasn't read* in (29) are to be derived from a nucleus containing a quantified noun.

One notices that the symbols for the relational constituents (*S, MV, O, IO, PO, Relator, Axis*) are not rewritten or deleted: they are part and parcel of the base-terminal strings. This has a specific purpose. As was pointed out in 3.3.3, and also in Seuren (1966) pp. 210–12, the points of attachment of many transformations are precisely these relational constituents. This remains equally true in the modified version of the base presented here: the effect of many transformations will be the incorporation of operators into what is ultimately going to be the sentence: they will in some way be connected with the relational constituents in the nucleus. For this reason it seems desirable to have actual symbols available in the deep structures for the transformations to operate on. The relational constituents thus form an integral part of the generative process and do not remain outside it in an isolated and disconnected set of definitions, as in Chomsky's model.

We still face the problem of selectional instruction, as explained in 3.2.1. In order not to complicate the problem unduly we shall limit ourselves to descriptive and restrictive relative clauses. It is by no means implied that the description of relative clauses is exhausted by this treatment. As was noted a few lines above, some surface structure relative clauses are derivable from existential deep structures. There are, furthermore, relative clauses referring not to a nominal antecedent, but, for instance, to a preceding nucleus,[1] as in:

(40)   yesterday I watched television, which is quite unusual for me

This kind of relative clause is probably best regarded as an optional variant of *and*-conjunction, so that the relative clause is equivalent to *and this* (i.e. my watching television) *is quite unusual for me*. As such it will be a variant of descriptive relative clauses, but numerous problems still remain.

The traditional and generally accepted distinction between restrictive and descriptive relative clauses will be taken as a basis for description. And it will also be assumed that, if the nucleus of a relative clause consists of a relative pronoun as the subject, followed by *be + adjective*, then the relative clause can be further condensed into an adjective. (Sometimes, as in *poor fellow, old friend*—at least in one of their meanings—this adjectivization is obligatory.)

In order, then, to illustrate how rules of selectional instruction can be introduced in such a way that the transformational component does not 'block' because of a faulty deep structure, we shall first revise rule (1) *xvii* as follows:

---

[1] There are other types of relative clause which look superficially similar to (40), but which refer not to a nucleus but to a proposition, such as *yesterday he watched television, which is quite unbelievable*. Here, *which* refers to 'that he watched television yesterday'. This example illustrates, again, the usefulness of the concepts of nucleus and proposition.

(1) *xvii'* n' → $\begin{cases} \text{QN}+\text{n} & \text{env} & \text{X}-\text{U}-\text{Y}- \\ (\text{?})\text{n} & \text{env} & \begin{cases} \text{QU} \\ \text{Qu} \end{cases} \text{X}- \\ (\text{QN})\text{n} & & \end{cases}$ $(\begin{cases} \text{Prop}_{rel} \\ \text{Sent}_{rel} \end{cases})$

That is, if the noun is followed by *Prop*$_{rel}$, the result will be a restrictive relative clause, such as:

(41)   that is the book I want

But if the noun is followed by *Sent*$_{rel}$, a descriptive relative clause will follow:

(42)   I finally found my brother, who was quietly reading a book

Restrictive relative clauses seem to lack their own sentence qualifier: they seem to be under the sentence qualifier of the main sentence. If we take, e.g.:

(43)   is that the book you want?

we cannot reasonably say that *you want* (*the book*) is asserted, questioned, ordered or suggested to be true. It is, indeed, part of the whole question. The same goes for imperatives:

(44)   get the book you want

which is analysable as 'I request that at this time you get the book you want'. Or with suggestions:

(45)   that is the book you want, isn't it?

Here we cannot say:

(46)   *that is the book you want, don't you?

Therefore, we represent restrictive relative clauses by *Prop*$_{rel}$, that is, a sentence but for the sentence qualifier.

Descriptive relative clauses, on the other hand, do have their own sentence qualifier. We can say both:

(47)   you finally found your brother, who was quietly reading a book, didn't you? (SUGG—ASS)

and:

(48)   you finally found your brother, who was quietly reading a book, wasn't he? (ASS—SUGG)

It seems, however, that not all sentence qualifiers are permissible in descriptive relative clauses: they cannot easily be under the imperative qualifier.[1] But the qualifiers of assertion, suggestion and question seem possible given any *SQL* of the main sentence:

(49) so you finally found your brother,—who was in the library? (ASS—QU)

(50) did you find your brother?—who was in the library (QU—ASS)

(51) did you find your brother,—who was in the library, wasn't he? (QU—SUGG)

(52) did you find your brother?—who was in the library? (QU—QU)

(53) go and get your brother, who is in the library   (IMP—ASS)

(54) go and get your brother, who is in the library, isn't he? (IMP—SUGG)

(55) go and get your brother,—who is in the library?   (IMP—QU)

The same distinction between restrictive and descriptive relative clauses as is made here is found in Chomsky (1966*a*) p. 38:

A restrictive relative clause is based on a proposition, according to the Port-Royal theory, even though this proposition is not affirmed when the relative clause is used in a complex expression. What is affirmed in an expression such as *men who are pious*, as noted above, is no more than the compatibility of the constituent ideas. Hence in the expression *minds which are square are more solid than those which are round*, we may correctly say that the relative clause is 'false', in a certain sense, since 'the idea of being square' is not compatible with 'the idea of mind understood as the principle of thought'. Thus sentences containing explicative as well as restrictive relative clauses are based on systems of propositions (that is, abstract objects constituting the meanings of sentences); but the manner of interconnection is different in the case of an explicative clause, in which the underlying judgment is actually affirmed, and a determinative clause, in which the proposition formed by replacing the relative pronoun by its antecedent is not affirmed but rather constitutes a single complex idea together with this noun. These observations are surely correct, in essence, and must be accommodated in any syntactic theory that attempts to make the notion 'deep structure' precise and to formulate and investigate the principles that relate deep structure to surface organization.

---

[1] Unless we regard certain relative clauses with *must* as representing underlying imperatives: *so you found your brother, whom you must now tell not to go out alone again*. We also find an imperative-like *must* in restrictive relative clauses: *this is the book you must buy*, but here it is not implied that it is the *speaker's* wish that the book be bought by the hearer. How these cases can be solved can at the moment only be a matter of speculation. Let us assume, for the time being, that imperatives are excluded from descriptive relative clauses. If this proves to be untrue, we only have to remove a restriction from the grammar.

A further difference between restrictive and descriptive relative clauses consists in their quantificational treatment. Descriptive relative clauses are not affected by rule (1) *xix*, i.e. they remain in the nucleus, whereas restrictive relative clauses are. That is, in:

(56)   this is a book I want

the relative clause must, for reasons of semantic interpretation, be transferred into the string of operators along with the quantifier and the transferred noun: (56) cannot adequately be rendered as:

(57)   I assert that at this time there is a book such that this is the book which I want

A more adequate reading is:

(58)   I assert that at this time there is a book which I want such that this is the book

This point becomes clearer when we take an imperative:

(59)   take any book you want

which is not:

(60)   I request that at this time there be an arbitrary book such that you take the book which you want

but rather:

(61)   I request that at this time there be an arbitrary book which you want such that you take the book

For this reason we modify rule (1) *xix* as follows:

$$(1) \quad xix' \quad X - \overline{T} - Y - QN + n \begin{Bmatrix} sg \\ pl \end{Bmatrix} (Prop_{rel}) - Z \rightarrow$$

$$\begin{Bmatrix} X - QN + n \begin{Bmatrix} sg \\ pl \end{Bmatrix} (Prop_{rel}) - \overline{T} - Y - n \begin{Bmatrix} sg \\ pl \end{Bmatrix} - Z \\ X - \overline{T} - QN + n \begin{Bmatrix} sg \\ pl \end{Bmatrix} (Prop_{rel}) - Y - n \begin{Bmatrix} sg \\ pl \end{Bmatrix} - Z \end{Bmatrix}$$

The rewriting of *Prop_{rel}* and of *Sent_{rel}* must now be 'guided' so as to ensure the selection of the antecedent noun again in any noun position in the relative clause, either in its nucleus, or in the last of a possible series of embedded object-clauses, such as are found in (12) and (15) of chapter 3. Moreover, if we assume that *IMP* must be excluded from descriptive relative clauses, we must prevent it from occurring in that position.

In order to make these provisions we introduce a new type of rule, exemplified by:

$$(1) \quad xxv \quad \text{Sent}_{\text{rel}} = \text{Sent} : ii \quad \text{SQL} \to \begin{Bmatrix} \text{ASS} \\ \text{QU} \\ \text{SUGG} \end{Bmatrix}$$

which is to be read as follows: '*Sent*$_{rel}$ is equivalent to *Sent*, i.e. is input to the same rules as *Sent*, with the exception of rule *ii*, which is as stated here.' This rule thus provides for the exclusion of *IMP* as a sentence qualifier for descriptive relative clauses.

The re-selection of the relativized antecedent noun either in the nucleus of the relative clause or in the final nucleus of a possible series of object-clauses must be organized by means of a recursive set of rules, as we saw in 3.2.1 (14): the nucleus of the relative clause must contain either (*a*) the antecedent noun or (*b*) an object-clause, the nucleus of which must again contain either (*a*) or (*b*). The application of such a set of rules ends, of course, when the antecedent noun is selected, since this is not subject to the condition of containing either (*a*) or (*b*). These rules can be formulated as follows:

$$(1) \quad xxvi \quad \begin{bmatrix} \text{Sent}_{\text{rel}} \\ \text{Prop}_{\text{rel}} \end{bmatrix} = \begin{bmatrix} \text{Sent} \\ \text{Prop} \end{bmatrix}:$$

$$x \quad [\text{V}] \overset{\text{L}}{\to} \text{v}-\text{X}[n_{s(\alpha)}] \twoheadrightarrow [\text{N}^{\text{X}}] \overset{\text{L}}{\to} \alpha$$

$$\text{v}-\text{O} \begin{Bmatrix} [\text{c}+\text{Prop}] \\ [\text{Nucleus}] \end{Bmatrix} \twoheadrightarrow$$

$$(a) \quad [\text{N}^{\text{O}}] \overset{\text{L}}{\to} \begin{Bmatrix} \text{c}+\text{Prop} \\ \text{Nucleus} \end{Bmatrix}$$

$$(b) \quad \text{Prop} = \text{Prop}_{\text{rel}}$$

$$(c) \quad \text{Nucleus} = \text{Nucleus}[\text{V}]:$$

$$x/xxvi$$

where: X stands for 'S', 'O', 'IO' or 'Axis';

   α for the antecedent noun, i.e. the noun preceding *Sent*$_{rel}$ or the first occurrence of *Prop*$_{rel}$;

   v—Q[p] for any verb in the lexicon entailing the selection of a relational constituent Q filled by *p*;

   $n_{s(\alpha)}$ for any subcategory of nouns such that $s(\alpha)$ is a set of features comprised by the features of the antecedent noun α;

   c for any clause qualifier (*Ass, Qu, Imp*);

   x/xxvi for: rule *x* as given in rule *xxvi*.

The rules (*b*) and (*c*) ensure the recursiveness of the set of rules, since both lead again to rule *x* as given in *xxvi*. Thus we have a generalized and formalized formulation of the conditions laid down in (14) of chapter 3.

5.2   A sample of the lexicon

The rules which have been given in the preceding section provide at least a provisional answer to the criticisms levelled in chapter 3 at the way of describing deep structure prevalent in the literature on transformational grammar. They also account, as far as is possible at the present stage of enquiry, for the new category of operators introduced in chapter 4. We shall now give a sample of lexical items, chosen more or less at random, so as to give a somewhat richer illustration of the way our grammar works.

5.2.1 Verbs. In this sample verbs are specified according to what selectional subclasses can figure non-deviantly as their subject, object, indirect object and prepositional object. In a fully-fledged lexicon they should also be specified according to their own intrinsic selectional features. Thus, for instance, *write* or *drink* will presumably have to be provided with a feature 'process', whereas other verbs, such as *sleep*, will have a feature like 'durative'. *Go* will have the features 'process' and 'direction'. These features will have to account for the possible addition of certain adverbial expressions. 'Process' will allow a verb to be associated with adverbs like *quickly*. 'Durative' will allow for adverbials such as *long* or *for a long time*. 'Direction' will let the verb be combined with prepositional phrases under the prepositions *into* or *towards*.[1] Presumably, such features will be carried along with the verbs when they undergo various forms of nominalization, so that they become noun features, which will be operative for the selection of nominalized constructions as subject, object, etc. to verbs. But the description of these intrinsic verb

---

[1] One notices that, for instance, *go into, look into, go over, look over* are sometimes best taken as verbs plus adverbial phrases. The following noun must be concrete and local: *we went into the church, we went over the bridge, we looked over the roof*. In these cases the noun in axis-position cannot figure as the subject of a passive sentence. But in other cases they must be regarded as verbs plus *PO*, so that the axis-noun can become the subject of a passive sentence: *we went into the difficulty, we went over the place, we looked into that possibility*. Here the axis-noun need not be concrete and local (see (62) *iii* and (62) *iv*). I am indebted to our research student Heather R. Bayes for bringing these examples to my attention.

features will involve a number of complications which cannot possibly be gone into here. Gruber's study (1967) provides an admirable instance of the kind of study that is required here. Unfortunately, such investigations are still extremely rare. We shall, therefore, disregard this aspect of verbs and concentrate only on their entailment features, i.e. the restrictions they entail on the selection of their subject, object, etc.

We now give the following verbs:

(62)   *i*   V   *drink* $\longrightarrow$ S[n_{an}]

$$*O[n_{lq}], \ [n_{c, vol, cont}]$$

$$*PO[\text{Relator}[p(\textit{from})] + \text{Axis } [n_{c, vol, cont}]]$$

(62)   *ii*   V   *eat* $\longrightarrow$ S[n_{an}]

$$*O[n_{vol}], \ [n_{c, vol, cont}]$$

$$*PO[\text{Relator}[p(\textit{from})] + \text{Axis}[n_{vol}], \ [n_{c, vol, cont}]]$$

(62) *i* is identical to (2), where it was explained that the lines indicate selective entailment; the asterisk optional choice (yes or no); the comma between two pairs of brackets optional choice (the one or the other). The *V* before each item indicates its rough-class-membership.

One might wonder whether the feature *vol* is sufficient in the object of (62) *ii*: should not there also be a feature 'edible'? The feature 'edible', however, should rather figure in the semantic description of the meanings of individual nouns, and it should then be specified further: edible for humans, edible for insects, etc. Just as animate beings may be said, without deviance, to drink liquids even if these are indigestible or harmful, they can be said to eat indigestible or harmful voluminous things. But to say that a man eats beauty is certainly deviant (see 5.4.2).

One might also wonder why a distinction is made in the object between n_{vol} and $n_{c, vol, cont}$, since, obviously, the former class comprises the latter. The reason for this distinction is that it enables us to differentiate between two possible meanings of a sentence such as *he ate two plates*, which is taken to say either that the subject emptied two plates, or that he actually swallowed them. In the former case *plates* falls under the class of concrete, voluminous, contentful nouns; in the latter it is just a voluminous noun. How precisely this distinction in meaning is to be recorded so that the generative process contains the information necessary for pinpointing the different meanings, is not clear (see 5.4.2). Presumably, this information can, in some way or other, be inserted. But it seems reasonable to suppose that the source of any such information will lie in the kind of object chosen for *eat*. And we can at least provide the discriminatory means necessary for the provision of any such information.

(62) *iii* V *go* —S[n_c]
(62) *iv* V *go* —S[n_{hum}]
$$\text{PO[Relator[p(}into\text{)]} + \text{Axis[}n_{a,\,pr}\text{], [}n_{a,\,solv}\text{]]}$$

In (62) *iii* it is not specified, in accordance with what was said earlier, that this verb may be combined with certain adverbs, such as *quickly* or *well*, with certain particles like *up* or *down*, and with certain adverbial prepositional phrases, the axis of which contains a concrete local noun, and the relator a preposition of direction. (62) *iv* is a different *go* from (62) *iii* (see p. 194, note 1): it requires a human subject and a prepositional object (which can become the subject of a passive sentence) with the preposition *into* and an axis noun characterized by the features 'abstract' and 'process', or 'abstract' and 'solvable' (such as *problem* or *difficulty*).

(62) *v* V *learn* —S[n_{an}]
$$\text{*O[}n_{par}\text{], [}n_{pr}\text{], [}n_{a,\,lg}\text{],}$$
$$\text{[(}how\text{) }to + \text{Nucleus], [Ass} + \text{Prop]}$$

Here, *par* stands for 'parameter', which is a feature of nouns like *distance, age, length*; *lg* stands for 'linguistic', which features in, for instance, *book, language, story, word*. *Nucleus* will have to be equated with *Nucleus[V]*, and will thus undergo treatment by rules (1) *x* and following. The subject of this nucleus will have to be identical with that of the embedding nucleus. This identity can be ensured in a simple way by stipulating somehow that no subject is selected for this nucleus. *Ass* is a clause qualifier corresponding to *ASS* in much the same way as *Qu* corresponds to *QU* and *Imp* to *IMP*. It is usually manifested by the conjunction *that*. *Prop* will be input to rule (1) *iii*.

(62) *vi* V *write* — $S[n_{hum}]$
  |
  $*O[n_{par}]$, $[n_{com}]$, $[Ass+Prop]$
  |
  $*IO[n_{an}]$
  |
  $*PO[Relator$

$*O[n_{lg}]$

$$\left\{ \begin{array}{l} [p\left\{ \begin{array}{l} (about) \\ (on) \end{array} \right\}\ ]+Axis[n] \\ [p((up)on)]+Axis[n_{sol}] \\ [(in)]+Axis[n_{sol}],\ [n_{nsol}] \end{array} \right\}$$

]

The subject is here required to be a human noun (although one might conceive of animals writing). There are two kinds of object. The one implies only the feature 'linguistic'. If this is chosen there can be no indirect object, although there may be a *PO*. The other, which does allow for an *IO*, is a parameter-noun, a *that*-clause, or a noun with the feature *com* ('communication'). All communication nouns are also linguistic nouns: the feature *com* distinguishes, for instance, *letter* or *message* from *book*, which lacks this feature. Both kinds of object allow for a *PO* with *about* or *on* followed by any noun (*I write on/about beauty*), or else the *PO* may contain (*up*)*on* plus a noun having the feature *sol* ('solid'), as in *I write on paper/the wall*, or *in* plus a noun having the feature *nsol* ('non-solid'), such as *water* or *air*, or again *sol* (*I write in the book*).

(62) *vii* V *see* — $S[n_{an}]$
  |
  $*O[n_{vol}]$, $[n_{par}]$, $[n_{pr}]$, $[n_{prop}]$, $[n_{solv}]$,

$$[Nucleus],\ [\left\{ \begin{array}{l} Ass \\ Qu \end{array} \right\}+Prop]$$

One new feature is introduced here: *prop* ('property'), which characterizes nouns such as *length, colour, beauty, relatedness, strength* (many of which are nominalizations). (It would have been very rewarding to incorporate the results of Gruber's study, 'Look and see' (1967), into the specification of (62) *vii*. Unfortunately, however, it was published too late to be taken into account.)

If the object is a nucleus, the regular surface form, in English, has either the *ing*-form or just the main verb in the nucleus. No qualifiers are generated now for the embedded nucleus, which is in accordance with the facts of the English language: embedded nuclei are tenseless (**I saw him having finished his work*); adverbials of time relate to the main clause

(*I saw him working yesterday*); negation is awkward if not ungram-matical, and has a comic effect (**I saw him not working*; **I definitely heard the clock not strike*); no modal auxiliaries occur (**I saw him being allowed to go*); the passive does occur (*I saw him being beaten by the police*).

As we saw, however, when discussing (266) of chapter 4, quantifiers occur freely in embedded nuclei. This follows from rule (1) *xvii*, where the introduction of a quantifier into the nucleus is made contingent upon the occurrence of a noun. The transposition rule (1) *xix* does not apply to embedded nuclei, since there is no tense qualifier. For reasons of semantic interpretation, however, it seems desirable not to leave the quantifiers in the embedded nucleus, but to transpose them to pre-nucleus position, thus indicating their scope. It is semantically awkward to have a structure such as:

$$I \text{ saw Nucleus}$$
$$|$$
$$\text{the cat catch E(mouse)}$$

We therefore add the following rule, to be inserted after (1) *xix*:

(1)   *xxvii* $X - QN + n \begin{Bmatrix} sg \\ pl \end{Bmatrix} - Y \to QN + n \begin{Bmatrix} sg \\ pl \end{Bmatrix} - X - n \begin{Bmatrix} sg \\ pl \end{Bmatrix} - Y$

where X and Y stand for any string, including null, of symbols not derived from SQL or QL.

It should be specified for the embedded nucleus that the main verb occurring in it must be a verb denoting an action that can be seen. That is, the verb must have a feature 'visible' or the like. But this would be one of the intrinsic features of verbs, which we have decided to leave out of consideration here.

The object can also be an embedded assertion or question. In order to allow for embedded *wh*-questions, rule (1) *xvii* has been formulated so as to comprise Qu in the context restriction for the specific question operator.

(62)   *viii* $V \text{ know } - S[n_{an}]$
$$|$$
$$*O[n_i], [\begin{Bmatrix} Ass \\ Qu \end{Bmatrix} + Prop]$$

The feature i ('individual', as opposed to 'mass') seems sufficient to characterize all non-deviant noun-objects of this verb.

(62) *ix* V *say* —— $S[n_{an}]$

$$O[n_{lg,\,el}],\ [\left\{\begin{array}{c} Ass \\ Imp \end{array}\right\} + Prop]\quad O[n_{par}],\ [Qu+Prop]$$

$$*PO[Relator[p(to)] + Axis[n_{an}]]$$

Here again, as with *write* (62) *vi*, there are two sorts of object: the one permits a prepositional object for the person spoken to, the other does not. The former kind of object can be a noun with both the features 'linguistic' and *el*, i.e. 'element'. The latter feature distinguishes element linguistic nouns, such as *word, phrase, sentence*, from non-element linguistic nouns like *book, letter*. This kind of object can also be an embedded assertion or imperative (see (323) and (324) in 4.3.7). The second kind of object is either a parameter noun (*length, age, distance, price*) or an embedded question. If the person spoken to must be mentioned the verb *tell* is used with an indirect object. (The *PO* of *say* is not an indirect object, as one might be inclined to think, since it always requires the preposition *to*, and since it never becomes the subject of a passive sentence. In this respect *say* behaves like *explain, indicate, point out*, etc.)

(62) *x* V *tell* — $S[n_{an}]$

$$O[n_i],\ [n_{par}],\ [n_{pr}],\ [n_{com,\,cont}],\ [\left\{\begin{array}{c} Ass \\ Qu \\ Imp \end{array}\right\} + Prop]$$

$$IO[n_{an}]$$

In the object, a distinction has been made between individual nouns, parameter nouns, process nouns and communication-content nouns. The reason for this is that these four kinds of object are semantically different. In all four cases the object is semantically equivalent to an embedded question, but the question is different according to the class of nouns employed. If the object is an individual noun (*city*), the embedded question is 'what/which individual *x* it is', as in: *can you tell me the city?*, which is equivalent to: *can you tell me what/which city it is?* If the object is a parameter noun, the question implied is 'what the value of the parameter *x* is', as in: *can you tell me your age?* If the object is a process noun, the question implied is 'what the process of *x* consists in', as in: *can you tell me the game?* And, lastly, if the object is a communication-content noun (*story, message, answer*), the question is 'what the content of the communication x is', as in: *can you tell me the story?* This explains the ambiguity which arises when the object-noun has two or more of these features at the same time, such as *game*, which has both *i* and *pr*. The sentence *can you tell me the game?* means either 'can you tell me how the game is played?' or 'can you tell me what/which game it is?' We have here a case analogous to *he ate two plates*, discussed with reference to (62) *ii*.

Perhaps, the description could be simplified by taking these objects as collapsed embedded *wh*-questions in which the asked-for information is precisely the feature of individuality, parameter value, process, or communication content. But so far there is no apparatus available to do so.

The verb *tell* can, furthermore, have an embedded assertion, question, or imperative as its object. It must be specified somehow that, in the latter case, the subject of *Prop* must be the same as the indirect object: *I told Jim that he must go* ⇒ *I told Jim to go*.

The indirect object referring to the person spoken to is obligatory, so that *tell* assumes the function of *say*, if necessary. This idiosyncrasy of the English language suggests, again (see chapter 3, note 5), that we should envisage the possibility of actual lexical items being introduced in, or along with, the transformational component, rather than having them as part of the deep structure description (see also below, where copula-verbs are discussed, and 5.4.2).

There is a class of verbs which take, or may take, the subject *it* in surface structures. These are the 'impersonal' verbs. Let us consider one example:

(62) xi V *seem* —O[Ass + Prop]
          |
          *PO[Relator[p(*to*)] + Axis[n_{an}]]]

We represent these verbs in the lexicon as never having a subject. This accounts automatically, as we have seen above, for the fact that these verbs do not occur in the passive. Transformationally, a subject *it* is supplied. Further transformations, however, should also allow for the subject of the *that*-clause to become the subject of the surface sentence, as in: *Archibald seems to have worked hard yesterday*, derived from: *it seems that Archibald worked hard yesterday*. If the embedded assertion contains the copula-verb *be* followed by an adjective in predicate nominal position, then, under certain conditions, the element *to be* can be deleted, whereby the word order is slightly modified. Thus: *it seems to me that this is wrong* ⇒ *this seems to me to be wrong* ⇒ *this seems wrong to me.* Or: *it seems to me that this is good for children* ⇒ *this seems to me to be good for children,* but not: **this seems good for children to me.*

This treatment of *seem* also automatically accounts for the fact that nuclei containing this verb cannot be transformed into derived nominals. If we took *Archibald* as the deep structure subject of *Archibald seems to have worked hard yesterday,* we should expect: **Archibald's seeming to have worked hard yesterday.* And since we have established the rule that derived nominalization is only possible for verbs with a subject, we also rule out **the seeming to me that this is wrong,* the ungrammaticalness of which is an argument against taking the *that*-clause as the subject of *seem*: *that this is true seems to me.*

5.2.2 Copula-verbs and adjectives. Let us now turn to copula-verbs. This category has been neglected so far so as not to complicate matters. They form a separate category for a variety of reasons. They do not allow for the passive, and they require a predicate nominal, which can be either an adjective or a noun phrase. We shall consider here only adjectives, since the problems of specifying non-deviant nouns in predicate nominals with respect to the nouns in subject position still seem to be beyond our reach at present.

In introducing copula-verbs into the grammar, we shall assume that there are two kinds of nucleus, the one introduced in rule (1) *iii,* and containing an 'ordinary' verb with or without other relational constituents, and the kind of nucleus containing a copula-verb plus an obligatory predicate nominal. The latter type also allows for a possible indirect object and/or prepositional object, but these do not make the nucleus passivizable. We shall, therefore, adapt rule (1) *iii* to:

(1) *iii'* $\quad$ Prop → QL + Nucleus $\begin{Bmatrix} [V] \\ [CV] \end{Bmatrix}$

where *CV* stands for the category of copula-verbs.

We now need a new rule, along with (1) *x,* for the selection of a copula-verb from the lexicon:

(1) *xxviii* $\quad$ [CV] $\overset{L}{\rightarrow}$ cv

Another new rule must now be added after (1) *xi* for the rewriting of Nucleus[cv]:

(1) *xxix* $\quad$ Nucleus[cv] →

$\qquad$ MV[cv] + PN[A] + *IO[N] + *PO[Relator[P] + Axis[N]] where *A* stands for 'adjective' and *PN* for 'predicate nominal'. (As was said above, nouns in *PN*-position are not considered.) No subject is generated by this rule for reasons that will become clear later: it appears that the adjective, rather than the copula-verb, must introduce the subject. The rule introducing the subject will be given below as (1) *xxxi*.

We also add a new rule of lexical selection, to be inserted immediately after (1) *xxix*, for the selection of adjectives, as allowed for by the copula-verb:

(1)   *xxx* $[A^{PN}] \xrightarrow{L} [a_s]$

Finally, rule (1) *xiv* must now be formulated so as to apply only to those nuclei which contain a non-copula-verb, that is, containing MV[v]. This can be done by adding further context restrictions to n_s^O and n_s^{IO} in the second part of rule (1) *xiv*. For n_s^O we add: env X – MV[v] + O—, and for n_s^{IO} : env X – MV[v] + *O[n] + IO—.

The category of English copula-verbs is not very large. It comprises such verbs as *be, become, get, go, grow, turn (into), run, look (like), resemble*. The *cv turn* requires the preposition *into*, and *look* requires *like*, if the *PN* is filled by a noun. (There are such exceptional cases as *to turn traitor*. One notices, however, that no determiner is allowed here. Perhaps the noun is to be taken as an adjective in such expressions.) *Resemble* can only be used with nouns.

The *cv*'s *become, get, go, grow, turn* all have roughly the same meaning, say, 'begin to be', but their use is restricted to certain classes of predicate nominals: *get* can be followed by adjectives like *old, dark, difficult, big*, or colour adjectives; *grow* can be followed by many adjectives that go with *get*, but less easily by, for instance, *difficult*; *go* goes with *blind, mad, wild*, etc., or colour adjectives; *turn* goes with, for example, *nasty, cold, sour*, and colour adjectives; *run* sometimes means 'begin to be', as in *my blood runs cold*, or *the river runs dry*, but sometimes it is equivalent to *be*, as in *run parallel, run wild*.

The restrictions of occurrence are notoriously difficult to describe in generalized rules: in many cases listing seems to be the only device. Yet they have to be described in any adequate grammar of English. Here again we see the possibility emerging of simplifying deep structure grammar and, at the same time, of making it more regular by specifying lexical items in an abstract way, that is, by means of bundles of semantic features rather than as actual lexical items, which are idiosyncratic, i.e.

idiomatic, for every particular language.[1] Of course, this would complicate the post-base treatment of sentences, but such a procedure would
have several advantages. It would separate semantic deviance clearly
from idiomatic oddity (*virtue drinks elephants*, as against *his hair is
becoming grey*); it would raise the semantic value of the base, in that it
would contain not only *all*, but also *only* the relevant semantic information for every sentence, without depriving it of its syntactic deep structure character; and, lastly, it would make the base more universal. But
again, we must postpone these considerations until more research has
been done and an adequate descriptive apparatus has been made
available (see also 5.4.2). For the moment, the safest procedure would
seem to concentrate on the precise analysis and description of a limited
number of languages. Too big a leap towards abstraction would lead to
mere speculation.

Let us now see how copula-verbs can be introduced into the lexicon.
Taking a simple copula-verb, *turn*, let us assume that it will be specified
in a way analogous to the verbs of (62). We will then have a lexical entry:

(63)   CV *turn* —S[n_{vol}]
       |
       PN[a_{col}]

where *a* stands for 'adjective' and *col* for the feature 'colour'. This form
of specification, however, which may seem satisfactory for such a simple
case as *turn* plus colour adjectives, leads to complications if we consider
other adjectives and less simple copula-verbs. Let us take the copula-
verb *be* followed by an adjective. Clearly, there is a close dependency
relation between the subject-noun and the adjective in *PN*-position. It
will, therefore, be necessary to set up a large number of pairs of classes
of subjects and classes of *PN*-adjectives for the copula-verb *be*. We must
then establish selectional sub-classes of adjectives in much the same way
as we do for nouns, i.e. by means of intrinsic features. This is simple
enough in the case of colour adjectives. But if we set out to do this for a

---

[1] A parallel argument for an abstract treatment of lexical items can be found in the use
of *be* as a copula-verb followed by a noun phrase. There is a regular difference, in
English, in the meaning of *be* according to whether it is followed by a definite or an
indefinite noun phrase. If the noun phrase is definite, *be* establishes an equivalence
relation. But if it is indefinite, *be* establishes a relation of inclusion within a class.
(In the latter case the indefinite article does not represent an existential quantifier.)
The base can be made simpler and semantically more adequate if two copula-verbs
are distinguished, both of which happen to be manifested by *be* in English (see
also 5.4.2).

greater variety of adjectives, we find that they require classification mainly in terms of possible subjects. Let us suppose, for example, that in one of the pairs of subjects and *PN*'s the subject is the class of animate nouns. *Be* will then have associated with it, in the lexicon, $S[n_{an}]$ in the following way:

(64)   CV *be* —$S[n_{an}]$
                     |
                 $\dot{P}N[n_s]$

We must now, however, specify the class of adjectives that can occur in *PN*-position with this class of subject-nouns. That is, we must give a specific value to *s* for *a* in *PN*. Let us take, at random, a few adjectives that admit of an animate subject: *active, healthy, great, calm, young, old, new, careful, blind, handy, blue*. We can try to set these off against those adjectives which cannot be used with animate subjects, such as *parallel, undue, effectual*, by allotting them a feature, say *x*. Just as in the case of selection restriction classes of nouns, the classes overlap: only a relatively small class of adjectives is restricted exclusively to animate nouns: *young, blind* (disregarding *a blind alley* and similar cases). But many adjectives that can be used with animate subjects can also be used with other kinds of subject. Thus, a statement can be said to be *calm*, or *old*, or *careful*, but also *parallel, undue*, or *effectual*. A parameter noun, such as *length*, can be combined with *great, old, new*, but also with *undue* or *effectual*; not, however, with *parallel*.

Let us assign the feature *y* to those adjectives that can occur with subject-nouns having the feature 'linguistic', and the feature *z* to those occurring with parameter nouns in subject position. We can now set up the following matrix for these adjectives with these noun classes:

(65)   active   x
       healthy   x
       great   x   z
       calm   x   y
       young   x
       old   x   y   z
       new   x   y   z
       careful   x   y
       blind   x
       handy   x   y   z
       blue   x

parallel	y	
undue	y	z
effectual	y	z

Such a matrix, however, lacks the justification of a matrix of a similar type set up for nouns. Noun features arranged in a matrix classify nouns according to their non-deviant occurrence in various positions: subject, object, etc. They recur in the specifications of many different verbs. Thus, as far as can be seen, they provide the simplest possible classification of nouns in various positions with respect to the verbs. The noun features, furthermore, are semantically interpretable in terms of intrinsic semantic properties. In the case of adjectives, however, they must be assigned a new feature, it seems, for every class of subject-nouns characterized by any noun feature, and possibly also for many classes of nouns characterized by a combination of features. The copula-verb *be* would then in principle, be associated, in the lexicon, with as many different subjects as there are noun features in something like the following way:

(66) CV *be* —$S[n_{an}]$
$$|$$
$PN[a_x]$

—$S[n_{lg}]$
$$|$$
$PN[a_y]$

—$S[n_{par}]$
$$|$$
$PN[a_z]$ etc.

The features x, y, z, etc..., however, characterizing the classes of permitted adjectives in *PN*-positions do nothing but reflect the features *an*, *lg*, *par*, etc...., respectively, of the nouns in subject-position. That is, these adjectival features are immediately predictable once the subject-noun features are given. And their sole interpretation is 'can be said of such and such subject-nouns'.

Supposing that this is generally true, the lexical entry *be* can be simplified to, for example:

(67) CV *be* —$S[n_s]$
$$|$$
$PN[a_s]$

with a general metarule stating that the adjective (which is selected first during the process of generation, since the new rule (1) *xxx* precedes rule (1) *xiv*) allows for any subject-noun having any feature or features specified for the selected adjective.

This means that, for the copula-verb *be*, the selection of the adjective in *PN*-position is 'free', i.e. not subject to any selectional restriction, and that the selection of the subject is dependent not on the verb, but on the adjective. As far as the copula-verb *be* is concerned, therefore, we could consider the possibility of modifying rule (1) *xxx* into:

(1) *xxx'* [A] $\overset{\text{L}}{\rightarrow}$ a

so that it would have the same form as rules (1) *x* and (1) *xxviii*. This would not be a viable procedure, however, for those copula-verbs for which the selection of the adjective is not free, such as *turn, get, go*, etc. We shall, therefore, leave (1) *xxx* as it stands. Under the interpretation given for this type of rule (see (1) *xii* and (1) *xiii*), the selection of the adjective will be free automatically whenever the lexicon gives no subscripts along with the slotfiller of *PN*. (Presumably, rule (1) *xxx'* would be adequate for all copula-verbs if, as has been suggested more than once above, they were to figure in deep structure in an abstract, purely semantic, representation.)

Even (67), however, is redundant, because the sub-class of permitted subject-nouns is now generally predictable from the selected adjective. We can do away with this redundance by leaving out the subject-specification for all copula-verbs. *Be* will now be given as follows:

(68) *i* CV *be* —PN[a]

The adjectives will now be listed in the lexicon in very much the same way as verbs. That is, they entail the selection of the subject-noun, and of nouns and prepositions in *IO* and *PO* (if any). Thus, the adjective *calm* will be listed as follows:

(69) *i* A *calm* —S[n_{an}], [n_{lg}], [n_{pr}], [n_{nsol}]

Or *new* will look something like:

(69) *ii* A *new* —S[n_c], [n_{par}], [n_{lg}], [n_{pr}], [n_{prop}]

                |
              *IO[a_{an}]

Here we see that the adjective can introduce an indirect object, as in *this book is new to me*.

In order to allow for the introduction of new relational constituents by adjectives we need a new rule in the grammar, to be inserted after (1) *xxx* and before (1) *xii*:

(1)   *xxxi*   PN[a] →

$$S[N] + PN'[a] + *IO[N] + *PO[Relator[P] + Axis[N]]$$

to be interpreted analogously to rule (1) *xi* (the priming of *PN* prevents recursion).

The interpretation of rules of the type $[X^Q] \xrightarrow{L} x_s$, as given above, in connection with rules (1) *xii* and (1) *xiii*, must now be adapted so as also to cover the selectional restrictions entailed by the copula-verb and the adjective on the relational constituents specified for them in the lexicon. The interpretation of rules of this type will now be: 'go to the lexicon; select an x_s from the category X such that the string of features s as attached to x in the lexicon comprises the string of features attached to the slotfiller of Q as specified for the selected v in the lexicon if Q is dominated by *Nucleus*[v], for the selected *cv* if Q is dominated by *Nucleus*[cv], and for the selected a if Q is dominated by *PN*[a]; or select the specific x if any specific x is given as the slotfiller of Q in the lexical specification of the selected v, *cv*, or a; or select any member of the class X in the lexicon if no features are attached to the slotfiller X of Q as specified for the selected v, *cv*, or a in the lexicon; write the x_s (i.e. with the complete series of features as given in the lexicon for x) for X in slot Q'.

We see that *IO*'s and *PO*'s can also be introduced by rule (1) *xxix*, which expands *Nucleus*[cv] into a string of relational constituents. This double possibility of expansion allows us to distinguish, in sentences with copula-verbs, between those indirect and/or prepositional objects which are dependent on the copula-verb, as in:

(70)   this looks wrong to me

and those dependent on the adjective:

(71)   this is new to me

It also allows for a double occurrence of these constituents, as in:

(72)   this looks to me to be new to him   (see (68) *iii*)

The sentence:

(73)   this looks new to him

is ambiguous in English, in that *to him* refers either to *looks* or to *new*. In Spanish the two different meanings are distinguished by a different position of the personal pronoun. In the former meaning (73) is translatable as:

(74)   esto le parece nuevo

but in the latter it becomes:

(75)   esto parece serle nuevo

It seems that the form of lexical specification as given for *be* in (68) *i*, can now be extended to all copula-verbs. *Turn*, for example, can now be given as follows:

(68)   *ii*   CV *turn* —PN[a_{col}], [a(*nasty*) (*cold*) (*sour*)...]

Generally, copula-verbs which are restricted to certain adjectives will have to be given in the lexicon with a list of these adjectives in *PN*-position, unless they can be grouped together in a non-*ad hoc* class, such as can be set up for the colour adjectives. But the possibility of setting up such classes seems to be an exception rather than a rule. Features characterizing these classes, such as *col*, are intrinsic features, and not selectional entailments. One of those features is also 'gradable', to be assigned to those adjectives which can occur in the comparative (*rich*, *big*, *old*, etc., but not, e.g. *dead* or *blind*).

Another feature that will probably have to be assigned to many adjectives is an indication of their being members of a pair of opposites: *young-old*, *new-old*, *hard-soft*, etc. This feature will be useful, for example, for the specification of a possible prepositional object of the copula-verb *turn*, disregarded in (68) *ii*, viz.: PO[p(*from*)+a]. This would account for sentences such as *the liquid turns from white to red*, or *the weather turned from warm to cold*, where *red* and *cold*, respectively, could conceivably be regarded as the predicate nominal with a transformationally added *to*. For such a *PO*, the selection of the adjective depends on the intrinsic feature or features of the adjective in *PN*-position: if it is a colour adjective, then the *PO* requires, equally, a colour adjective; if it is *nasty* or *cold*, the *PO* requires their respective opposites. It is not clear, however, how this opposition feature, or indeed all intrinsic adjectival features, can be incorporated into the grammar in an adequate way.

In having intrinsic features along with selectional entailments adjectives resemble verbs, which, as we have seen above, will also have to be classified according to their intrinsic features. And, as with the verbs, we shall also, in this study, leave these features aside.

The form of lexical specification employed in (68) *i* and (68) *ii* seems viable for copula-verbs in general. Thus, we can specify *look* in the following way:

(68)   *iii*   CV *look* —PN[a]

$$*\text{IO}[n_{an}]$$

The optional indirect object is found in (70), (72) and (73). In (72), the element *to be* is regarded as the product of a transformational insertion, obligatory under certain conditions. Possibly, this solution is not maximally simple and will have to be reconsidered in the light of an overall description of the lexicon: on the face of it there seem to be arguments for treating this *look* on a par with *seem*, as in (62) *xi*, but with an *as if*-clause instead of an embedded assertion in the object. (70) would then be a transform of a deeper:

(76)   it looks to me as if this is wrong

and (72) would be derived from:

(77)   it looks to me as if this is new to him

Semantically, however, such a description of *look* appears inadequate in a number of cases. Thus, for example:

(78)   Archibald looks pale

is not equivalent to:

(79)   it looks as if Archibald is pale

But:

(80)   Archibald seems pale

is equivalent to:

(81)   it seems that Archibald is pale

For the moment we can take it that there are two different verbs *look*, one the copula-verb (68) *iii*, and the other an impersonal verb like *seem*.

Now that we have introduced new rules for copula-verbs and adjectives, we must take account of these in the rest of the grammar. Notably, rule (1) *xxvi*, which ensures the repetition of the antecedent noun in relative clauses, or the selection of an embedded object-clause which is 'heir to' the instructions for relative clauses, must be extended so as also to cover noun selections entailed by copula-verbs and adjectives. We

14   SON

therefore add, after the colon of rule (1) *xxvi*, the following two rules as they are modified when applied within a relative clause:

$$xxviii \quad \left\{ \begin{array}{l} [\text{CV}] \overset{\text{L}}{\rightarrow} \text{cv—X}[n_{s(\alpha)}] \\ [\text{A}^{\text{PN}}] \overset{\text{L}}{\rightarrow} \text{a—X}[n_{s(\alpha)}] \end{array} \right\} \twoheadrightarrow [\text{N}^{\text{X}}] \overset{\text{L}}{\rightarrow} \alpha$$

5.2.3 Nouns. We have not given, so far, any nouns in the lexicon apart from (4) and (6) in 5.1. Let us repeat these here and add some more nouns to the list:

(82)   *i*   N *water*   c   m   vol   nsol   lq
(82)   *ii*   N *cup*   c   i   vol   cont

The specification given for *water* will also be valid for *milk, ink, wine, petrol*, and, in general, for all nouns referring to liquids. Of course, an adequate lexicon will have to differentiate further among the various liquids, and it will have to do so in the most economical way possible, using a coherent set of descriptive terms. But this further differentiation does not seem to have a bearing on the non-deviance of the sentences of English. And since we limit ourselves in this study to those features that ensure non-deviance, we shall not go into the problems of further semantic specification (see 5.4.2).

In the same way, the specification given for *cup* will also cover such items as *glass, box, mug, chest, jar, vase*, etc. And, in general, the specifications of nouns presented in this section will be valid not only for the nouns given but for whole classes of semantically similar nouns.

It must be taken into account, furthermore, that the features assigned to individual nouns here are the result of an investigation into an extremely limited lexicon. The sample of the lexicon that served as a basis for the present results is, in fact, somewhat larger than the set of items discussed in this chapter, but it does not exceed a total of about two hundred. One must expect, therefore, that more features will have to be added as work progresses. (Whether and to what extent the number of new features required will decrease or increase as more and more items are taken into account, is a question that cannot be decided here.) So, for example, for the limited purpose of this restricted lexicon, the item *air* is specified as follows:

(82)   *iii*   N *air*   c   m   vol   nsol

But presumably, if we take the verb *fly* into account, we shall have to add a feature like 'rarefied' or 'gaseous', since this verb requires a gaseous noun in its *PO*: one does not fly non-deviantly through water.

Here follows a tentative and incomplete specification of some more items:

(82) *iv* N *conversation* c/a i/m pr lg cont

where the slanted line indicates that both features can be taken to specify this item, regardless of the other features.

(82) *v*   N *letter* c i vol sol lg com
(82) *vi* N *book*   c i vol
              a i lg   cont

where the two sets of features reflect two meanings, or senses, of the same item, as in *the book is new*, which is equivalent either to 'this volume has not been perused', or to 'the text of this book was composed recently'.

(82)							
vii	N *story*	c/a	i	lg	com	cont	
viii	N *language*	a	i/m	lg			
ix	N *word*	c/a	i	par	lg	com	el
x	N *question*	c/a	i	lg	solv		
xi	N *problem*	a	i	lg	solv		
xii	N *bread*	c	m	vol	sol		
xiii	N *loaf*	c	i	vol	sol		
xiv	N *man*	c	i	vol	an	hum	
xv	N *distance*	a	m				
		a	i	par			
xvi	N *age*	a	m				
		a	i	par	prop		
xvii	N *colour*	a	i/m	prop			
xviii	N *beauty*	a	i/m	prop			
xix	N *length*	a	m				
		a	i	par	prop		
xx	N *game*	a	i	pr			
		c	i	vol			

One notices that *game* in the sense of '(flesh of) wild animal' is excluded, since this would require the feature *m* instead of *i* in the bottom row.

(82)					
xxi	N *change*	a	m	pr	
		a	i	pr	par
xxii	N *price*	a	i	par	

In the feature specification employed here no account has been taken of the predictability of some features in terms of others. Thus, it seems

predictable throughout the category of nouns that the features 'voluminous', 'solid', 'non-solid', 'liquid', will all imply the feature 'concrete',
and similarly that 'parameter' will imply the features 'abstract' and
'individual'. When more information is available, it will probably be
profitable to set up rules permitting the derivation of 'concrete' from
'voluminous', 'solid', etc. or of 'abstract' and 'individual' from 'parameter'. These rules will then be part of the general interpretation of
selectional entailment by the verbs. But for the present too little material
is available to make this procedure pay.[1]

For the sake of convenience a list of the features introduced, with their
interpretations, is given here:

a	—	abstract	an	—	animate
c	—	concrete	hum	—	human
i	—	individual	par	—	parameter
m	—	mass	pr	—	process
vol	—	voluminous	solv	—	solvable
lq	—	liquid	prop	—	property
sol	—	solid	lg	—	linguistic
nsol	—	non-solid	com	—	communication
cont	—	contentful	el	—	element

5.2.4 Prepositions. The only category of lexical items which has not
been investigated in any detail so far in this study, although mentioned
in the rules and the lexicon, is the category of prepositions. Here again,
we have a category of a complex character, and most of the questions
must be left open. In the limited framework of the rules and lexical
items presented here, the prepositions did not cause difficulty, because
they occur only in *PO*'s and *by*-phrases, where the choice of the prepositions is limited to specifically mentioned items. If, however, we introduce
other adverbial expressions, such as those of place and time, we must
set up selection restriction rules for prepositions and their axis-nouns.
We shall not do so here, since too little is known about this area of
grammar and lexicon to give sufficiently specific rules.

So much seems clear, however, that prepositions are similar to verbs
and adjectives in that they require a selectional subcategorization system
in terms of both intrinsic features and features of selectional entailment

---

[1] Katz ((1966) pp. 229–33) also discusses the predictability of certain features in terms
of others. His suggestion that this would help us to discover the 'semantic categories'
of a language is interesting but rather speculative.

on their axis-nouns. It is for this reason that the selection of the preposition in *PO*-position by rule (1) *xii* is made to precede the selection of nouns in various positions by the rules (1) *xiii* and (1) *xiv*.

Some intrinsic features seem obvious for certain prepositions, such as 'place', 'time', 'motion', 'rest'. The selection of prepositions in terms of their intrinsic features seems to depend on entailment by the verbs, which, in turn, seems to be connected with intrinsic verb-features. Thus we want to regard *he was sleeping towards the faculty building* as deviant. On the other hand, although we accept *he was sleeping in the faculty building* as non-deviant, we want to reject, for instance, *he was sleeping in the problem*. This suggests that, once the preposition has been selected, the selection of its axis-noun depends again on restrictions entailed by the preposition.

One also notices that the construction may change according to the noun selected in the axis-position. Thus in *I wrote in the book* the prepositional phrase is a *PO* (in accordance with (62) *vi*), but in *I wrote in the garden* the non-deviant structural interpretation is to take *in the garden* as an adverbial of place functioning as an operator ('while being in the garden'). We may, of course, have ambiguities here, as in *I wrote on the platform*, or *I will sleep in that bed*. In one interpretation they are equivalent to *the platform was written on by me* and *that bed will be slept in by me*, respectively; in another they allow for preposing of the adverbial phrase: *on the platform I wrote* and *in that bed I will sleep*. The former of these two sentences can mean, moreover, that the platform is the topic written about, so that *on the platform* is another of the possible *PO*'s of this verb.

We shall not, however, pursue these investigations any further here.

5.3 Summary of deep structure rules

At the end of this chapter on deep structure rules, let us summarize the rules given, incorporating all modifications and additions:

(83) *i* Sent → SQL + Prop

    ii SQL → $\begin{Bmatrix} \text{ASS} \\ \text{QU} \\ \text{IMP} \\ \text{SUGG} \end{Bmatrix}$

    iii Prop → QL + Nucleus $\begin{Bmatrix} [\text{V}] \\ [\text{CV}] \end{Bmatrix}$

iv QL → (NEG) Tense

v Tense → $\begin{cases} \text{T} & \text{env IMP(NEG)—} \\ \text{T (Modal)} \end{cases}$

vi Modal → M (Neg) Tense

vii T → $\left\{ \begin{array}{l} \left\{\begin{array}{l}\text{Pres}\\\text{Fut}\\\text{Perf}\end{array}\right\} \quad \text{env IMP (NEG)—} \\ \text{Pres} \\ \text{Fut} \\ \text{Perf} \\ \text{Past} \\ \text{U} \end{array} \right\}$

$viii$ NEG → Neg (Neg) (Neg)

ix M → $\begin{cases}\text{Poss}\\\text{Nec}\\\text{Perm}\end{cases}$

x [V] $\overset{\text{L}}{\to}$ v

xi [CV] $\overset{\text{L}}{\to}$ cv

xii Nucleus[v] →
      *S[N] + MV[v] + *O[N] + *IO[N] + *PO[Relator[P] + Axis[N]]

$xiii$ Nucleus[cv] →
      MV[cv] + PN[A] + *IO[N] + *PO[Relator[P] + Axis[N]]

xiv [A^{PN}] $\overset{\text{L}}{\to}$ a_s

xv PN[a] → S[N] + PN′[a] + *IO[N] + *PO[Relator[P] + Axis[N]]

xvi [$P^{Relator}$] $\overset{\text{L}}{\to}$ p_s

$xvii$ $\begin{cases}[N^O]\\{[N^{IO}]}\\{[N^{Axis}]}\end{cases} \overset{\text{L}}{\to} n_s$

$xviii$ [N^S] $\overset{\text{L}}{\to}$ n_s

      [N^S] → $\left[\begin{array}{l} n_s^O \text{ env } X - MV[v] + O— \\ n_s^{IO} \text{ env } X - MV[v] + *O[n] + IO— \\ n_s^{Axis} \text{ env } X - MV[v] + PO[Relator[p] + Axis—] \end{array}\right] →$

      (a) $\begin{bmatrix}O[n_s]\\IO[n_s]\\Axis[n_s]\end{bmatrix} → \begin{cases}\varnothing\\AgPhr[Relator[p(by)] + Axis[N^S]]\end{cases}$

(b) $[N^S] \overset{L}{\to} n_s$

(c) $MV[v] \to Pass + MV'[v]$

xix $n_1 \to n_i' \begin{Bmatrix} sg \\ pl \end{Bmatrix}$

xx $n \to n' + sg$

xxi $n' \to \begin{Bmatrix} QN+n & env\ X-U-Y- \\ (\imath)n & env\ \begin{Bmatrix} QU \\ Qu \end{Bmatrix} Z- \\ (QN)n \end{Bmatrix} (\begin{Bmatrix} Prop_{rel} \\ Sent_{rel} \end{Bmatrix}).$

where X and Y stand for any string not derived from *Modal*; Z for any string; no recursion between *xxi* and *xix* and *xx*

xxii $\begin{Bmatrix} QU \\ Qu \end{Bmatrix} -X-\imath+n \begin{Bmatrix} sg \\ pl \end{Bmatrix} (Prop_{rel})-Y \to$

$\begin{Bmatrix} QU \\ Qu \end{Bmatrix} \imath+n \begin{Bmatrix} sg \\ pl \end{Bmatrix} (Prop_{rel})-X-n \begin{Bmatrix} sg \\ pl \end{Bmatrix} -Y$

xxiii $X-\overline{T}-Y-QN+n \begin{Bmatrix} sg \\ pl \end{Bmatrix} (Prop_{rel})-Z \to$

$\begin{Bmatrix} X-\overline{T}-QN+n \begin{Bmatrix} sg \\ pl \end{Bmatrix} (Prop_{rel})-Y-n \begin{Bmatrix} sg \\ pl \end{Bmatrix} -Z \\ X-QN+n \begin{Bmatrix} sg \\ pl \end{Bmatrix} (Prop_{rel})-\overline{T}-Y-n \begin{Bmatrix} sg \\ pl \end{Bmatrix} -Z \end{Bmatrix}$

where X, Y and Z stand for any string including null

xxiv $X-QN+n \begin{Bmatrix} sg \\ pl \end{Bmatrix} (Prop_{rel})-Y \to$

$QN+n \begin{Bmatrix} sg \\ pl \end{Bmatrix} (Prop_{rel})-X-n \begin{Bmatrix} sg \\ pl \end{Bmatrix} -Y$

where X and Y stand for any string, including null, of symbols not derived from *SQL* or *QL*

xxv $QN+n \to \begin{Bmatrix} A & env\ X-U-Y- \\ A \\ E \end{Bmatrix} n'(Neg)$

where X and Y as in *xxi*

xxvi $A+n_i' \to \begin{Bmatrix} A(arb)\ (num)n_1 & env—sg \\ A((arb)num)n_1 & env—pl \end{Bmatrix}$

xxvii $A+n_m' \to A(arb)n_m$

xxviii $E + n_i' \rightarrow \begin{cases} E(mult)n_i & env—pl \\ E(arb(num))n_i & env \\ E(num)n_i \end{cases} \begin{pmatrix} QU \\ Qu \\ IMP \\ Imp \\ Neg \end{pmatrix} Z—$

where Z stands for any string

xxix $E + n_m' \rightarrow \begin{cases} E(arb)n_m & env \\ E(mult)n_m \end{cases} \begin{pmatrix} QU \\ Qu \\ IMP \\ Imp \\ Neg \end{pmatrix} Z—$

where Z stands for any string

xxx $Sent_{rel} = Sent : ii \quad SQL \rightarrow \begin{cases} ASS \\ QU \\ SUGG \end{cases}$

xxxi $\begin{bmatrix} Sent_{rel} \\ Prop_{rel} \end{bmatrix} = \begin{bmatrix} Sent \\ Prop \end{bmatrix} :$

$\begin{cases} x & [V] \overset{L}{\rightarrow} v—X[n_{s(\alpha)}] \\ xi & [CV] \overset{L}{\rightarrow} cv—X[n_{s(\alpha)}] \\ xiv & [A^{PN}] \overset{L}{\rightarrow} a—X[n_{s(\alpha)}] \end{cases} \twoheadrightarrow [N^X] \overset{L}{\rightarrow} \alpha$

or: $x \quad [V] \overset{L}{\rightarrow} v—O\begin{Bmatrix} [c+Prop] \\ [Nucleus] \end{Bmatrix} \twoheadrightarrow$

(a) $[N^O] \overset{L}{\rightarrow} \begin{Bmatrix} c+Prop \\ Nucleus \end{Bmatrix}$

(b) $Prop = Prop_{rel}$

(c) $Nucleus = Nucleus \begin{Bmatrix} [V] \\ [CV] \end{Bmatrix} : x, xi, xiv/xxxi$

where X stands for 'S', 'O', 'IO' or 'Axis';

     α for the antecedent noun;

     $\left.\begin{matrix} v \\ cv \\ a \end{matrix}\right\}—Q[p]$ for any verb, copula-verb or adjective in the lexicon entailing the selection of Q filled by p;

     $n_{s(\alpha)}$ for any subcategory of nouns such that $s(\alpha)$ is a set of features comprised by the features of the antecedent noun α;

     c for any clause qualifier (*Ass, Imp. Qu*);

     x, xi, xiv/xxxi for: rules *x, xi* and *xiv* as given in rule *xxxi*.

5.4 Conclusion

By way of conclusion two basic points emerging from this study will be commented upon: the adequacy of the grammatical model presented here, and, more specifically, its relevance for the description of meanings.

5.4.1 Adequacy. The deep structure rules and the form of lexical specification presented in this chapter are the result of the criticisms levelled against Chomsky's model of the base in chapter 3, and of the analysis performed in chapter 4, where the category of operators was set up as an answer to a variety of descriptive problems. Necessarily, not all observations made in chapter 4 could be incorporated into the rules and the lexicon given here: the grammatical regularities on which we concentrated here are so general and fundamental to the language, and so intimately connected with a large variety of other regularities, that their complete description can only be given in the context of a much wider study. Only by carefully and gradually extending and revising the description as it exists so far, in interaction with systematic and detailed research into sub-parts of the language, can we hope to arrive eventually at a reasonable degree of adequacy.

We seem justified, however, in asserting that we have provided an apparatus of greater simplicity, generality and semantic adequacy than Chomsky's deep structure model can be said to possess, and allowing for at least as wide a range of data to be accounted for.

The greater simplicity[1] is perhaps most conspicuous in the procedure of lexical selection. We can dispense with Chomsky's strict subcategorization rules and selectional rules: the intrinsic and selectional entailment features are all given in the lexicon, and their proper effect is ensured by metarules in the theory of the grammar. Another advantage of simplicity

[1] Simplicity is taken in an intuitive sense, which it proves very hard to make more precise. The difficulty of defining simplicity in any precise way is not surprising, and should not worry us. So far no two or more exhaustive and adequate linguistic descriptions have been made available to be compared as to their relative simplicity. And instances of partial descriptions covering the same ground and equally adequate in all respects other than their simplicity are still extremely rare. It seems that, given this situation, we must not commit ourselves to premature formulae, but rather rely on an intuitive idea of simplicity until this can be made explicit and precise on the basis of a sufficient number of different competing descriptions. We can only forecast that simplicity will turn out to be not just a function of the number of symbols employed in the rules, but also of the range of sentences covered by the same rule (generality, see 1.4.3) and hence of the number of rules required to describe the sentences of a language or some specific subset of these.

is that our grammar enables us to distinguish sentences, propositions and nuclei in a straightforward way. It may, furthermore, be expected that the transformational component, about which little has been said, will be considerably simplified by its now being able to operate on symbols indicating relational constituents.

A gain in simplicity, generality and semantic adequacy is achieved, for instance, by the treatment of the passive. It does not need a dummy *by*-phrase for passive sentences without agent phrase. It automatically excludes from passivization sentences with impersonal verbs or copula-verbs. And, by being restricted to the nucleus, it eliminates such semantic irregularities as are signalled by Chomsky: *nobody in the room knows two languages* versus *two languages are known by nobody in the room*.

Derived nominals represent another instance of greater simplicity and generality. These can now be derived by a uniform procedure from base-terminal nuclei, which automatically accounts for their tenselessness.

A higher degree of semantic adequacy is achieved, in general, by the introduction of operators. There is now a much more general correspondence between semantic and grammatical regularities, and the semantic interpretation of the sentences generated can now be read immediately from their deep structure, without the complication of projection rules. There is a clear separation of the lexical items and their grammatical relations on the one hand, and all scope-possessing elements on the other. Our description permits us to distinguish consistently those ambiguities which are regular for the language. In particular, semantic adequacy is enhanced by our treatment of the passive (see above) and of negation (which is accounted for by Klima in a semantically inconsistent way).

The claim that the range of data accounted for is at least as wide as the coverage of data in Chomsky's terms, is substantiated by the fact that, as far as could be checked (much of the research done by Chomsky and his fellow-workers is still unpublished), all grammatical phenomena described so far in Chomskian terms can be described in terms of the apparatus presented here.

5.4.2 Meaning. Finally, some remarks remain to be made on the possible implications of our work for a theory of meaning and semantic description.[1] Some introductory remarks were made in 3.4.2. A fuller statement can now be made in the light of chapter 4 and the present chapter.

It has often been stated that, essentially, meanings cannot be described in language. Sometimes they can be demonstrated by ostensive definitions, but any description in terms of a language, natural or artificial, is bound to have its own meaning in turn, a description of which will again have its own meaning, etc. If this is true, we can only set up sets of synonymous expressions, and, on the face of it, it is hard to see why certain synonyms should be regarded as representing 'the' meaning rather than others. Thus, we may give a number of synonyms for, for instance:

(84) *i*   water is wet

such as:

(84) *ii*   wetness is a property of water
(84) *iii*   water has the property of wetness
(84) *iv*   liquid H_2O has the property of loose adhesion
(84) *v*   for all x, if x is water, x is wet
(84) *vi*   I assert that for all water it is true that water is wet

And if we take other languages into account, the number of synonyms becomes very large indeed:

(84) *vii*   Wasser ist nass
           etc.

It is to a large extent arbitrary to take any of these synonymous expressions as representing what must be the meaning of (84) *i*. Yet one notices that sometimes people have preferences for certain synonyms, which they regard as giving the meaning of an expression. Thus, a native speaker of German will take (84) *vii* as a description of the meaning of (84) *i*. In general, when one comes across an expression which one does not, or not fully, understand, one will want a synonymous expression that one does understand. This, however, does not apply to the linguist,

---

[1] The following remarks arise from a seminar in semantics conducted in the University of Cambridge in 1967–8, where my proposals concerning deep structure were discussed. I am particularly indebted to Dr Mary Hesse and Dr Karen Sparck Jones for their contributions.

whose aim is not the understanding of expressions (which is a function of language-users), but their description.

Quite generally, in all studies of meaning, it must be borne in mind that meanings are not facts that serve as a basis for research and against which a theory can be tested. That is, meanings do not themselves provide evidence. It is only the *understanding* of sentences by language-users which can be taken as basic evidence. Understanding is part of the language-users' know-how. The *specification* of meanings is a result of the linguist's activity. Accordingly, the safest method for a descriptive linguist is to ask the language-user only whether he understands two given sentences as the same or not, not *what* a given sentence means.

The question is now whether for the theoretical purpose of description we can find for each sentence of a given language one specific synonym which can be considered 'favourite' for the linguist, i.e. which for him, within his terms, can be said to represent the meaning of this sentence. The set of all favourite synonyms will then constitute a *favourite synonymous language*.

Suppose we have, for a natural language L, a set L_f of non-homonymous expressions and that for every sentence S_i of L there is a set

$$F_i\{F_{i_1}, F_{i_2}, ..., F_{i_n}\} \quad (1 \leqslant n)$$

of semantically different expressions in L_f such that S_i can be syntactically derived from every member of F_i and such that every member of F_i is synonymous with S_i in at least one of the meanings of S_i; and suppose that there is no set L_f' of non-homonymous expressions related to L in the same way as L_f but permitting simpler derivations for every S_i; suppose, furthermore, that all synonymous sentences of L have one common source expression in L_f;—then, presumably, the expressions of L_f constitute the favourite synonymous language for L for the purpose of linguistic description. L_f permits the simplest possible syntactic specification of L; it distinguishes different meanings of the sentences of L by relating every different meaning to a different source in L_f, and it accounts for synonymy by positing one common source for all synonymous sentences. If, moreover, L_f satisfies the conditions that it satisfies for L, for all natural languages as well, then L_f constitutes a syntactic and semantic universal of language.

The conditions imposed on L_f are extremely heavy, and it is not *a priori* clear that an L_f can be constructed for any language, let alone for all languages. But one notices that L_f comes very close to what has been called deep structure. In setting up our deep structure hypothesis we have taken all conditions of L_f into account, except that it provide one common source for every set of synonymous English sentences. Our deep structure hypothesis permits a direct reading of its expressions in a way which distinguishes clearly between different meanings of the same sentence, at least as far as the grammatical structure is concerned. A separate semantic component has now lost much of its significance: the deep structures can be taken as their own semantic interpretation.

Since, among the synonymous sentences (84) *ii*–(84) *vi*, it is (84) *vi* that represents most faithfully the most adequate deep structure analysis of (84) *i* available so far, we can say that (84) *vi* comes closest to the ideal favourite synonym of (84) *i*. It is clear, however, that (84) *vi* is not the favourite synonym we are looking for. For one thing, it has not been demonstrated that other synonyms, such as (84) *ii*–(84) *v*, can be derived from (84) *vi* by maximally simple transformational rules. Yet it is not at all unreasonable to expect that this can be done. (84) *ii* and (84) *iii* have a fair chance of being transformationally related to (84) *i*. The derived nominal of the nucleus of (84) *i* is *the wetness of water*. We might, conceivably, set up transformational rules similar to those of derived nominalization, but applying to the whole sentence with all its operators, and converting this into sentences of the form (84) *ii* or (84) *iii*. It is clear, moreover (see 3.4.1, p. 82, note 1), that there is a deep structure identity between *have* and certain occurrences of *be*.

(84) *iv* has the same grammatical structure as (84) *iii*, but differs in the choice of lexical items. It is doubtful whether, and if so how, it belongs to the English language. But the problems of lexical specification will be returned to below.

As for (84) *v*, it is also debatable whether it is proper English. It is, perhaps, best regarded as an Angloid version of the logical language of predicate calculus. As such it is easily derivable from (84) *vi* by means of some simple and general rules deleting those elements which are regarded as irrelevant in predicate calculus (such as the sentence qualifier), and providing specific forms for quantifiers.

Another reason why (84) *vi* cannot be regarded as a representative of the favourite synonymous language for English is its lack of semantic specifications of lexical items. This does not disturb us in the case under consideration, since *water* and *wet* are not homonymous in English, nor do they have clear synonyms. Some homonymous lexical items will be disambiguated by our grammar, such as *ball* in, for instance:

(85)   the ball was colourful

It will be remembered that in the deep structure apparatus set forth above the selectional features of the nouns have never been deleted, and are, therefore, part and parcel of the base-terminal products. Actually, (84) *vi* is not a precise representation of the deep structure version of (84) *i*, since it does not contain these features. A more genuine representation is:

(86)   ASS U A(water$_{c,m,vol,nsol,lq}$) : water$_{c,m,vol,nsol,lq}$ be wet

Accordingly, (85) will be represented as:

(87)   ASS Past : ball$_{c,1,vol}$ be colourful

or as:

(88)   ASS Past : ball$_{c,1,pr}$ be colourful

The difference in feature specification of *ball* accounts for the homonymy of (85).

This solution, however, is not always available. Let us take, for instance, the homonymous sentence:

(89)   the bank is green

The deep structure representation of (89) is:

(90)   ASS Pres : bank$_{c,1,vol}$ be green

for both meanings of (89). It may be objected that the system of selectional feature specification set up here is based only on a very limited sample of the lexicon, and that, therefore, we must expect there to be more features in an ultimate specification of the complete lexicon. But even so, it is not *a priori* clear that we shall then have a means of distinguishing all lexical homonyms. We must reckon with the possibility that, in order to distinguish all lexical homonyms, we shall have to introduce more features than just those necessary for ensuring non-deviance. Studies of isolated cases, such as *bachelor* by Katz and Postal ((1964) p. 14), show that a complete homonym-distinguishing system of feature specification will become fairly elaborate and will come close to a unique characterization of each item.

Let us suppose that we have such a homonym-distinguishing specificational system. The deep structure language will then fulfil the requirement of distinguishing all homonymous sentences of the language, relating each meaning to a different deep structure source expression. There will, however, still be one requirement of L_f that is not complied with: the deep structure language will not always provide a common source for synonymous expressions in the language. To take a simple example:

(91)   Cynthia broke her shinbone

and:

(92)   Cynthia broke her tibia

which must be considered perfect synonyms, will still have different deep structure representations. Even though the set of features attached to *tibia* may be the same as that associated with *shinbone*, there will still be the difference between the two actual lexical items *tibia* and *shinbone*.

We are, admittedly, simplifying the problem, in that such perfect synonyms as *tibia* and *shinbone* are relatively rare. Much more common are 'incidental' synonyms, i.e. synonyms in certain environments, but not in others, such as *landscape* and *scenery*, which are commutable without change in meaning in many contexts, but not in, for instance:

(93)   Archibald bought a landscape

The problem of how to account for incidental synonyms has never been solved, and no attempt is made here to solve it. What interests us here, however, is that in those contexts where they are interchangeable without difference in meaning, our deep structure language does not provide a common source for the synonyms, so that our deep structure language cannot be identical with the L_f we are seeking to establish.

Ideally, this last difficulty can be overcome if we extend the system of lexical specification to cover the whole lexical meaning of each item. That is, we might be able to go further than the specification needed for the distinction of homonyms, and describe a set of individual lexical meanings in terms of some consistent and maximally simple system of specificational features. It will then no longer be necessary to select actual items from the lexicon: they will be selected during the process of transformation from deep into surface structure. The relation of unambiguous synonymy between each deep structure expression and a sentence in the language will then be ensured by the complete specification of every lexical meaning. And if there are synonyms in the lexicon (either perfect or incidental), it will be up to the transformational component to choose among them. This, it seems, provides another, strong, argument in favour of a procedure whereby the selection of lexical items is excluded from the base, apart from the support lent to this view by various considerations above.

The requirements set up for a favourite synonymous language embody a programme for future research following from the work that has been done so far in deep structure. The concept of deep structure emerging from this study originated in Chomsky's model of deep structure as set forth in his *Aspects of the Theory of Syntax* (1965). Application to English of his requirements for a base grammar led to a concept of deep structure of higher semantic relevance than could be foreseen at the outset. This may be regarded as a continuation of the development which led from the original idea of kernel to the semantically determined deep structure proposed by Katz and Postal (1964) and endorsed by Chomsky (1965). We now see reasons for regarding deep structure not only as semantically determined, in that the transformations do not affect any semantic change, but also as providing for the language under description a synonymous language with certain clearly definable advantages over other sets of synonymous expressions. This result leads us to envisage a descriptively ideal synonymous language, which will contain not only all, but also only semantic information, and which will provide us with an important universal insight into the nature of human language.

Bibliography

Austin, J. L. *Philosophical Papers*. Edited by J. O. Urmson and G. J. Warnock. Oxford 1961.

Ayer, A. J. *Philosopical Essays*. London 1954.

Bach, E. *An Introduction to Transformational Grammars*. New York 1964.

Bazell, C. E. 'Meaning and the morpheme', *Word 18* (1962) pp. 132–42.

Bloomfield, L. *Language*. New York 1933.

Bocheński, I. M. 'The problem of universals', *Logico-Philosophical Studies*, edited by Albert Menne, pp. 118–36. Dordrecht 1962*a*.

    Formale Logik. Freiburg–München 1962*b*.

Bolinger, D. L. *Interrogative Structures of American English*. University Alabama 1957.

    'Linguistic science and linguistic engineering', *Word 16* (1960) pp. 374–91.

Carnap, R. *The Logical Syntax of Language*. London 1964⁶.

Chomsky, N. *Syntactic Structures*. The Hague 1957.

    'Some methodological remarks on generative grammar', *Word 17* (1961) pp. 219–39.

    Current Issues in Linguistic Theory. The Hague 1964*a*.

    'Degrees of grammaticalness', *The Structure of Language, Readings in the Philosophy of Language*, edited by J. A. Fodor and J. J. Katz, pp. 384–89. Englewood Cliffs 1964*b*.

    Aspects of the Theory of Syntax. Cambridge, Mass., 1965.

    Cartesian Linguistics, A Chapter in the History of Rationalist Thought. New York–London 1966*a*.

    Topics in the Theory of Generative Grammar. The Hague 1966*b*.

    Remarks on Nominalization. Unpublished, 1967*a*.

    'Some general properties of phonological rules', *Language 43* (1967*b*) pp. 102–28.

Cook, W. A. *On Tagmemes and Transforms*. Washington, D.C., 1964.

Dixon, R. M. W. *Linguistic Science and Logic*. The Hague 1963.

Doherty, P. C. and A. Schwartz, 'The syntax of the compared adjective in English', *Language 43* (1967) pp. 903–36.

Drange, Th. *Type Crossings. Sentential Meaninglessness in the Border Area of Linguistics and Philosophy*. The Hague 1966.

Elson, B. and Velma Pickett, *An Introdution to Morphology and Syntax*. Santa Ana, California, 1962.

Ewing, A. C. 'Meaninglessness', *Mind 46* (1937) pp. 347–64.

Fillmore, Ch. J., 'A proposal concerning English prepositions', *Report on the 17th Annual Round Table Meeting on Linguistics and Language Studies*.

Monograph Series on Languages and Linguistics, Number 19 (1966), Georgetown University, Institute of Languages and Linguistics, pp. 19–33.

Fowler, H. W. *A Dictionary of Modern English Usage*. Oxford 1965².

de Groot, A. W. *Inleiding tot de Algemene Taalwetenschap*. Groningen 1964².

'The construction Subject-Predicate in English; primary and secondary semantic functions', *Symbolae Linguisticae in Honorem Georgii Kuryłowicz*, Polska Akademia Nauk—Oddział w Krakowie, Prace Komisji Językoznawstwa Nr. 5, Wrocław–Warszawa–Kraków 1965, pp. 93–102.

Gruber, J. S. 'Look and see', *Language 43* (1967) pp. 937–47.

Hare, R. M. 'Imperative sentences', *Mind 58* (1949) pp. 21–39. Also in: *The Language of Morals*. Oxford 1952.

Harris, Z. S., *Methods in Structural Linguistics*. Chicago 1951.

Hockett, C. F. *A Course in Modern Linguistics*. New York 1958.

'Language, Mathematics, and Linguistics', *Current Trends in Linguistics, Vol. III, Theoretical Foundations*, edited by Th. A. Sebeok, pp. 155–304. The Hague 1966.

Hornby, A. S. *A Guide to Patterns and Usage in English*. London 1966¹⁰.

Huddleston, R. 'More on the English comparative', *Journal of Linguistics 3.1* (1967) pp. 91–102.

Jespersen, O. *Negation in English and Other Languages*. Copenhagen 1917.

The Philosophy of Grammar. London 1924.

Essentials of English Grammar. London 1933.

Joly, A. *Negation and the Comparative Particle in English*. Quebec 1967.

Katz, J. J. 'Semi-sentences', *The Structure of Language, Readings in the Philosophy of Language*, edited by J. A. Fodor and J. J. Katz, pp. 400–16. Englewood Cliffs 1964*a*.

'Mentalism in linguistics', *Language 40.2* (1964*b*) pp. 124–37.

The Philosophy of Language. New York–London 1966.

and J. A. Fodor. 'The structure of a semantic theory', *Language 39.2* (1963) pp. 170–210.

and P. M. Postal. *An Integrated Theory of Linguistic Descriptions*. Cambridge, Mass., 1964.

Kerner, G. *The Revolution in Ethical Theory*. Oxford 1966.

Klima, E. S. 'Negation in English', *The Structure of Language, Readings in the Philosophy of Language*, edited by J. A. Fodor and J. J. Katz, pp. 246–323. Englewood Cliffs 1964.

Kneale, W. and M. *The Development of Logic*. Oxford 1962.

Koutsoudas, A. *Writing Transformational Grammars, an Introduction*. New York 1965.

Kraak, A. *Negative Zinnen. Een Methodologische en Grammatische Analyse*. Hilversum 1966.

Kruisinga, E. *A Handbook of Present-Day English, Part II, English Accidence and Syntax 3*. Groningen 1932.

Lees, R. B. *The Grammar of English Nominalizations*. Supplement to *International Journal of American Linguistics 26* (1960*a*). Also: The Hague 1963.

Review of D. L. Bolinger (1957), *Word 16* (1960*b*) pp. 119–25.

'Grammatical analysis of the English comparative construction', *Word 17* (1961) pp. 171–85.

Levelt, W. J. M. 'Generatieve grammatica en psycholinguistiek I, inleiding in de generatieve grammatica', *Nederlands Tijdschrift voor de Psychologie 21.5* (1966) pp. 317–37.

'Generatieve grammatica en psycholinguistiek II, psychologisch onderzoek', *Nederlands Tijdschrift voor de Psychologie 21.6* (1966) pp. 367–400.

Lewis, C. I. *An Analysis of Knowledge and Valuation.* La Salle, Illinois, 1946.

Liddell, H. G. and R. Scott, *A Greek–English Lexicon.* Oxford 1951.

Longacre, R. E. 'String constituent analysis', *Language 36* (1960) pp. 63–88.

Grammar Discovery Procedures. The Hague 1964.

Lyons, J. 'Towards a "notional" theory of the "parts of speech"', *Journal of Linguistics 2.2* (1966) pp. 209–36.

Matthews, P. H., 'Problems of selection in transformational grammar', *Journal of Linguistics 1.1* (1965) pp. 35–47.

Review of Chomsky (1965). *Journal of Linguistics 3.1* (1967) pp. 119–52.

Mehler, J. 'Some effects of grammatical transformations on the recall of English sentences', *Journal of Verbal Learning and Verbal Behavior 2* (1963) pp. 346–51.

Miller, G. A. 'Some psychological studies of grammar', *American Psychologist 17* (1962) pp. 748–62.

'Language and psychology', *New Directions in the Study of Language*, ed. E. H. Lenneberg, pp. 89–107. Cambridge, Mass., 1966[2].

Nuchelmans, G. 'Taaldaden', *Forum der Letteren VIII* (1967) pp. 208–23.

Ogden, C. K. and I. A. Richards, *The Meaning of Meaning. A Study of the Influence of Language upon Thought and of the Science of Symbolism.* London 1923.

Palmer, H. E. *English Intonation with Systematic Exercises.* Cambridge 1922.

Pap, A. 'Types and meaninglessness', *Mind 69* (1960) pp. 41–54.

Pike, K. L. *Language in Relation to a Unified Theory of the Structure of Human Behavior.* Second, revised edition. The Hague 1967.

Pilch, H., 'Comparative constructions in English', *Language 41* (1965) pp. 37–58.

Postal, P. *Constituent Structure: a Study of Contemporary Models of Syntactic Description. International Journal of American Linguistics 30.1* (1964). Part III. Also: The Hague 1964.

Prior, A. N., 'Entities', *Australasian Journal of Philosophy 32* (1954) pp. 159–68.

Formal Logic. Oxford 1955.

Quine, W. V. O. *Mathematical Logic.* Cambridge, Mass., 1951.

Word and Object. Cambridge, Mass., 1960.

From a Logical Point of View. Cambridge, Mass., 1961[2].

Quirk, R. and J. Svartvik. *Investigating Linguistic Acceptability.* The Hague 1966.

Rescher, N. 'On the logic of chronological propositions', *Mind 75* (1966) pp. 75–96.

Ross, J. R. *A Proposed Rule of Tree-Pruning*. Report MIT, Cambridge, Mass. Unpublished.

Russell, B. *A Critical Exposition of the Philosophy of Leibniz*. Cambridge 1900.

Savin, H. B. and E. Perchonock, 'Grammatical structure and the immediate recall of English sentences', *Journal of Verbal Learning and Verbal Behavior 4* (1965) pp. 348–53.

Seuren, P. A. M. Review of Longacre (1964). *Foundations of Language 2* (1966) pp. 200–12.

'Negation in Dutch', *Neophilologus 51.4* (1967) pp. 327–63.

Smith, C. S. 'A class of complex modifiers in English', *Language 37* (1961) pp. 342–65.

Staal, J. F. 'Generative syntax and semantics', *Foundations of Language 1* (1965) pp. 133–54.

'Some semantic relations between sentoids', *Foundations of Language 3* (1967a) pp. 66–88.

Word Order in Sanskrit and Universal Grammar. Dordrecht 1967b.

Straumann, H. *Newspaper Headlines. A Study in Linguistic Method*. London 1935.

Vendler, Z. 'Each and every, any and all', *Mind 71* (1962) pp. 145–60.

Wells, R. S. 'Immediate constituents', *Language 23* (1947) pp. 81–117.

von Wright, G. H. *An Essay in Modal Logic*. Studies in Logic and the Foundations of Mathematics. Amsterdam 1951.

Ziff, P. *Semantic Analysis*. New York 1960.

'On understanding "understanding utterances"', *The Structure of Language, Readings in the Philosophy of Language*, edited by J. A. Fodor and J. J. Katz, pp. 390–9. Englewood Cliffs 1964.

Index